Publisher: Dan Bolton

Senior Editor: Jill Hughart

Editor: Jonathan Ekedahl

Editorial Assistance: Paige Cline, Reneé Harris, Alfredo Ramirez, Robert Gonzales, Jessica Meyerson, Clarice Abert, Samantha Wood, Charlotte Freeman, Jesse Mackey

Manager of Finance & Administration: Stefanie Mount

Director of Editorial and Production: Dale E. Norley

Director of Sales and Marketing: Brian McOwen

Account Manager: Jeff Bounds, Heather Wimett

Art Coordinator/Restaurant Maven: Marjorie V. Goldberg

Database Management: Aaton Cohen-Sitt

Technical Support: Jim Dennis

Graphic Design & Production: Donna Greiner

A Division of Reed Elsevier, Inc.

Marc Teren
CEO

Brian Nairn
President and COO

Dan Hart
Vice President of Finance

Rose Einstein
Group Publisher

Giles Goodhead
Managing Director

Telephone 323/460-6304 or 800/545-2411. Facsimile 323/460-6314.

http://www.la411publishing.com
email: jekedahl@la411.cahners.com

Table of Contents

Somewhere along the path of expressing
myself through music, sound and
photography, I discovered another art.
The art of choosing how we see things.
The art of living more freely.

Beauty too exists by choice.
One can see some things to be beautiful,
or no things...

...or everything.

turn

This exposure started at
11:30 PM December 31, 1999 and
ended at 12:30 AM January 1, 2000.
It is of the constellations Orion
(upper right) and Canis Major
(lower left), which includes
Sirius, the brightest star
after the Sun. It was taken
from Zion National Park, Utah.
The trees were lit by campfire.

photography
by
billy mallery

323.462.4862

Dining

Bakeries

B & L Gourmet
8556 W. Third St.   (310) 271-8333
Los Angeles, CA 90048
Mon - Fri 7am - 6pm, Sat 7am - 5pm

Known around town for the best pecan "alligators." Cookies by the pound and exquisite European cakes. Devotees of the cocoa bean adore the chocolate truffle, but the hazelnut is an uncanny confrere.

Breadworks
7961 W. Third St.   (323) 930-0047
Los Angeles, CA 90048
Mon - Sat 8am - 6pm

Gourmet breads and rolls baked fresh daily. Choose from rosemary, country white, potato, honey sunflower, jalapeno, sun-dried tomato, olive and nine-grain. If bread is the staff of life, this is the source. Two-for-one specials from 5pm-6pm.

Brentwood Bread Co.
11640 San Vincente Blvd.   (310) 826-9400
Los Angeles, CA 90049
Mon - Sat 7am - 7pm, Sun 7am - 5pm

Ambrosian gourmet breads available at the shop, local farmers' market and Trader Joe's. Varieties include great white, herb garden, cranberry zest, sourdough and cinnamon walnut. Giant cookies are divine.

Brooklyn Bagel Bakery
2217 W. Beverly Blvd.   (213) 413-4114
Los Angeles, CA 90057
Mon - Sun 7am - 11pm

Authentic New York-style bagels a coast beyond anything the chain stores have to offer. Thirty-seven varieties including water, egg, onion and blueberry. Get there early for bagels fresh from the oven.

Buona Forchetta
2229 S. Barry Ave.   (310) 477-2229
Los Angeles, CA 90064
Mon - Fri 6am - 2pm, Sat 6am - 1pm

It's almost impossible to believe that these melt-in-your-mouth breads contain no sugar, added fat or dairy. The retail store carries kalamata olive, foccacia rosemary, hazelnut sage, panne osso, fogasse, rustico, integrale and plain baguettes. Some of these varieties cannot be found in grocery stores and are well worth the special trip.

Cake & Art
8709 Santa Monica Blvd.   (310) 657-8694
West Hollywood, CA 90069
Mon - Sat 10am - 6pm

From Schwarzenegger to Spielberg, everyone's a fan of Glenn von Kickel's work. A veritable Guggenheim of an "edible art experience." His specialty is portraits, from the Beatles to Hanson. He once made an 800 lb., 12 ft. tall three-horse carousel carrot cake! No matter what the size, the cakes taste as good as they look.

The Cake Collection
2221 S. Barry Ave.   (310) 479-7783
Los Angeles, CA 90064
Mon - Fri 9am - 5pm, Sat 10am - 4pm

Old-fashioned bakery creates hand-crafted works of art in butter cream and cake. From traditional to whimsical. Muffins, cookies, deep-dish apple pie and even good ol' Rice Crispies squares.

Cliff's Gourmet Goodies
4712 Admiralty Way, PMB 118   (310) 874-8629
Marina Del Rey, CA 90292

A custom wholesale bakery, Cliff makes everything from cookies and brownies to low-fat, healthy treats. Catering, gift baskets and delivery available.

Diamond Bakery
335 N. Fairfax Ave.   (323) 655-0534
Los Angeles, CA 90036
Mon - Sat 5:30am - 6:30pm, Sun 5:30am - 5pm

The original Jewish bakery and a staple in the Fairfax neighborhood. Unbelievably delicious corn-rye and raisin pumpernickel breads. Bubkas galore!

Emil's Swiss Pastry
1567 Barry Ave.   (310) 277-1114
Los Angeles, CA 90025
Mon 7am - 4pm, Tue - Sat 7am - 5:30pm

Luscious fruit tarts with creamy custard and apple strudels lure in the crowds. Tiramisu to die for plus every kind of Danish and cake known to modern civilization -- plus a few to discover.

La Brea Bakery

624 S. La Brea Ave.   (323) 939-6813
Los Angeles, CA 90036
Mon - Fri 7:30am - 6pm, Sat 8am - 6pm, Sun 8am - 4pm

Though you can find these breads in just about any market these days, it's still worth a trip to the original shop to discover the various baked and prepared delicacies on hand. Daily staples include summer camp coffee cake with creme fraîche, ginger scones, butter croissants, brownies and chocolate cookies. Also look for chocolate, dried apricot or lemon panetone. Occasional treats include Normandy apple tart and Viennese Danish.

La Conversation

638 N. Doheny Dr.   (310) 858-0950
West Hollywood, CA 90069
Mon - Wed 7am - 7pm

Ooo-la-la, baby. Fresh croissants as close as you can get to a Paris cafe. Sample the macadamia hearts dipped in chocolate or indulge in a hazelnut teacake. Just try to pass on a mousse tart.

LA Desserts

113 N. Robertson Blvd.   (310) 273-5537
Los Angeles, CA 90048
Mon - Sat 10am - 5pm

This is the birthplace of The Ivy, where all its desserts are made on the premises at LA Desserts and anyone can walk in, buy a pecan square and take home a little piece of of the famed eatery without spending a fortune. Divine chocolate chip cookies. Keep a sharp eye out for celebrity sightings at this perennially trendy eatery.

Mäni's Bakery

519 S. Fairfax Ave.   (323) 938-8800
Los Angeles, CA 90036
Mon - Fri 6:30am - Midnight, Sat - Sun 7:30am - Midnight

Healthy delights for the calorie-conscious, fat-fighter and sugar-scrimper, indulging those cravings without tomorrow's regrets. Giant chocolate-dipped cookies, fresh breads and muffins, and even soy lattes at this bakery/coffee house. Many dairy-free items, too.

Michel Richard

310 S. Robertson Blvd.   (310) 275-5707
Los Angeles, CA 90048
Mon - Sat 8am - 10pm, Sun 9am - 4pm

Monsieurs et mesdames, relax after a hard day of antique shopping on Robertson with an eclair filled with coffee custard or a slice of chocolate truffle cake soaked in raspberry sauce. Don't worry -- you deserve it.

Miss Grace Lemon Cake Co.

255½ S. Beverly Dr.   (800) 367-2253
Beverly Hills, CA 90210   (310) 281-8096
Mon - Sat 8am - 6pm

Hand-squeezed lemons, fresh-cracked eggs and the finest ingredients go into these well-loved lemon cakes. Though there are 15 other flavors from which to choose, the lemon cakes account for 90% of their business. Try one and you'll know why.

Old Town Bakery

166 W. Colorado Blvd.   (626) 793-2993
Pasadena, CA 91105
Mon - Thu 7:30am - 3pm, Fri - Sat 7:30am - 11pm, Sun 7:30am - 9pm

Lounge on the sunny patio while savoring homemade blueberry scones or sit indoors and watch them being baked. Award-winning triple-chocolate flourless cake for that special occasion or impression-making event.

Paris Pastry

1448 Westwood Blvd.   (310) 474-8888
Los Angeles, CA 90024
Mon - Sat 7am - 6pm

In easy distance to your stake on the map, their Florentine cookies are available in Bergdorf Goodman and fine Las Vegas hotels. But go right to the source for things baked and sumptuous and discover why it's the next best thing thing to jetting to Paris for patisseries francaises, meringues, and thin lace cookies. Almonds, cream, chocolate and Swiss hazelnut paste are de rigeur.

Regal Cake Gallery

1068 S. Fairfax   323-938-2286
Los Angeles, CA 90019
Mon - Fri 9am - 6pm, Sat 9am - 5pm, Sun 9am - Noon
Web: www.regalcakegallery.com

Test delicious free samples as you peruse their albums and life-size examples in search of the perfect cake for your special occasion. Experienced representatives available to help you personalize your cake needs.

Rosebud Cakes

311 S. Robertson Blvd.   (310) 657-6207
Beverly Hills, CA 90211
Tue - Sat 10am - 5pm

Nothing says 'festive' quite like a cake. Original designs are works of art, created in a theme, mood or style to complement any occasion. As heavenly on the inside as they are beautiful on the outside. Exotic fillings and icings like whipped creme and chocolate ganache, white chocolate Bavarian creme with raspberry, or "The Most" blanket white, marble or hazelnut cakes. Banana, lemon, poppyseed and angelfood present a myriad of possibilities, too. Tiramisu is a showstopper and custom-made wedding cakes are a specialty. Two weeks advance notice required.

Sweet Lady Jane

8360 Melrose Ave.   (323) 653-7145
West Hollywood, CA 90069
Mon - Sat 8:30am - 11:30pm

Three-berry cake with fresh strawberries, raspberries and blackberries fly off the shelves as fast as the fudge-filled five-layer chocolate "blackout" cake. Specializing in wedding cakes. Stop in anytime for a lemon cream cheese puff or as a nightcap since they're open late.

Viktor Benes Pastries on 3rd

8718 W. Third St.   (310) 276-0488
Los Angeles, CA 90048
Mon - Sat 6am - 7pm

European-style bakery with assorted Danish: cheese, cinnamon raisin, poppy seed. Wide assortment of cakes, breads and rolls. Conveniently located across the street from Cedars Sinai in case of a pastry emergency.

Zen Bakery

10988 W. Pico Blvd.   (310) 475-6727
Los Angeles, CA 90064
Mon - Sat 7am - 3pm, Sun 8:30am - 1pm

Over 25 years as a health food bakery, Zen offers 12-24 different varieties of muffins daily. Scones, cinnamon rolls, sesame rolls and whole-wheat sesame bread round out the menu. All muffins are sweetened with white grape juice, are low in fat and high in fiber.

Astro Family Restaurant

2300 Fletcher Dr. (323) 663-9241
Los Angeles, CA 90039

Breakfast 24 hours a day. Incredibly diverse crowd (from punks to families). Recently reupholstered booths don't take away from the original '60s diner feel. Laid back atmosphere. Greek style eggs fit for the gods to go gaga over.

Beverly Hills Hotel Coffee Shop

Beverly Hills Hotel, 9641 Sunset Blvd. (310) 276-2251
Beverly Hills, CA 90210

With a capacity of only 19 and known for its breakfasts (served all day), the competition for a stool at the counter is fierce, especially on the weekends. Alliances are formed and deals are sealed over waffles, pancakes, salads and sandwiches. Gossip as delicious as the food and famous faces as plentiful as the coffee.

Blueberry's

510 Santa Monica Blvd. (310) 394-7766
Santa Monica, CA 90401

Blueberry pancakes-what else? Also blueberry pies, scones, ice tea and lemonade. Try the blue special blueberry pancakes topped with blueberry ice cream and homemade blueberry compote.

Caffe Latte

6254 Wilshire Blvd. (323) 936-5213
Los Angeles, CA 90048

Tiny, homey neighborhood in-spot for over 10 years. Specializes in roasting high-quality, small-estate coffees from all over the world. The busy weekend crowds are queuing up for the Yucatan scramble or cappuccino pancakes.

Charlie's Coffee Shop

Farmers Market, 6333 W. Third St. (323) 933-0616
Los Angeles, CA 90036

Regulars come from all over to get their fix of Charlie's French toast. Thick slices melt in your mouth. Plus, there's all the atmosphere of historic Farmers' Market.

Clifton's

648 S. Broadway (213) 627-1673
Los Angeles, CA 90014

Since 1932, serving breakfast the old-fashioned way: hot cakes, oatmeal and chicken livers. Breakfast specials draw in young downtown loft dwellers. Eggs are served any way you like 'em or try a Mexican chorizo omelet. Odd decor includes redwoods and a waterfall.

Coffee Table

2930 Rowena Ave. (323) 644-8111
Los Angeles, CA 90039

Mondrian and mosaic decor, full of bright colors at this Silverlake cafe. Home-cooked meals from French toast to pot roast. Even the breakfast granola is made from scratch. Save space for an individual banana creme pie or tiramisu cheese cake.

Duke's Tropicana Coffee Shop

8909 Sunset Blvd. (310) 652-9411
West Hollywood, CA 90069 (310) 652-3100

The only place to go for breakfast after a night out on the town. Dine with equally hung over patrons on humongous portions of delicious morning grub. Rub elbows with a true cast of Hollywood characters. Many T.V. & movie stars.

Hollywood Hills Coffee Shop

6145 Franklin Ave. (323) 467-7678
Los Angeles, CA 90028
Breakfast: Mon - Sun, Lunch: Mon - Sun, Dinner: Mon - Sun
All Major Credit Cards, Reservations: No

Old-school coffee shop serving American fare with a California twist. Tile flooring leads to the bright red stooled counter. Choose the brick-walled dining room for more privacy. Servers make sure there's never an empty coffee cup. Breakfast all day, highlighted by specials such as cinnamon croissant French toast.

Hugo's

8401 Santa Monica Blvd. (323) 654-3993
West Hollywood, CA 90069 (323) 654-3994

A regular spot for industry insiders, both the well-known and the not-so-recognizable power players. Fresh-squeezed vegetable and fruit juices are the perfect accompaniment to breakfast pastas, pumpkin pancakes or "desauno fuerte" (a potato pancake with spinach, poached eggs and cheese). New tea and herb room offers 100 varieties, plus feng shui, free psychic readings and plug-ins for laptops.

Jinky's

14120 Ventura Blvd. (818) 981-2250
Sherman Oaks, CA 91423

Breakfast for late-risers served well into the afternoon every day. Sample the Southwestern specialties: Yucatan quesadilla, Santa Fe scramble eggs and gourmet chili (five flavors). Pancakes from scratch for the mild at heart.

John O'Groats

10516 Pico Blvd.   (310) 204-0692
Los Angeles, CA 90064
Breakfast: Mon - Sun, Lunch: Mon - Sun, Dinner: Wed - Sat
Visa/MC, Reservations: No

Family-friendly home style eatery with a touch of country charm. Scottish plaids and local art from nearby elementary schools adorn the walls. Ham is known to tip over the plate while mile-high pancakes are served in a pond of syrup. Feel free to linger under the impatient eyes of those who are waiting in the endless brunch line while you devour finger-lickin' fried chicken and fresh-from-the-oven buttermilk biscuits.

Kokomo Cafe

Farmers Market, 6333 W. Third St.   (323) 933-0773
Los Angeles, CA 90036

Crowds continue to wait in line during weekends at this Farmers' Market upstart. Maybe it's because of the huge stacks of plain or buckwheat pancakes with fresh strawberries or bananas baked right in. Eggs sardou straight out of N'Awlins are in constant demand as is the accompanying slabs of coffee cake.

Maxwell's Cafe

13329 Washington Blvd.   (310) 306-7829
Los Angeles, CA 90066
Mon - Sun 6am - 2pm
Web: www.maxwellscafe.net

Tiny storefront on an unassuming block of Washington serves up creative and delicious breakfasts, drawing in local Venetians. Surly waitresses are adored by all as they dish up "garbage omelets" stuffed with ham, avocado, tomato, onion, spinach, mushroom, cheese and topped with Spanish sauce. Turn of the century pics of Venice. Cater to both vegetarians and meat lovers alike.

Nate 'n Al's

414 N. Beverly Dr.   (310) 274-0101
Beverly Hills, CA 90210
Breakfast: Mon - Sun, Lunch: Mon - Sun, Dinner: Tue - Sun
All Major Credit Cards, Reservations: No

Lox and eggs don't get any better. The "phattest" brisket outside New York and the chicken soup is sure to cure what ails you. Expect long lines for weekend brunch.

The Newsroom

120 N. Robertson Blvd.   (310) 652-4444
Los Angeles, CA 90048
Breakfast: Mon - Sun, Lunch: Mon - Sun, Dinner: Mon - Sun
All Major Credit Cards, Reservations: No

Casual atmosphere with respectable magazine stand, TV news monitors and sunny patio. Eclectic, healthy menu with many vegetarian selections. Juices, smoothies, teas, coffees and cocktails. Gigantic pancakes with daily special fillings and soups served in giant hollowed-out bread shells.

The Original Pantry Cafe

877 S. Figueroa St.   (213) 972-9279
Los Angeles, CA 90017
Mon - Sun, 24 Hrs.

Since 1924, this landmark owned by Mayor Richard Riordan (who sold the air rights so no one will ever tear it down). Americana at its best: eggs, bacon, sausage, French toast and hot cakes.

Pann's Restaurant

6710 La Tijera Blvd.   (310) 670-1441
Los Angeles, CA 90045
Breakfast: Mon - Sun, Lunch: Mon - Sun, Dinner: Tue - Sun
All Major Credit Cards, Reservations: No

Restored to its original 1958 splendor, Pann's is a favorite among the churchgoing Sunday crowd. Waffles'n'wings and homemade meat loaf plopped alongside a pool of gravy tempts even the most abstinent vegetarian.

Rae's Restaurant

2901 Pico Blvd.   (310) 828-7937
Santa Monica, CA 90405
Breakfast: Mon - Sun, Lunch: Mon - Sun, Dinner: Mon - Sun
Cash Only, Reservations: No

People have been waking up over these bountiful breakfasts since 1958. Classic greasy spoon serving notable pancakes, egg combos and vegetable omelets. Dinners are satisfying with Rae's signature chicken fried steak and hefty pork chops.

S & W Country Diner

9748 Washington Blvd.   (310) 204-5136
Culver City, CA 90232
Breakfast: Mon - Sun, Lunch: Mon - Sun
Cash Only, Reservations: No

Two adjoining storefronts create a down-home diner serving everything from eggs Benedict to green chile enchiladas. Locals and Sony execs fill every mismatched chrome and wood chair, but feel free to tarry over a Sam's Special: hot chocolate with vanilla coffee topped with a dollop of whipped cream.

Snug Harbor

2323 Wilshire Blvd. (310) 828-2991
Santa Monica, CA 90403
Mon - Sun 6am - 3pm

Snuggle up to this adorable little '40s style diner with outside patio. "Stack Factory," offers a variety of pancakes (blueberry, chocolate and seven-grain). "Garage Seal" omelet is a veggie favorite filled with tofu, mushrooms, tomatoes, bell peppers and jack cheese.

Swingers

8020 Beverly Blvd. (323) 653-5858
Los Angeles, CA 90048
Mon 6am - 2am, Tue - Sun 6am - 4am
All Major Credit Cards, Reservations: No

A scene where being seen takes priority over the cuisine. Vinyl stools, booths and groovin' tunes from the CD jukebox. Just try to concentrate on the menu while a leggy waitress takes your order. The inexpensive breakfast burrito (black beans, eggs and cheese) is a popular dish. Burgers (including ostrich) are respectable and there's a surprisingly decent selection of veggie meals (tofu sauté). For dessert, polish off a brownie sundae and wash it down with either a "rocket shake" (chocolate shake blended with espresso beans) or a "swinger zinger" (coffee drink).

Urth Caffe

8565 Melrose Ave. (310) 659-0628
West Hollywood, CA 90069
Breakfast: Mon - Sun, Lunch: Mon - Sun, Dinner: Mon - Sun
All Major Credit Cards, Reservations: No

Known for organic coffee and the thickest soy lattes in town, Urth serves up complete breakfasts each morning and is open late into the evening. Owners Shallom and Jilla dote on every detail and want your stay to be among the most pleasurable experiences of your day. Fantastic tea selection with free advice on how to heal what's ailing you. Patio dining.

Ethnic & Gourmet Markets

Bay Cities Importing

1517 Lincoln Blvd. (310) 395-8279
Santa Monica, CA 90401
Mon - Sat 7am - 7pm, Sun 7am - 6pm

Behind their large glass display case is a wide selection of hot and cold Italian entrees, ranging from vegetarian lasagna to stuffed eggplant, served up by super efficient, super friendly counter clerks. Bay Cities features fresh made pasta, imported olive oil and hard to find wines. Small section of French and Middle Eastern products.

Beverly Hills Juice Club

8382 Beverly Blvd. (323) 655-8300
Los Angeles, CA 90048
Mon - Fri 8am - 6:30pm, Sat 10am - 6pm

The freshest, most delicious juices in town. Especially tasty is their apple/lemon/ginger concoction (single, double or triple). Try Bananamana, the ice cream alternative.

Bezjian's Grocery

4725 Santa Monica Blvd. (323) 663-1503
Los Angeles, CA 90029
Mon - Sat 11am - 7pm, Sun 11am - 5pm

Extensive selection of Middle Eastern and Indian groceries but their renowned specialty is sourdough bread (along with 31 other varieties) sold at some of the local farmers' markets.

Bharat Bazaar

11510 W. Washington Blvd. (310) 398-6766
Los Angeles, CA 90006
Wed - Mon 11am - 7pm

Whole spectrum of dals (lentils), rice, chutneys and imported Indian dried foods and ready-made sauces.

Caviarteria of California, Inc.

158 S. Beverly Dr. (310) 285-9773
Beverly Hills, CA 90212 (800) 287-9773
Mon - Sat 10am - 5:30pm

A miniature version of it's grownup New York sister store sells Caspian Sea caviar (salty sevruga, nutty-flavored osetra or the prized creamy beluga) and an assortment of American sturgeon, trout roe and salmon roe. Scottish smoked salmon to smoked boar available. Will ship anywhere in the US.

Delmarus Lox

9340 W. Pico Blvd.   (310) 273-3004
Los Angeles, CA 90035
Mon - Fri Noon - 6pm, Sat 9am - 6pm, Sun 9am - 3pm

Delicate smoked fish flown in daily from, where else? New York. Try the smoked sturgeon, which despite its name tastes incredibly like smoked turkey. Bargain prices for such high quality.

Elat Market

8730 W. Pico Blvd.   (310) 659-9253
Los Angeles, CA 90035
Mon - Sun 8am - 8pm

Middle Eastern market specializing in hard-to-find items, fresh challah and good grocery selection. Grains, beans, rice and spices. Impressive displays of whole fresh fish.

Gourmet Grub To Go

1627 Montana Ave.   (310) 451-2021
Santa Monica, CA 90403
Mon - Fri 9am - 5pm, Sat 10am - 5pm

Mainstays include turkey burgers, pastas, rice and vegetable dishes. Specials may include pot stickers, turkey meatloaf or chicken piccatta all prepared with no salt, little oil but plenty of flavor. Daily low fat specials.

India Sweet House

5992 W. Pico Blvd.   (323) 934-5193
Los Angeles, CA 90035
Mon - Sun 11am - 9pm

A no-frills, paper plate shop with authentic vegetarian Indian food at inexpensive prices. While snacking on an aloo paratha (flat bread stuffed with potato), you may hear store owner Jagdish's story of how he carefully transported his mother's dahi (yogurt) culture to America.

Owens Market

9769 W. Pico Blvd.   (310) 553-8181
Los Angeles, CA 90035
Mon - Sun 9am - 6pm

Known for their high quality cuts of beef, Owens can special order anything you need for your dinner party. Stocks everything from gourmet and ethnic foods to wines and spirits. Refrigerated delivery and house accounts available.

Santa Monica Seafood

1205 Colorado Ave.   (310) 393-5244
Santa Monica, CA 90404
Mon - Fri 9am - 8pm, Sat 9am - 7pm

In business for 60 years providing high quality fresh fish. Thirty different varieties of seafood offered daily along with tastings and cooking demos. Prepared entrees, including sushi, sandwiches and clam chowder for those too tired to cook. Don't forget to ask about their party platters.

Say Cheese

2800 Hyperion Ave.   (323) 665-0545
Los Angeles, CA 90027
Mon - Sun 8am - 6:30pm

Feeling continental? Head over and choose from more than 100 cheeses including farmhouse stilton, morbier or St. Agur. Creamy or stinky, whatever your pleasure. Full assortment of pastas, mustards and gourmet items. Cafe serves sandwiches made on La Brea Bakery bread.

Surfas

8825 National Blvd.   (310) 559-4770
Culver City, CA 90232
Mon - Fri 9am - 5:30pm, Sat 9am - 5pm

Mostly imported high end gourmet bargains. Unusual beans, imported French and Belgian chocolates, caviar, cheeses, oils and vinegars, smoked salmon, fresh pastas. Prices 1/3 below retail. Frozen fruit purées are a particular treat.

Farmers' Markets

Beverly Hills
200 N. Cañon Dr., At Wilshire Blvd.   (310) 285-2535
Beverly Hills, CA 90210

Sundays - 9am to 1pm

Burbank
Third St., At Orange Grove Ave.   (626) 308-0457
Burbank, CA 91501

Saturdays - 8am to 12:30pm

Costa Mesa
88 Fair Dr., At Orange County Fairgrounds   (714) 573-0374
Costa Mesa, CA 92626

Thursdays - 9am to 1pm

Culver City Farmer's Marker
9070 Venice Blvd, At Culver Blvd.   (310) 253-5775
Culver City, CA 90232

Tuesdays - 3pm to 7pm

Dana Point
Golden Lantern, At Dan Point Harbour Dr.   (714) 573-0374
Dana Point, CA 92629

Wednesday - 2pm to 7pm

Eagle Rock
Eagle Rock, At Colorado Blvd.   (818) 774-0755
Los Angeles, CA 90041
Fri 5pm - 9pm

Fridays - 5pm-9pm

Glendale
100 N. Brand Blvd., At Broadway   (626) 449-0179
Glendale, CA 91201

Thursdays - 9:30am to 1:30pm

Hermosa Beach
Valley Dr., At 10th Ave.   (310) 379-1488
Hermosa Beach, CA 90254

Fridays - noon to 4pm

Hollywood
Ivar St., At Hollywood Blvd.   (323) 936-8143
Hollywood, CA 90028

Sundays - 8:30am to 1pm

Huntington Beach
Fifth St., At Walnut Ave.   (714) 573-0374
Huntington Beach, CA 92605

Fridays - 2pm to sunset

Irvine
Bridge, At Campus   (714) 573-0374
Irvine, 92602

Saturdays - 9am to 1pm

Long Beach
North Promenade, At Broadway   (562) 433-3881
Long Beach, CA 90801

Fridays - 10am to 4pm

Long Beach
Norwalk Blvd.   (562) 433-3881
At El Dorado Shopping Center
Long Beach, CA 90801

Saturdays - 7:30am to 11:30am

Pasadena
363 E. Villa St., At Villa Park   (626) 449-0179
Pasadena, CA 91106

Tuesdays - 9:30am to 1:30pm

Pasadena
Sierra Madre Blvd., At E. Victory Park   (626) 449-0179
Pasadena, CA 91050

Saturdays - 8:30am to 12:30pm

Santa Monica
2640 Main St., At Ocean Park Blvd.   (310) 458-8712
Venice, CA 90291

Sundays - 9:30am to 1pm

Santa Monica
Third St., At Arizona Ave.   (310) 458-8712
Santa Monica, CA 90401

Wednesdays - 9am to 2pm

Santa Monica
Third St., At Arizona Ave.   (310) 458-8712
Santa Monica, CA 90401

Saturdays - 8:30am to 1pm

Santa Monica
Pico Blvd., At Cloverfield Blvd.   (310) 458-8712
Santa Monica, CA 90404

Saturdays - 8am to 1pm

Thousand Oaks
Wilbur Rd., At Thousand Oaks Blvd.   (805) 529-6266
Thousand Oaks, CA 91358

Thursdays - 3pm to 6:30pm

Torrance
2200 Crenshaw Blvd., At Wison Park   (310) 781-7520
Torrance, CA 90503

Tuesdays - 8am to 1pm
Saturdays - 8am to noon

Tustin
El Camino Real, At Third St.   (714) 573-0374
Tustin, CA 92780

Wednesday - 9am to 1pm

Venice
Venice Blvd., At Venice Way   (310) 399-6690
Venice, CA 90291

Fridays - 7am to 11am

Ventura
Main St., At Mills Rd.   (805) 529-6266
Ventura, CA 93001

Wednesdays - 10am to 1pm

Ventura
Santa Clara St., At Palms   (805) 529-6266
Ventura, CA 93001

Saturdays - 8:30pm to noon

Ventura
Valencia Blvd., At College of the Canyons   (805) 529-6266
Ventura, CA 93001

Sundays - 8:30pm to noon

West Hollywood
7377 Santa Monica Blvd.   (323) 848-6502
At Plummer Park
West Hollywood, CA 90069

Mondays - 9am to 2pm

Westwood
Weyburn Ave., At Westwood Blvd.   (310) 208-6115
Westwood, CA 96137

Thursdays - 2pm to 7pm

360° Restaurant & Lounge — American
6290 Sunset Blvd.   (323) 871-2995
Hollywood, CA 90028
Dinner: Mon - Sat
Web: www.360hollywood.com

This stylish penthouse restaurant & lounge offers a stunning panorama of the entire city, a selection of a solid new American cuisine, a comfortable lounge that features dancing to LA's hottest dee jays and live entertainment.

5 Dudley — Eclectic
5 Dudley Ct.   (310) 399-6678
Venice, CA 90291
Dinner: Tue - Sat
All Major Credit Cards, Reservations: Yes

Casual, small bistro that has captured the hearts and palates of local gourmands with its nouveau rustic cuisine. The open kitchen changes menus weekly and is not afraid to experiment. The chefs personally create each item from pasta to dessert. While there is a French influence, hints of Mexican, Thai and even Danish cooking are evident. Excellent wine choices.

Ago — Italian
8478 Melrose Ave.   (323) 655-6333
West Hollywood, CA 90069
Lunch: Mon - Fri, Dinner: Mon - Sun
All Major Credit Cards, Reservations: Yes

Two-level seating amidst modern architecture. Weekdays, power lunches dominate. Night crowds are elegant and sophisticated to match the cuisine. Raw artichoke salad with walnut and parmesan is a popular appetizer. Favorite entrees include bistecca alla fiorentina, T-bone steak cooked in a wood-burning oven or homemade ravioli. Extensive wine list.

Allegria — Italian
22821 Pacific Coast Hwy.   (310) 456-3132
Malibu, CA 90265
Lunch: Mon - Sun, Dinner: Mon - Sun
All Major Credit Cards, Reservations: Yes

From the folks that brought you Locanda Veneta, country-style Italian cooking with a Venetian slant. Romantic restaurant in hues of burgundy and gold with covered, heated outdoor patio. Casual elegant atmosphere invites you to dress up or down as you dine on Tuscan delights. Whole boneless chicken is grilled and roasted to perfection, served with an aged vinegar reduction. Or sample the Allegria pizza, one of their homemade thin-crusted pizzas, topped with wild mushrooms, roasted pine nuts and chopped grilled chicken. Crema di vaniglia is a must for dessert with vanilla creme in a luscious caramel sauce. Superb wine list with many Italian vintages to choose from.

Alto Palato — Italian
755 N. La Cienega Blvd.   (310) 657-9271
Los Angeles, CA 90038
Lunch: Fri, Dinner: Mon - Sun
All Major Credit Cards, Reservations: Yes

Upscale Italian in a comfortable room. Try a thin crusted pizza like the rucola e prosciutto but save room for the homemade gelato. Pleasant private party room.

Amazon Bar & Grill	**Caribbean**
14649 Ventura Blvd. (818) 986-7502
Sherman Oaks, CA 91423
Lunch: Mon - Sun, Dinner: Mon - Sun
Web: www.amazonbarandgrill.com
All Major Credit Cards, Reservations: Yes

Preserve the rain forest! A simulated jungle from floor to ceiling complete with a giant waterfall and shooting stars. Healthy Caribbean menu includes black salmon in a spicy West Indian pepper sauce, a satisfying blend of sweet and hot sensations. Wash it down with a micro brewed Ale-a-Gator. Happy Hour everyday from 4-7 and live entertainment Friday and Saturday.

Asia de Cuba	**Asian**
Mondrian Hotel, 8440 Sunset Blvd. (323) 848-6000
West Hollywood, CA 90069
Lunch: Mon - Sun, Dinner: Mon - Sun
All Major Credit Cards, Reservations: Yes

Serious mood lighting offsets the signature white design pervading this tony, after-dark experience atop LA. Named for its Asian and Latin-fused drinks and dishes, toast with a Rumba-Bumba over Lobster Mai-Tai and other entrees meant to be shared in this energizing atmosphere. Specialty cocktails, fresh sangria and sake exotica are as imaginative, fun and colorful as the food. Outdoor dining available.

Atlantic	**California/French**
8256 Beverly Blvd. (323) 951-1949
Los Angeles, CA 90048
Dinner: Mon - Sat
All Major Credit Cards, Reservations: Yes

Christopher Ciccone designed the interior which resembles a 30's/40's stlye New York restaurant and bar. The cuisine is cal/french specializing in steaks, seafood and lobster. Also chicken, vegetarian, salads and appetizers.

Aunt Kizzy's Back Porch	**Soul Food**
4325 Glencoe Ave. (310) 578-1005
Marina Del Rey, CA 90292
Lunch: Mon - Sun, Dinner: Mon - Sun, Brunch: Sun
Amex, Reservations: No

Massive amounts of finger lickin' Southern chow: mac'n'cheese, greens, and pork chops smothered with gravy. Sunday brunch packs a full house of athletes, college students and families. Photos and framed accolades by celebs make interesting reading during your wait.

Barney Greengrass	**Deli**

9570 Wilshire Blvd., 5th Fl.   (310) 777-5877
Beverly Hills, CA 90212
Breakfast: Mon - Sun, Lunch: Mon - Sun
All Major Credit Cards, Reservations: Yes

Unmistakably the best smoked fish in the city flown in daily fresh from New York. While the sturgeon is out of this world, an abundance of East-coast delicacies, including authentic bagels (chewy, with a tasty crust), are featured. Elegant rooftop dining indoors or on the shaded patio.

Bistro 45	**California**

45 S. Mentor Ave.   (626) 795-2478
Pasadena, CA 91106
Lunch: Tue - Fri, Dinner: Tue - Sun
Web: www.bistro45.com
All Major Credit Cards, Reservations: Yes

Housed in a 1935 Art Deco building, this California-French bistro features a seasonal menu designed by a team of five chefs (French, Japanese, American, Central and South American). Generous portions. Sashimi-grade ahi in a black and white sesame seed crust or double-cut Australian lamb chop are current favorites. 600 wines on an award-winning menu.

The Bistro Garden At Coldwater	**Continental**

12950 Ventura Blvd.   (818) 501-0202
Studio City, CA 91604
Lunch: Mon - Fri, Dinner: Mon - Sun
Web: www.bistrogarden.com
All Major Credit Cards, Reservations: Yes

A true continental dining experience within a sky lit room filled with power brokers. The gazebo-like interior replicates the feeling of being outside while dining indoors. During the day white sunlight floods the room, and at night, twinkly lights create a romantic and picturesque environment. Seasonal menu with fresh seafood and game entrees.

The Boathouse Restaurant & Beach Club	**Seafood**

301 Santa Monica Pier   (310) 393-6475
Santa Monica, CA 90401
Lunch: Mon - Sun, Dinner: Mon - Sun

Historical Santa Monica at its finest, this restaurant features great steaks and seafood, free live entertainment seven days a week and an unsurpassed view of the coast.

...a hip new place for a drink or a bite

on Restaurant Row

(debuting winter 2001 at Le Meridien at Beverly Hills)

𝒱isit PANGAEA Bistro

...where Hollywood meets Cannes

(featuring a photo exhibition of 50 years at the Cannes Film Festival)

Le Meridien at Beverly Hills

465 SOUTH LA CIENEGA BOULEVARD AT CLIFTON WAY, LOS ANGELES, CA 90048
TELEPHONE 310-247-0400
www.lemeridienbeverlyhills.com

Border Grill — Mexican
1445 Fourth St.   (310) 451-1655
Santa Monica, CA 90401
Lunch: Tue - Sun, Dinner: Mon - Sun
All Major Credit Cards, Reservations: Yes

Mary Sue Milliken and Susan Feniger have gained a reputation as the grand dames of California Mexican cuisine. Known for their green corn tamales, empanadas and panuchos (corn tortilla stuffed with black beans, chicken, pickled onion and avocado). The marinated skirt steak served with moros corn relish and flour tortillas is a mucho-requested favorite. Two story murals on brightly colored walls are just part of the lively atmosphere. Over 30 super-premium tequilas to select from.

Ca' Brea — Italian
346 S. La Brea Ave.   (323) 938-2863
Los Angeles, CA 90036
Lunch: Mon - Fri, Dinner: Mon - Sat
All Major Credit Cards, Reservations: Yes

Casually elegant country decor at this multi-floored eatery serving Northern Italian fare. Bigoletti all' aragosta e fruitti di mare is a popular pasta tossed with lobster, clams, and shrimp, but especially succulent is the whole boneless chicken infused with wine and spices. Adjourn with crema de vaniglia, a brulee-like custard drizzled with soft caramel sauce.

Ca' del Sole — Italian
4100 Cahuenga Blvd.   (818) 985-4669
North Hollywood, CA 91602   (818) 753-8889
Lunch: Mon - Fri, Dinner: Mon - Sun, Brunch: Sun
Web: www.cadelsole.com
All Major Credit Cards, Reservations: Yes

Experience the true ambience and décor of a Venetian country inn. With hand-picked ceramic art, Venetian masks and antique copper pots, this quaint restaurant offers traditional Venetian and Northern Italian cuisine at an outstanding value.

Cadillac Cafe — American
359 N. La Cienega Blvd.   (310) 657-6591
Los Angeles, CA 90048
Breakfast: Sat - Sun, Lunch: Mon - Sun, Dinner: Mon - Sun
Web: www.cadillaccafe.com
All Major Credit Cards, Reservations: Yes

Comfort food with a twist. Known for their home style meat loaf with blackened crust and garlic mashed potatoes and turkey sundaes in a bowl. Perhaps the only place in the city where you can order deviled eggs and a four cheese fondue (served with potato, green apple, French pickles and bread for dunking). No one leaves without sampling the milk-chocolate bread pudding. Full bar breakfasts on weekends.

● Cafe Noir — Mediterranean
At Le Meridien   (310) 246-2039
465 S. La Cienega Blvd.
Los Angeles, CA 90046
All Major Credit Cards, Reservations: Yes

The buzz is already strong for the newly opened Cafe Noir in Le Meridien at Beverly Hills. Destined to become one of the entertainment industry's hottest new "must-be-seen" places with its sexy decor, outstanding food and cocktails, Cafe Noir joins Le Meridien's Pangaea Bistro for Mediterranean cuisine at its best. It's where Hollywood meets Cannes.

Cafe Pranzo — Italian
8514 W. Third St.   (310) 652-7755
Los Angeles, CA 90048
Lunch: Mon - Fri, Dinner: Mon - Sun
All Major Credit Cards, Reservations: Yes

Casual trattoria noted for its penne arrabiatta and winner of the best vegetarian lasagna in town, filled with finely chopped crunchy vegetables and a béchamel sauce. As the weather turns cool, order the ossu bucco (veal shank).

Campanile — California
624 S. La Brea Ave.   (323) 938-1447
Los Angeles, CA 90036
Lunch: Mon - Fri, Dinner: Mon - Sat, Brunch: Sat - Sun
All Major Credit Cards, Reservations: Yes

Housed in Charlie Chaplin's former office space. A gorgeous bell tower facade (Campanile is Italian for bell-tower) sits above the building. Chef Mark Peel serves Californian rustic cuisine with Mediterranean flair. A signature dish is grilled prime rib with olive tapenade. Nancy Silverton, a James Beard pastry chef award winner, creates phenomenal desserts including pannacotta, a cooked cream Italian custard.

Capo — Italian
1810 Ocean Ave.   (310) 394-5550
Santa Monica, CA 90401
Dinner: Tue - Sat
All Major Credit Cards, Reservations: Yes

Rustic yet elegant Tuscan style bistro. All pastas are prepared in-house, the gnocchi patate is outstanding. Dry-aged prime N.Y. cut is prepared over an open hearth and served with an herb infused sauce. Candied bread pudding or a lemon filled cannoli completes any evening.

Cayo
American
39 S. El Molino Ave.   (626) 396-1800
Pasadena, CA 91107
Lunch: Fri, Dinner: Tue - Sat
Web: www.cayorestaurant.com
All Major Credit Cards, Reservations: Yes

Pasadena's dining scene got a lot brighter with the addition of chef/proprietor Claud Beltran's Cayo. He has been thrilling guests with his imaginative rethinking of classic cuisine executed with assurance, consistency and dazzling preparation at this elegant and comfortable restaurant. It's a place that strikes the right balance between serious gastronomy and fun.

Celestino Ristorante
Italian
141 S. Lake Ave.   (626) 795-4006
Pasadena, CA 91101
Lunch: Mon - Fri, Dinner: Mon - Sat
All Major Credit Cards, Reservations: Yes

Hearty rustic Italian cuisine served in an elegant homelike dining room with antique decor. Start with insalata primavera with grilled eggplant, roasted pepper and goat cheese. Capelli d'angelo, angel hair pasta with fresh tomato and basil is a top pick, as is the tortelloni stuffed with pumpkin in a cream and sage sauce. The dessert table reminds you to leave room for tiramisu.

The Century Supper Club
Supper Club
10131 Constellation Blvd.   (310) 553-6000
Los Angeles, CA 90067
Dinner: Fri - Sat
Web: www.centuryclub.com
All Major Credit Cards, Reservations: Yes

Sophisticated dining under soft lighting. Chef Caesar Dominguez's contemporary fare features lobster ravioli, jambalaya, chicken Provençal and grilled or sautéed Pacific salmon. Reservations highly recommended.

Chart House
American
231 Yacht Club Way   (310) 372-3464
Redondo Beach, CA 90277
Dinner: Mon - Sun
Web: www.chart-house.com
All Major Credit Cards, Reservations: Yes

A sumptuous feast from land and sea, where the steak and seafood specialties are as impressive as the ocean and sunset views from every seat in the house. This wonderfully casual dining experience has an imaginative menu of appetizers and entrees. Slow-roasted prime rib available in two cuts, steamed lobster tail with herb and citrus butter, sesame crusted salmon, and of course, New England clam chowder and coconut shrimp are among the many selections. Will open early to accommodate private parties on the facility's private stretch of beach with a menu plan to meet your requirements. (Also located at 18412 Pacific Coast Hwy., Malibu; 13950 Panay Way, Marina Del Rey.)

Chaya Brasserie
French-Japanese
8741 Alden Dr.   (310) 859-8833
Los Angeles, CA 90048
Lunch: Mon - Fri, Dinner: Mon - Sun
All Major Credit Cards, Reservations: Yes

The staff is outfitted in BCBG designs. Inside contemporary design mixes bamboo and Japanese prints with French bistro stylings. Chef Shigefumi Tachibe combines French and Japanese cooking to create rich yet subtle delights. Some of the best sushi in town and a special menu which changes weekly. Seafood dishes are a sure bet but the most requested entree is the sliced roasted venison with black peppercorns and chestnut puree. Exclusive wine list with hard-to-find favorites and superb quality.

Chi Dynasty
Chinese
2112 Hillhurst Ave.   (323) 667-3388
Los Angeles, CA 90027
Lunch: Mon - Sun, Dinner: Mon - Sun
Web: www.chidynasty.com
All Major Credit Cards, Reservations: Yes

Favorite spot among locals for Chinese chicken salad over the last twelve years. Try the orange crispy beef and garlic string beans. Traditional mandarin cuisine in a modern setting.

Chinois on Main — Eclectic

2709 Main St.   (310) 392-9025
Santa Monica, CA 90405
Lunch: Wed - Fri, Dinner: Mon - Sun
All Major Credit Cards, Reservations: Yes

Loud, noisy and fun. Wolfgang Puck's signature restaurant can seat guests at the chef's counter where you can watch them prepare whole sizzling catfish. Make sure you try the Chinois chicken salad. Go with a group and order family style.

● Cicada — Italian

617 S. Olive St.   (213) 488-9488
Los Angeles, CA 90014   (213) 488-9951
Lunch: Mon - Fri, Dinner: Mon - Sat,
All Major Credit Cards, Reservations: Yes

The experience begins as your car pulls up to the exquisite Art-Deco Oviatt building. A former men's haberdashery, the walls are lined with hundreds of dark wooden drawers. Majestic gold-leaf ceiling and mezzanine-style second floor contribute to the "Old Hollywood" ambiance. Start with seared tuna or fried calamari. Raviolis filled with portabello mushroom or spinach and ricotta gnocchis are favorite dishes. Choosing a wine from their award-winning list may prove difficult.

Cienega — New American

730 N. La Cienega Blvd.   (310) 358-8585
West Hollywood, CA 90069
Dinner: Tue - Sun
All Major Credit Cards, Reservations: Yes

Casual elegant dining in one of three main rooms or the picturesque courtyard which are also available for private functions. Chef Rainer Schwarz offers a special three-course tasting menu at bargain prices on Tuesdays. The regular menu features prime items and platters for two: cote de boeuf with portabello mushroom pan jus and fennel roasted whole fresh fish.

Ciudad — Latin

445 S. Figeroa St.   (213) 486-5171
Los Angeles, CA 90071
Lunch: Mon - Fri, Dinner: Mon - Sun
Web: www.ciudad-la.com
All Major Credit Cards, Reservations: Yes

Mary Sue Milliken and Susan Feniger's new downtown restaurant brings Latin cuisine with menus from South America, the Caribbean, Spain and Portugal. The atmosphere is light and colorful in tones of banana, avocado, mocha and spice to match the cuisine. Dishes vary from traditional home-cooking to contemporary creations based on authentic ingredients. The dessert menu is overwhelming with delightful cakes and pastries which are pure temptation as you enter the space. Lively "happy hour" runs daily from 3-7pm with overflowing rum drinks and "cuchifrito" (Spanish for little fried things) tapas-like snacks.

Clay Pit — Indian

145 S. Barrington Ave.   (310) 476-4700
West LA, CA 90049
Lunch: Mon - Sun, Dinner: Mon - Sun
All Major Credit Cards, Reservations: Yes

Brentwood locale serving traditional northern Indian cuisine. Tandoori dishes include baby rack of lamb and broiled pork chops. The sea bass is amongst the best in town. No ghee is used in any dishes and a multitude of curries are offered. Traditional Indian desserts and drinks.

Cowboy Sushi — Japanese

911 Broxton Ave.   (310) 208-7781
Los Angeles, CA 90024
Lunch: Mon - Sun, Dinner: Mon - Sun
All Major Credit Cards, Reservations: No

If sushi is the only thing worth eating, this is the only place worth going. All you can eat (hour time limit) when you sit at the bar and made to order by attentive chefs. Fresh, fabulous and exotic. House specialties include Dynamite and shrimp-asparagus handrolls. "Stuff" menu also included in one low lunch or dinner price.

Crustacean — French-Vietnamese

9646 Santa Monica Blvd.   (310) 205-8990
Beverly Hills, CA 90210
Lunch: Mon - Fri, Lunch: Mon - Sat
All Major Credit Cards, Reservations: Yes

One of the prettiest rooms in all of Beverly Hills with a walkway atop a 6,000 gallon sunken aquarium, sweeping draperies and a bi-level dining room with a zen-like feel despite the crowds anxious to dine on An's garlic noodles. Signature dishes feature colossal (really!) tiger prawns, assorted Dungeness crab dishes and roasted lobster in tamarind sauce. The bar features Asian martinis, Asian tapas and live music. Note: there is a strictly enforced dress code, but it only adds to the elegance of the entire experience.

Da Pasquale — Italian

9749 Santa Monica Blvd.   (310) 859-3884
Beverly Hills, CA 90210
Lunch: Mon - Fri, Dinner: Mon - Sat
All Major Credit Cards, Reservations: Yes

Hailed the preeminent cook in LA by her husband Pasquale, Ana Mora creates Napolitan cuisine. Pasquale himself bakes bread and pizzas from recipes handed down from his grandfather. The result, light and fluffy flavored with garlic and olive oil. Italian food for Italians cooked home-style and made-to-order. Try their spaghetti brimming with mussels and clams "the way mama made it."

Dal Rae
American

9023 E. Washington Blvd.   (562) 949-2444
Pico Rivera, CA 90660
Lunch: Mon - Fri, Dinner: Mon - Sun
All Major Credit Cards, Reservations: Yes

Blue collar types, from police chiefs to factory workers, take a load off in black leather booths dating back fifty years. Fancy food just like Ma used to make when Pa brought the boss home for dinner: pepper steak that's smooth as velvet smothered in onions, cherries jubilee and their famous Crab Louis.

Dominick's
American

8715 Beverly Blvd.   (310) 652-7272
Los Angeles, CA 90048
Dinner: Mon - Sat
All Major Credit Cards, Reservations: Yes

Dominick's has been around for the last 50 years or so. In its latest incarnation, Jon Sidel has stepped in to work his magic. Comfortable, traditional booth seating encompasses a small bar. Large outdoor patio. American faire features fresh seafood and excellent steaks.

Dr. Hogly Wogly's &
Tyler Texas BBQ
SoulFood

8136 N. Sepulveda Blvd.   (818) 782-2480
Los Angeles, CA 90045
Lunch: Mon - Sun, Dinner: Mon - Sun
All Major Credit Cards, Reservations: No

Authentic Texas-style BBQ served tender, juicy and hanging off the plate. Smoky dark decor. Beans, pie and sauce are sweet and plentiful. Expect to wait among fellow carnivores on the outside patio.

Drago
Italian

2628 Wilshire Blvd.   (310) 828-1585
Santa Monica, CA 90403
Lunch: Mon - Fri, Dinner: Mon - Sun
All Major Credit Cards, Reservations: Yes

Elegant yet relaxed. Signature Italian entrees include spaghetti al cartoccio cooked with seafood in foil, and ostrich breast with red cherries. Industry crowd, reservations recommended for lunch and dinner. Private rooms and wine cellar available.

Duke's Malibu
California

21150 Pacific Coast Hwy.   (310) 317-0777
Malibu, CA 90265
Lunch: Mon - Sun, Dinner: Mon - Sun, Brunch: Sat - Sun
All Major Credit Cards, Reservations: Yes

Offering spectacular ocean views, Duke's Malibu extends the spirit of aloha to all guests. Dine in the romantic main room or grab a casual meal and cocktail in LA's only "Barefoot Bar". Specializing in Pacific Rim preparations of Hawaiian fresh fish, crowds from all over So Cal flock to enjoy such favorites as Big Island pork ribs glazed with homemade mango BBQ sauce. Tuesday nights feature the best fish tacos around. Banquet and wrap party facilities.

El Cholo
Mexican

1025 Wilshire Blvd.   (310) 899-1106
Santa Monica, CA 90401
Lunch: Mon - Sun, Dinner: Mon - Sun
All Major Credit Cards, Reservations: No

A branch of the original restaurant on Western opened in 1927. This version is housed in a traditional hacienda-style building with beautiful pottery and greenery. From May-September, everyone shows up for the green corn tamales, an LA favorite for over 70 years. Private party rooms.

Electric Lotus
Indian

4656 Franklin Ave.   (323) 953-0040
Los Angeles, CA 90027
Lunch: Mon - Sun, Dinner: Mon - Sun
Web: www.electriclotus.com
All Major Credit Cards, Reservations: No

Located near ultra-cool Vermont, serving Indian village cuisine prepared in authentic spicy style. No dairy or ghee used. All dishes cooked with little or no olive oil. Sample their chana masala (the beans are cooked for at last 24 hours) or chicken curry with cashew nuts. Happening Sunday brunch buffet and live classical Indian music Friday and Saturday evenings.

Empress Pavilion — Chinese

988 N. Hill St.   (213) 617-9898
Los Angeles, CA 90012   (213) 626-1007
Lunch: Mon - Sun, Dinner: Mon - Sun
All Major Credit Cards, Reservations: Yes

Come and enjoy an authentic Cantonese dining experience featuring Hong Kong style seafood and an extensive selection of dim sum at Los Angeles' premier Chinese restaurant. Many dishes highlight live seafood and seasonal vegetables. Specialties of the Empress Pavilion include prawns with honey-glazed walnuts, Dungeness crab with garlic and flat noodles and mango pudding. Whether it is a small gathering in one of our intimate private rooms or a large group in our main dining room, our staff is at your service to assure you of a truly memorable experience.

Encounter — Eclectic

209 World Way   (310) 215-5151
Los Angeles, CA 90045
Lunch: Mon - Sun, Dinner: Mon - Sun
All Major Credit Cards, Reservations: Yes

Dome shaped and mysteriously hovering over the middle of LAX, this architectural marvel maintains a futuristic optimism evident in the decor and serves award-winning cuisine. "Groovy galactics" interested in "jet-set" dining. Enjoy a bird's eye view of the airport and its environs. Reservations suggested.

exIncendo — California

6282 Hollywood Blvd.   (323) 465-3257
Los Angeles, CA 90028
Breakfast: Mon - Sun, Lunch: Mon - Sun, Dinner: Tue - Sun
All Major Credit Cards, Reservations: No

Do lunch in the loft or dinner after the theatuh at this arty, New York style café where salads are big, fresh and creatively designed, the pizzas and calzones are unique and the sandwiches are so much more than two slices of bread and stuff in between. Interesting uses for eggplant, goat cheese and other exotics. Hand-rolled bread sticks, giant cookies and other treats are baked daily on the premises. Extensive breakfast menu, too. Admirers of the sunny pastel exIncendo ceramics upon which menu selections are presented may purchase them along with other lovely things at the adjoining shop.

Farfalla — Italian

143 N. La Brea Ave.   (323) 938-2504
Los Angeles, CA 90036
Lunch: Mon - Fri, Dinner: Mon - Sun
All Major Credit Cards, Reservations: Yes

Dine on thin-crusted pizza from their wood-burning oven. Live jazz and blues Wednesday through Friday. Casually elegant with shapes and colors of old world Mediterranean villas. Large portions of pasta served in handsome ceramic bowls. Bar F2 is a local gathering spot.

The Farm of Beverly Hills — American

439 N. Beverly Dr.   (310) 273-5578
Beverly Hills, CA 90210
Breakfast: Mon - Fri, Brunch: Sat - Sun, Lunch: Mon - Sun, Dinner: Mon - Sun
All Major Credit Cards, Reservations: Yes

Casual Nantucket-style eatery tucked in among the high-power designers of Beverly Hills. Meat is butchered onsite, all breads (even the hamburger buns) and desserts baked fresh daily and only the highest quality produce is used. Insiders demand the Cobb salad with applewood smoked bacon, but know to leave room for a killer brownie.

Fred's 62 — Eclectic

1850 N. Vermont Ave.   (323) 667-0062
Los Angeles, CA 90027
Breakfast: Mon - Sun, Lunch: Mon - Sun, Dinner: Mon - Sun
All Major Credit Cards, Reservations: No

Retro diner/noodle shop with decor and grub hip enough to lure the Eastside 24-7 crowd, but with a price range to fit anyone's budget. Food brought to you by Fred Eric the same creator of the famed VIDA. Try their Thai cobb salad, served with a spicy sesame dressing or their homemade apple crisp a la mode. What ever you are craving the folks at Fred 62 can satisfy it.

Grand Central Market

317 S. Broadway   (213) 624-2378
Los Angeles, CA 90013
Mon - Sat 9am - 6pm, Sun 10am - 6pm

This downtown open-air market carries everything from Mexican to Chinese and anything in-between. Hot entrees and patio seating make shopping a little easier. Forty different vendors with all the fresh produce, meats and fish you need.

Granita   Seafood

23725 W. Malibu Rd.   (310) 456-0488
Malibu, CA 90265
Dinner: Mon - Sun, Brunch: Sat - Sun
All Major Credit Cards, Reservations: Yes

Soft lighting, textured glass, custom-glazed tiles in organic shapes and an outdoor koi pond lend an aquatic feel of Barbara Lazaroff's meticulously designed space. Chef Jennifer Naylor's seasonal menus feature fresh seafood from the Pacific Northwest, New England and France. Pastry chef Darcy Tizio creates irresistible desserts. Trademark granitas (Italian ice) provide limitless possibilities like pomegranate, blood orange, and espresso.

Guelaguetza   Mexican

11127 Palms Blvd.   (310) 837-1153
Los Angeles, CA 90034
Breakfast: Mon - Sun, Lunch: Mon - Sun, Lunch: Mon - Sun
All Major Credit Cards, Reservations: No

Mole (chocolate chile sauce) is to Oaxacan cooking what gravy is to Southern cuisine. Fortunately, Guelaguetza lavishes in this tradition; yellow mole filled empanadas and chicken entrees doused with mole negro, will elate your taste buds. Cantaloupe colored walls and serape covered tables make for a festive dining experience. The horchata with cactus fruit puree and chopped pecan topping is a must.

Gumbo Pot at the Original Farmers Market   Cajun

6333 W. Third St.   (323) 933-0358
Los Angeles, CA 90038
Breakfast: Mon - Sun, Lunch: Mon - Sun, Dinner: Mon - Sun
Visa/MC, Reservations: No

Charles Myer's original New Orleans stand remains a local favorite, serving up dishes made from fresh and imaginative ingredients. Order a bowl of gumbo, po'boy or muffelatta with sweet potato salad or try a plate of crayfish. Mardi Gras is an annual fête celebrated with live N'Awlins-style music.

Hal's Bar & Grill   American

1349 Abbot Kinney Blvd.   (310) 396-3105
Venice, CA 90291
Brunch: Sat - Sun, Lunch: Mon - Sun, Dinner: Mon - Sun
All Major Credit Cards, Reservations: Yes

For eleven years, this bar and grill has served the industry and neighborhood locals alike. Cool art, notable margaritas and a famed Caesar salad. Menu changes weekly. Private dining room upstairs. Live jazz Sunday and Monday nights.

Hirozen Gourmet   Japanese

8385 Beverly Blvd.   (323) 653-0470
Los Angeles, CA 90048
Lunch: Mon - Sat, Dinner: Mon - Sat
All Major Credit Cards, Reservations: No

Always a line at this Japanese eatery. Order from the daily specials menu (seaweed or salmon skin salad, Chilean sea bass, rock cod). Supreme sushi. Friendly and knowledgeable waitresses will help you select.

Home   American

1760 Hillhurst Ave.   (323) 669-0211
Los Angeles, CA 90027
Breakfast: Mon - Sun, Lunch: Mon - Sun, Dinner: Mon - Sun
All Major Credit Cards, Reservations: No

Come back home where cooking is as American as their apple pie. Housed in a two-story "home" with white stone and green trim. Dine in the living room, den, kitchen or, of course, the dining room. Large front yard stone patio invites diners to enjoy the canopy of two ancient oak trees.

Hugo Molina   California

1065 E. Green St.   (626) 449-7820
Pasadena, CA 91106
Lunch: Mon - Fri, Dinner: Mon - Sun
All Major Credit Cards, Reservations: Yes

Chef Hugo Molina blends California cuisine with Caribbean and Latin flavors. Atmosphere is casual and open, airy interior with blonde woodwork, soft colors and lots of flowers. Crab cakes ladled with lobster lemon grass cream are a good choice as is the African pheasant or the grilled lamb chops. Don't leave without sampling their decadent chocolate tower.

The Hump   Japanese

3221 Donald Douglas Loop South   (310) 313-0977
Third Floor, Santa Monica, CA 90405
Lunch: Mon - Fri, Dinner: Mon - Sun
All Major Credit Cards, Reservations: Yes

Named for the Himalayans over which pilots flew in the '30s, this intriguing sushi bar is exotically themed with a WWII ambiance that harkens back to the mystery and allure of Casablanca. An 800-ft observation deck and nearby beacon add to this unique dining experience. Not the least of it is the sushi itself; sit at the bar and watch as the best of the West Coast plus Tokyo imports become works of edible art in the skilled hands of chef-artistes.

I Cugini   Italian
1501 Ocean Ave.   (310) 451-4595
Santa Monica, CA 90401
Lunch: Mon - Sun, Dinner: Mon - Sun
All Major Credit Cards, Reservations: Yes

A dreamy ocean view from their main patio. Choose between fresh Italian seafood served whole or very thin-crusted pizza baked in their wood-burning oven. Rustic murals in warm earth tones and natural wood offer an unpretentious environment. Don't forget to order a fresh baked cookie or biscotti.

Indo Cafe   Indonesian
10428 1/2 National Blvd.   (310) 815-1290
Los Angeles, CA 90034
Lunch: Tue - Sun, Dinner: Tue - Sun
All Major Credit Cards, Reservations: No

Small casual Indonesian cafe. Chicken saté (skewered seasoned chicken), spiced coconut beef or the Indonesian staple gado-gado salad with peanut sauce in generous portions. Traditional Rijstafel (nine course meal) served once a week.

Jiraffe   California
502 Santa Monica Blvd.   (310) 917-6671
Santa Monica, CA 90401
Lunch: Tue - Fri, Dinner: Tue - Sun
Web: www.jirafferestaurant.com
All Major Credit Cards, Reservations: Yes

Mix a French bistro with rustic American cuisine, add down-to-earth service and you've got Jiraffe. An established favorite among locals. Tasting menu changes monthly. Bright and airy ambiance with a quiet loft upstairs.

Jitlada   Thai
5233 Sunset Blvd.   (323) 667-9809
Los Angeles, CA 90027
Lunch: Tue - Sun, Dinner: Tue - Sun
All Major Credit Cards, Reservations: Yes

There's about a zillion little Thai restaurants on the stretches of Sunset and Hollywood east of Vine all the way down to Vermont. And most of them are great. Jitlada has become somewhat of an established favorite serving their notorious whole catfish and a multitude of spicy (hot, hot, hot!) dishes. If you find yourself unable to breathe, reach for a cooling Thai iced coffee instead of water--instant refreshment!

Joan's On Third
8350 W. Third St.   (323) 655-2285
Los Angeles, CA 90048
Lunch: Mon - Sun, Dinner: Mon - Sun

A gourmet marketplace offering both prepared and specially selected packaged foods. Divine desserts (decadent brownies, cappuccino nut torte, lemony lemon bars), imported cheeses and salami, sandwiches, salads and baked goods. Prepared entrees include pesto crusted salmon, grilled maple rosemary chicken and more.

Jones Hollywood   American
7205 Santa Monica Blvd.   (323) 850-1726
West Hollywood, CA 90046   (323) 850-1727
Dinner: Mon - Sun, Lunch: Mon - Fri
All Major Credit Cards, Reservations: Yes

Match the black'n'white rock'n'roll photos on the wall to the rock'n'rollers dressed in black and white dining at the tables, gazing adoringly at 144 bottles of Jack Daniels above the bar. Nouveau comfort food, grilled N.Y. steak and fish finished with good ol' apple pie for dessert.

Jozu   California
8360 Melrose Ave.   (323) 655-5600
West Hollywood, CA 90069
Dinner: Mon - Sun
All Major Credit Cards, Reservations: Yes

Subtle, elegant and cozy with attentive service at this California-Pacific dining room. Aficionados can choose from 12 different sakes, but the owner is known to have special sakes on hand. Start with tempura squash blossoms and progress to roast Chilean sea bass.

Kass Bah   California
9010 Melrose Ave.   (310) 274-7664
West Hollywood, CA 90069
Lunch: Mon - Fri, Dinner: Mon - Sat
All Major Credit Cards, Reservations: Yes

"This could be the beginning of a beautiful friendship," dining at this upscale eatery and tribute to Rick's Place. Skylights, wood paneling and a private Moroccan room plumped with pillows. Tuna tartare with soy ginger vinaigrette or a filet mignon with garlic mashed potatoes are sure bets.

Kokekokko — Japanese

3560 E. Second St.
Los Angeles, CA 90012
(213) 687-0690
Dinner: Mon - Sat
All Major Credit Cards, Reservations: No

Yakitori (chicken on skewers) is the main course at Kokekokko (Japanese for "cock-a-doodle-doo"), hence the name. Arguably the best chicken in town-what a sushi bar is to fish, this place is to chicken. As you enter, one of the friendly waiters will inform you that they ONLY serve chicken. Order the combo plate, big enough for two.

L'Arancino Cucina Siciliana — Italian

8908 Beverly Blvd.
Los Angeles, CA 90048
(310) 858-5777
Dinner: Mon - Sun
All Major Credit Cards, Reservations: Yes

Massive skylights, butterscotch marble, olive booths and white-walled paneling create a light drenched, airy space. At night mahogany trimmed walls, low lighting and candlelit tables spawn a warm and inviting golden hue over the restaurant. Outdoor patio is complete with banana trees. Creative twists on classic Sicilian favorites such as roasted rabbit in sweet and sour sauce and spaghetti all bottarga with dried cured tuna roe.

La Luz del Dia — Mexican

W-1 Olvera St.
Los Angeles, CA 90012
(213) 628-7495
Lunch: Tue - Sun, Dinner: Tue - Sun
Cash Only, Reservations: No

On the corner of Olvera Street, a refuge from downtown's urban chaos. Corn tortillas are hand-patted and carnitas (shredded pork) are tender and flavorful. During the holidays the place is packed with families filling their plastic trays with traditional sweet tamales and warm champurrado (a thick corn based chocolate beverage.)

Legal Grind, Inc.
Coffee & Counsel — Bagels, Coffee & Desserts

2640 Lincoln Blvd.
Santa Monica, CA 90405
(310) 452-8160
(818) 788-8058
Breakfast: Mon - Sun, Lunch: Mon - Sat
Web: www.legalgrind.com
All Major Credit Cards, Reservations: No

Sip a steaming "Cafe Law-te" as your appointed lawyer offers advice ($20 consultation fee). Saturday morning features a legal trust expert, and Wednesday evening is family law. Self-help reading material including child custody guidelines, copyright issues and how to fight traffic tickets. Document preparation with low flat fees. California State Bar certified. Redwood deck and ivy-covered lattice make this meeting space a relaxed alternative to the sometimes stuffy law office. (Also at The Coffee Junction in Tarzana, 19221 Ventura Blvd.)

Les Deux Cafes — French

1638 N. Las Palmas Ave.
Hollywood, CA 90028
(323) 465-0509
Lunch: Mon - Fri, Dinner: Mon - Sun
All Major Credit Cards, Reservations: Yes

One of the hardest restaurants to crash. Organic French fare featuring a seasonal menu with daily specials including fish, beef, poultry, fresh produce, house made desserts and pasta dishes. Lush gardens surround the 1904 Hollywood bungalow. Cabaret frequently hosts unannounced musical performances.

The Lobster — American

1602 Ocean Ave.
Santa Monica, CA 90401
(310) 458-9294
Lunch: Mon - Sun, Dinner: Mon - Sun
Web: www.thelobster.com
All Major Credit Cards, Reservations: Yes

Housed in the famous historical landmark site as the original Lobster of 1923, the newer version offers expanded seating, elegant regional American seafood and VIEWS. Casual atmosphere (abide by the old adage "shoes and shirt must be worn") specializing in Maine Lobster and tempting seafood entrees like Jumbo Lump Crabcakes or halibut with lobster and Sauce Americaine. Steak and poultry served.

Locanda Veneta — Italian

8638 W. Third St.
Los Angeles, CA 90048
(310) 274-1893
Lunch: Mon - Fri, Dinner: Mon - Sat
All Major Credit Cards, Reservations: Yes

Chef Masimo Ormani keeps the celebrity crowds coming back with gratifying favorites and seasonal specialties. Chicken and duck dumplings sautéed with onion confit marmalade is a welcome appetizer. Sample the Spaghetti with lentils, roasted tomatoes and spinach or their signature whole, boneless, free-range chicken grilled with balsamic vinegar sauce and guaranteed to melt in your mouth. End with an elegant pear tart in caramel sauce. The atmosphere is straight out of Venice, sundown tones reminiscent of antique frescoes-entirely romantic.

Lucques — California-French

8474 Melrose Ave. (323) 655-6277
West Hollywood, CA 90069
Dinner: Tue - Sun
All Major Credit Cards, Reservations: Yes

Chef Suzanne Goin has lured the crowds in with her French based cuisine highlighted by Mediterranean and California influences. The menu changes every six to eight weeks to reflect the freshest and finest the seasons have to offer as does the Sunday night prix-fixe dinner which restyles weekly. The warm room is highlighted by a working fireplace and pretty terrace. Small boutique wineries round out the wine list.

Maison Akira — French-Japanese

713 E. Green St. (626) 796-9501
Pasadena, CA 91101
Lunch: Tue - Fri, Dinner: Tue - Sun
All Major Credit Cards, Reservations: Yes

French trained Japanese chef Akira Hirose has created a menu of nouvelle cuisine that is light, precise and fine. The restaurant is formal yet cozy, French with a touch of Japanese in the good luck yen coins found throughout the space. Begin with sashimi with wasabi caviar. Signature dishes include Chilean sea bass marinated in miso with vegetables Provençal and quail stuffed with foie gras and dried fruit. Nothing equals the flourless chocolate cake for dessert.

McCormick & Schmick's — Seafood

2 Rodeo Dr. (310) 859-0434
Beverly Hills, CA 90210
Lunch: Mon - Sun, Dinner: Mon - Sun

This fish house offers the widest assortment of the freshest seafood available in Southern California. More than 35 varieties of fish, shellfish and oysters are brought in daily from around the world. Located in the Italian renaissance style piazza known as Two Rodeo, McCormick & Schmick's is perfect for an intimate dinner or large event.

Mélisse — New American

1104 Wilshire Blvd. (310) 395-0881
Santa Monica, CA 90401
Lunch: Wed - Fri, Dinner: Mon - Sun
Web: www.melisse.com
All Major Credit Cards, Reservations: Yes

Timeless European-styled restaurant with antique sofas and fireplaces. The garden room has a retractable skylight and bubbling fountain. Chef Josiah Citrin uses only the freshest ingredients and the menu changes daily. There are three different prixe-fixe menus ranging from a vegetarian's delight to a nine-course feast with slow roasted meats carved tableside. The wine list is predominantly Californian and French.

Mexico City — Mexican

2121 Hillhurst Ave. (323) 661-7227
Los Angeles, CA 90027
Lunch: Wed - Sun, Dinner: Mon - Sun
All Major Credit Cards, Reservations: Yes

'50s Naugahyde decor where Los Feliz locals chow down on simple yet flavorful Mexican cuisine. Mole (chocolate/chili sauce) like only a Mexican mother could make and salsas that'll have you speaking Spanish after the first bite.

Michael's — California

1147 Third St. (310) 451-0843
Santa Monica, CA 90403
Lunch: Tue - Fri, Dinner: Tue - Sat
All Major Credit Cards, Reservations: Yes

Elegantly casual atmosphere with art-adorned interior dining room and enchanting outdoor garden. Innovative California cuisine utilizing the freshest ingredients. Favorite entrees include filet of Mediterranean dorade with cipollini onion caponata or Sonoma duck prosciutto salad with Ligurian olive vinaigrette. Award winning wine list with 450 selections. Three private rooms accommodate 10-40 guests.

Mimosa — French

8009 Beverly Blvd. (323) 655-8895
Los Angeles, CA 90048
Lunch: Mon - Fri, Dinner: Mon - Sat
All Major Credit Cards, Reservations: Yes

Simple storefront bistro serving regional French cuisine in a celebrity filled setting. After 9pm, the clientele changes to young upwardly mobile Angelenos; their coteboeuf (a hefty two pound prime rib steak) and the seafood bouillabaisse remain popular and hearty.

Mirabelle — American

8768 Sunset Blvd. (310) 659-6022
West Hollywood, CA 90069
Breakfast: Mon - Sun, Lunch: Mon - Sun, Dinner: Mon - Sun
All Major Credit Cards, Reservations: Yes

Sunset Strip staple serves contemporary American fare including thick-cut swordfish with lime chardonnay and dry-aged prime New York steak. Wednesday lunch special, chicken meatballs over angel hair pasta, attracts the crowds. Distinct patio bar is fashioned from hammered copper and wood pillars. Dinner served till 1:30am.

Mistral   French
13422 Ventura Blvd.   (818) 981-6650
Studio City, CA 91604
Lunch: Mon - Fri, Dinner: Mon - Sat
All Major Credit Cards, Reservations: Yes

This French bistro bakes a remarkable soufflé and dishes up luscious mussels along with other seafood specials. Tuna and steak tartare as well as the authentic onion soup are local favorites. Interior design features wood-paneled walls, chandeliers and a San Francisco bar circa 1920. Large wine list from Napa Valley and the Central Coast.

Miyagi's   Japanese
8225 Sunset Blvd.   (323) 650-3524
West Hollywood, CA 90069
Dinner: Mon - Sun
All Major Credit Cards, Reservations: Yes

Former Roxbury location turned mega rockin' sushi house. Three levels of seven different sushi bars and five liquor bars. Indoor and outdoor dining surrounded by several cascading waterfalls and Japanese gardens. Vast cityscapes viewed from the third floor. Big screen televisions kick out the latest music videos.

Mulberry St.   Italian
347 N. Cañon Dr.   (310) 247-8998
Beverly Hills, CA 90210
Lunch: Mon - Sun, Dinner: Mon - Sun
Visa/MC, Reservations: No

Cathy Moriarity's N.Y. style pizza available by the pie or by the slice. Crunchy thin crust with the right amount of gooey mozzarella. Out of this world cheeseless, vegetarian pizzas. (Also at 240 S. Beverly Dr. in Beverly Hills, and at 17040 Ventura Blvd. in Encino.)

Musso & Frank Grill   Continental
6667 Hollywood Blvd.   (323) 467-7788
Hollywood, CA 90028
Breakfast: Tue - Sat, Lunch: Tue - Sat, Dinner: Tue - Sat
All Major Credit Cards, Reservations: Yes

Thursday's chicken pot pie is excellent at this retro Hollywood institution. For breakfast try the flannel cakes, large thin pancakes served till 3pm. At the counter, watch Manny dazzle the crowd with his magic tricks. Cocktail hour offers the best martinis in town, served in a glass decanter packed on ice and delivering quite a punch.

Netty's   California
1700 Silverlake Blvd.   (323) 662-8655
Los Angeles, CA 90026
Lunch: Mon - Sat, Dinner: Mon - Sat
Visa/MC, Reservations: No

California cuisine with daily specials like fresh tuna, flank steak or roasted bell pepper with smoked mozzarella sandwiches. All pasta comes with to-die-for pesto bread and green salad. Dine on the patio or call ahead to have your order ready for take out.

Off Vine   California
6263 Leland Way   (323) 962-1900
Hollywood, CA 90028
Lunch: Mon - Fri, Dinner: Mon - Sun, Brunch: Sun -
All Major Credit Cards, Reservations: Yes

Fresh California cuisine served in a lovely turn-of-the-century cottage with a garden setting tucked away from the core of Hollywood. Popular for pre and post-theatre dining. Chocolate or Grand Marnier soufflé is almost obligatory, but one portion is plenty for two.

Pastis   French
8114 Beverly Blvd.   (323) 655-8822
Los Angeles, CA 90048
Dinner: Mon - Sun
All Major Credit Cards, Reservations: Yes

Named for an aperitif served in the South of France and true to its name, Provençal cooking is brought to the fore. Using little or no dairy, the menu changes seasonally. Bouillabaisse is a favorite choice, but make sure to sample their signature dessert: lavender creme brulée. Lovely room with antique armoires and Moroccan lanterns. Small, comfortable outdoor patio.

Philippe The Original   American
1001 N. Alameda St.   (213) 628-3781
Los Angeles, CA 90012
Breakfast: Mon - Sun, Lunch: Mon - Sun, Dinner: Mon - Sun
Cash Only, Reservations: No

The oldest restaurant in Los Angeles just celebrated its 90th birthday. Looking very much the way it did 90 years ago with sawdust on the floors and simple seating arrangements. Wooden phone booths line one wall. Known for their French Dip which was invented by accident when a waiter dropped a sandwich in meat drippings. Equally popular are their pickled eggs and pickled pig feet. Ample selection of seasonal fruit pies tops off a great meal.

Posto   Italian
14928 Ventura Blvd.   (818) 784-4400
Sherman Oaks, CA 91403
Lunch: Tue - Fri, Dinner: Mon - Sat
All Major Credit Cards, Reservations: Yes

The best contemporary Italian cuisine in Sherman Oaks, hands down. Extraordinary pasta inventions, such as open ravioli stuffed with quail smothered in a creme and black truffle sauce; and homemade spinach spaghetti with wild mushrooms. Earthy interior tones and soft lighting provided by the legion of candles lend to a warm atmosphere where appropriate attire ranges from a suit and tie to jeans.

R23   Japanese
923 E. 2nd St. #109   (213) 687-7178
Los Angeles, CA 90013
Lunch: Mon - Fri, Dinner: Mon - Sat
All Major Credit Cards, Reservations: Yes

A little Tribeca, a little Soho, a lot of fresh sushi served on 4 ft. long marble slabs and an unexpectedly modern take on other Japanese delicacies like steamed salmon cakes and crab casserole. Exposed brick, industrial windows and a loft-high ceiling add to the NYC vibe of this intimate establishment that was part of a manufacturing complex in a past life. Reservations are the only thing that will get you a table where you'll sit on a surprisingly durable cardboard chair.

The Raymond Restaurant   American
1250 S. Fair Oaks Ave.   (626) 441-3136
Pasadena, CA 91105
Lunch: Tue - Fri, Dinner: Tue - Sun, Brunch: Sat - Sun
All Major Credit Cards, Reservations: Yes

American cuisine served in a romantic historic bungalow with three patios. Raymond Curry (chicken, lamb or beef) is a Pasadena luncheon staple. Prix-fixe menus Tuesday through Thursday and Sundays. Splendid weekend brunch.

Real Food Daily   Vegetarian
414 N. La Cienega Blvd.   (310) 289-9910
Los Angeles, CA 90048   (310) 451-7544
Lunch: Mon - Sun, Dinner: Mon - Sun
All Major Credit Cards, Reservations: No

Clean whole foods cuisine served in a stylish, comfortable, natural ambiance. LA's only vegan restaurant raises the standards of vegetarian cooking using certified organic produce. Organic wine, beer and coffee. Full menu and excellent daily specials which use the freshest seasonal ingredients. To-Go, delivery & catering available. Call or check the website for daily specials. (Original location at 514 Santa Monica Blvd., SM).

Rebecca's Santa Monica   Mexican
101 Broadway   (310) 260-1100
Santa Monica, CA 90401
Lunch: Mon - Sun, Dinner: Mon - Sun, Brunch: Sat - Sun
All Major Credit Cards, Reservations: Yes

Imagine sitting on the patio with an ocean view and a giant wraparound bar stocked with 200 tequillas-it's all here! Rebecca's newest Santa Monica locale serves up signature lobster enchiladas and duck relleno, not to mention oversized shrimp and papaya salads, but make sure you splurge on the mocha flan before heading back to the bar for a nightcap with the hordes of margarita fans. Private parties-no problem, bring your favorite bachelorette for an evening to remember.

Röck   Eclectic
13455 Maxella Ave., #102   (310) 822-8979
Marina Del Rey, CA 90292
Lunch: Mon - Fri, Dinner: Mon - Sun
Web: www.rockenwagner.com
All Major Credit Cards, Reservations: Yes

Eclectic menu amidst Modern comfort. Dine at the counter fashioned from recycled detergent bottles or below one of the futurist plastic ball fixtures. Small dishes are served like dim sum, choose one or all. Innovative salads and entrees. The calamari ciabatta comes with white anchovies or go all out with their famed veal schnitzel (with fries, of course). Seafood paella is served family-style. Bring a friend and an appetite.

Saddle Peak Lodge   American
419 Cold Canyon Rd.   (310) 456-7325
Calabasas, CA 91302
Dinner: Wed - Sun, Brunch: Sun
All Major Credit Cards, Reservations: Yes

Continental cuisine served high above Malibu in a lodge with intimate dining rooms, fireplaces, gardens and views. Unusual menu features medallions of venison, arries ranch ostrich and other gamely delights. Romantic Sunday brunch.

Sagebrush Cantina   American
23527 Calabassas Rd.   (818) 222-6062
Calabasas, CA 91302
Lunch: Mon - Sun, Dinner: Mon - Sun, Brunch: Sun -
All Major Credit Cards, Reservations: No

Rockin' cantina with enormous outdoor dining area surrounded by plants, lights and the owner's collection of circus banners. Sawdust covered wooden planks offer a casual and very social atmosphere. Try Cajun tacos or fresh Maine lobster. Live music nightly (usually classic rock cover bands!). Divine Sunday brunch serves everything from caviar and crab legs to champagne and vodka shots. Summer Sunday afternoons are biker days.

Skewers — Eclectic

8939 Santa Monica Blvd.
W. Hollywood, CA 90069
(310) 271-0555
Lunch: Mon - Sun, Dinner: Mon - Sun
All Major Credit Cards, Reservations: Yes

Down to earth eclectic restaurant specializing in a wide range of grilled skewers such as teriyaki, Thai, Mediterranean and many other kinds of chicken, as well as swordfish, salmon, Cajun shrimp, filet mignon and lamb. Impressive selection of appetizers and salads. One-of-a-kind hummus bar accentuates meals. Delivery and catering available. (Also at 617 S. Central Ave., Downtown.)

Solstice — California-French

7313 Beverly Blvd.
Los Angeles, CA 90036
(323) 525-0405
Dinner: Tue - Sun
All Major Credit Cards, Reservations: Yes

Hugo Veltman, formerly of Patina, has brought French-California cuisine to this cozy spot decorated in warm blues and yellows right down to the bud vases on the tables. While the menu changes seasonally, his signature potato crusted whitefish in a mild curry, and crispy duck breast in a caramel sauce have already made their mark. Even the divine desserts like ice cream and sorbet are made by hand.

Spago Hollywood — California

1114 Horn Ave.
West Hollywood, CA 90069
(310) 652-4025
Dinner: Tue - Sun
All Major Credit Cards, Reservations: Yes

Featuring Wolfgang Puck's interpretations of California cuisine, including fresh fish, trademark pizza and unusual items brought in from local farms. All pastas, desserts and breads made on the premises. Casual chic interior is complemented by a revolving contemporary art display, housing pieces by Jim Dine, Andy Warhol and Tony Curtis. The front of the restaurant overlooks the LA Basin, while the rear houses a lushly landscaped atrium.

The Standard — New American

8300 Sunset Blvd.
W. Hollywood, CA 90069
(323) 650-9090
Breakfast: Mon - Sun, Lunch: Mon - Sun, Dinner: Mon - Sun
Web: www.standardhotel.com
All Major Credit Cards, Reservations: Yes

Few hotels serve food 24/7 but here you can eat where you sleep without watching the clock. Menu features extra breakfast items. Make the scene in the restaurant after hours or make your own behind closed doors. Either way, modern comfort food like raw ahi tuna pizza with wasabi and daikon and steak frites with red wine mushroom sauce will quell that ravenous 4am appetite. But your name doesn't have to be in the guest registry to grab a table and scarf a killer Hollywood chopped salad with blue cheese or have an 'O' over a coffee cup creme brulee or traditional bana split.

Stevie Joe's Lounge & Supper Club — American

10433 National Blvd.
Los Angeles, CA 90034
(310) 837-5245
(310) 837-5232
Lunch: Mon - Fri, Dinner: Tue - Sun
Web: www.steviejoes.com
All Major Credit Cards, Reservations: Yes

"Spy Chic" supper club reminiscent of the early '60s, filled with dark velvets, leopard prints and plush leather booths. Martinis are de rigeur at the 30 foot bar, which attracts industry regulars to their hip happy hours. Chef Alle Thiam serves upscale "New Americana" cuisine, with live jazz & blues. Perfect for your next party or event.

The Stinking Rose, A Garlic Restaurant — Italian

55 N. La Cienega Blvd.
Beverly Hills, CA 90211
(310) 652-7673
Lunch: Mon - Sun, Dinner: Mon - Sun
Web: www.thestinkingrose.com
All Major Credit Cards, Reservations: Yes

It's almost all garlic all the time at the Beverly Hills edition of San Francisco's world famous eatery. Specialties include THE SLAB-True "USDA Prime" Prime Rib-40 ounces of succulent beef, THE CRAB-over two pounds of whole, garlic roasted, Dungeness crab in their secret garlic sauce, garlic encrusted baby back ribs and ever-popular forty-clove garlic chicken. Full bar, four unique dining rooms, open until 11:00 pm every day of the year.

Tahiti — World

7910 W. Third St.   (323) 651-1213
Los Angeles, CA 90048
Lunch: Tue - Fri, Dinner: Mon - Sun
All Major Credit Cards, Reservations: Yes

Elegant tropical settings accentuated by cascading waterfalls and large leopard-skinned booths. Incredible world cuisine specialties inspired by owners' former Indigo restaurant. Their newest addition is the tiki lounge, for drinks or dinner or request the heated patio complete with bamboo garden and tiered fountain.

The Tam O'Shanter Inn — American

2980 Los Feliz Blvd.   (323) 664-0228
Los Angeles, CA 90039
Lunch: Mon - Fri, Dinner: Mon - Sun, Brunch: Sun
Web: www.lawrysonline.com

Crackling fireplaces. Cozy rooms. Scottish cheer. The first member of the Lawry's fine dining family, the Tam has earned a rare reputation, where the warmth and intimacy of the ambiance is heralded on the same level as the award-winning foods.

Tanino — Italian

1043 Westwood Blvd.   (310) 208-0444
Los Angeles, CA 90024
Lunch: Mon - Sat, Dinner: Mon - Sun
All Major Credit Cards, Reservations: Yes

Another elegant newcomer situated in Westwood Village. Inside dark wood and travertine stone accentuate the original 1929 ceilings painted by the same artists who created The Biltmore's. Start with the burrata-abutter mozzarella salad, linguini ai fruitti di mare or spaghetti with baby squid, all equally satisfying. Ossobuco is served year-round. All desserts made on the premises as are the pastas.

A Thousand Cranes — Japanese

120 S. Los Angeles St.   (213) 253-9255
Los Angeles, CA 90012
Lunch: Mon - Fri, Dinner: Mon - Sun, Brunch: Sun -
All Major Credit Cards, Reservations: Yes

What lacks in interior design makes up in its works of sushi art. Pleasant view overlooking New Otani's Japanese garden. Sushi and tempura bars serve such favorites as maguro (tuna sashimi) and shiromi (whitefish of the day). Other delicacies include the shabu-shabu, the filet mignon steak and the salmon teriyaki. Boasts the finest Japanese brunch in SoCal.

Toi On Sunset — Thai

7505 1/2 Sunset Blvd.   (323) 874-8062
Los Angeles, CA 90046
Lunch: Mon - Sun, Dinner: Mon - Sun
All Major Credit Cards, Reservations: Yes

Trendy Thai food establishment offers cheap lunch deals including pad Thai amid lava lamp retro-chic. Campy flicks on the telly or blaring rock music on the hi-fi can't compete with the curry dishes. (Also at 1120 Wilshire Blvd. in Santa Monica.)

Twin Palms — California

101 W. Green St.   (626) 577-2567
Pasadena, CA 91105
Lunch: Mon - Sun, Dinner: Mon - Sun, Brunch: Sun -
All Major Credit Cards, Reservations: Yes

White sails billowing from two ancient palms form a shaded oasis in Old Town Pasadena. California coastal cuisine. Local ingredients abound on the menu. Live music most nights. Sunday evening Swing and Sunday Gospel brunch.

Typhoon — Eclectic

3221 Donald Douglas Loop South   (310) 390-6565
Santa Monica, CA 90405
Lunch: Mon - Sun, Dinner: Mon - Sun
All Major Credit Cards, Reservations: Yes

Eat Pan-Asian cuisine while watching aviation action through Typhoon's large picture windows. Wide variety of entrees, including dim sum, satays (strips of grilled pork, lamb, chicken on sticks), deep fried catfish, pad Thai, and mi-goreng (Indonesian stir fried noodles). Wood paneling and aero-vistas lend a romantic feel during the evening dining hours. Located at the Santa Monica Airport.

Valentino — Italian

3115 Pico Blvd.   (310) 829-4313
Santa Monica, CA 90405   (310) 315-2791
Lunch: Fri - , Dinner: Mon - Sat
All Major Credit Cards, Reservations: Yes

Gourmet Italian such as their famous risotto and pappardelle (long egg pasta) with wild greens, fresh tomatoes and aged ricotta. Branzino (sea bass) is imported directly from the Mediterranean. Subdued contemporary interior of winter greys, greens, pinks and beige accented with richly colored fabrics from Missoni.

Vermont Restaurant — New American

1714 N. Vermont Ave.
(323) 661-6163
Los Angeles, CA 90027
Lunch: Tue - Fri, Dinner: Tue - Sun
All Major Credit Cards, Reservations: Yes

Stylishly handsome cafe with beautiful lighting and outdoor seating. Contemporary American cuisine includes hearty, healthy portions of grilled meat and fish. Seasonal menu items and nightly specials. Small, bold, international wine list.

Wolfgang Puck Cafe — California

8000 W. Sunset Blvd.
(323) 650-7300
Los Angeles, CA 90046
Lunch: Mon - Sun, Dinner: Mon - Sun
All Major Credit Cards, Reservations: Yes

Puck's favorite recipes are made with only the freshest, premium ingredients. Signature dishes include Chinois Chicken Salad, world-famous wood-fired pizzas, special soups, farm-fresh salads, fresh pastas and classic entrees. The vibrant casual decor created by Barbara Lazaroff is as clever as the food. For lunch, dinner, happy hour seven days a week, whatever your craving or budget. (Also at Universal City Walk, Santa Monica, El Segundo, Ontario Mills and four locations in Orange County.)

Yamakasa — Japanese

1900 N. Highland Ave.
(323) 882-6524
Los Angeles, CA 90068
Lunch: Mon - Fri, Dinner: Mon - Sun
All Major Credit Cards, Reservations: No

Elevates the strip mall concept to a new level of respectability. Minimalist decor, maximum sushi and sashimi plus generous portions of other traditional fare. Set the mood with delicately seasoned miso soup followed by light, crisp tempura and an assortment of rather amazing sushi art.

Yujean Kang's — Chinese

67 N. Raymond Ave.
(626) 585-0855
Pasadena, CA 91103
Lunch: Mon - Sun, Dinner: Mon - Sun
All Major Credit Cards, Reservations: Yes

Gourmet Chinese cuisine served in a traditional setting complete with classic Chinese paintings. Highlights from the kitchen include the tea smoked duck with pancake and the veal with matchstick yam. Elegantly presented vegetarian meals such as tofu sheets smothered with assorted mushrooms. (Also at 8826 Melrose Ave. in West Hollywood, with a more modern design.)

● Zach's Italian Cafe

10820 Ventura Blvd.
(818) 762-4225
Studio City, CA 91604

This charming hideaway has a country home type atmosphere with both indoor and patio dining. Their menu has something for everybody from the best calamari to an award winning antipasta salad to a delicious chicken and eggplant parmigiana to a homemade tiramisu that's to die for. There are many other salads, entrees, subs and pizzas to choose from.

Zen Grill — Asian

8432 W. Third St.
(323) 655-9991
Los Angeles, CA 90048
Lunch: Mon - Sun, Dinner: Mon - Sun
All Major Credit Cards, Reservations: Yes

A welcome addition to Third Street dining. Exquisitely prepared multi-Asian food at more than reasonable prices. Sashimi tuna rice towers drizzled with wasabi and the delicately steamed shrimp rice dumplings are immensely satisfying, but don't stop there. Try the laksa, a rich curry noodle soup with shrimp, tofu and sprouts or the roasted garlic spinach fried rice loaded with whole garlic cloves. Lovely decor of russet walls, gorgeous wood tables and vintage Japanese prints. (Also at 14543 Ventura Blvd. Sherman Oaks.)

Entertainment

Catering

Alex Gourmet Catering
18047 Saticoy St. (818) 895-6633
Reseda, CA 91335 (818) 708-1930

Expert in film, TV, and commercial-related catering, including the nourishment of on-location casts and crews, wrap parties and premieres. Will enhance event themes with creative, customized menus. Filet mignon, lobster and crab legs are favorites among clients and chef.

Allegria
22821 Pacific Coast Hwy. (310) 456-3132
Malibu, CA 90265

Allegria can cater your next event at your home, party site or in their own romantic restaurant. Gourmet Tuscan fare can be prepared in your home complete with chef and professional staff, or brought in pre-prepared. Catering menus for various price ranges. Throw a party on their heated covered patio. They will assist in all your floral and decorating needs. Wrap parties, Bar-Mitzvahs, wedding rehearsals, graduations and wedding receptions (they're just 1/4 mile from Pepperdine's famous wedding chapel).

Another Time, Another Place
(310) 472-3369

Tea for two or 42. A traditional and complete English afternoon tea right down to the bone china and good silver. Gatherings are transported to a bygone era resplendent with customary antiques, linens and flowers. Homemade three-course respite includes delicate finger sandwiches, scones with Devon cream and jam, and an irresistible array of sweets. Alice and the Mad Hatter gladly accept the invitation.

Arie Atlas Presents
(323) 466-7258

Striking an exquisite balance between menu planning/execution and visual design, whether an intimate party for friends or the social event of the season. Casual chic. Lofty elegance. Either way, it will be a gracious event with seamless coordination of every element, thinking beyond standard thoughts, doing the undoable. Astutely determines needs, creates a mood, an atmosphere with imaginative menus, blends of colours, textures, flavours in food, props and theme. Will take care of every thing. Or just one thing. Will plan, design, coordinate, cater and make it all happen. Whatever the occasion calls for. Exceeds requirements always with sensational form following ingenious function.

Black Tie Event Productions, LLC

5741 Buckingham Pkwy., Ste. D   (310) 337-9900
Culver City, CA 90230
Web: www.blacktie-event.com

Offering in-house fine food catering, ABC licensed bar catering, event staffing and full service production for all special events.

Bonne Bouffe Catering

1521 Venice Blvd.   (310) 397-1660
Venice, CA 90291

Custom design for your event. Complete catering and party planning. Fresh dishes prepared with a variety of ethnic touches, vegetarian or oil-free. Famous for their desserts, the selection of 30 cheesecake variations are so divine that competitors buy them wholesale. In the area? Stop on by for a slice of heaven.

● Breakfast! Rise & Shine/Rise & Shine Lunch Catering

7401 W. 88th Pl.   (310) 649-0906
Los Angeles, CA 90045

They allow their clients to simply relax and enjoy the festivities with their award winning cuisine and personalized service. Menu and pricing are customized to each clients tastes and budget.

Bruce's Gourmet Catering, Inc.

13631 Saticoy St.   (818) 764-3181
Panorama City, CA 91402

Will orchestrate all peripherals and props from A to Z to make your party or event spectacular. Full-service catering where the food makes meaningful statements. Honey Lime Chicken, Sundried Tomato Basil Brie Tart, Blinis & Caviar, Stuffed Jumbo Mushrooms with spinach and cheese, and Chicken Medallions with goat cheese and red peppers are just a few of the gorgeous hors d'oeuvres originals from an extensive menu that also includes 36 unique salads, and many pork, lamb, beef, fish and pasta entrées. Event planning of any size is as creative as the cuisine.

Cadillac Cafe

359 N. La Cienega Blvd.   (310) 657-6591
Los Angeles, CA 90048   (323) 953-3649
Web: www.cadillaccafe.com

Innovative cuisine for cocktail/wrap parties. They provide appetizer trays, lunch/dinner delivery and boxed meals.

Cafe Sushi

8459 Beverly Blvd.   (323) 651-4020
Los Angeles, CA 90048
Mon - Sun, , Mon - Sun,

On-site or in-house catering for any size event at home or business. Have sushi chefs design artistic culinary creations for your guests. Portable sushi case ensures that the fish remains fresh.

A California Brain Freeze

(888) 525-8423

Web: www.californiabrainfreeze.com

Gourmet frozen drink bar will liven up any event with its eye-pleasing setup (decorated with lush fruits and flowers) and its delectable drinks. Fruit smoothies, blended coffee drinks, heavenly milkshakes and sinful sundae bars. Even has margarita and daiquiri bars to accompany your spirits.

California Celebrations, Inc.

4051 Glencoe Ave., Ste. 7   (310) 305-8849
Marina Del Rey, CA 90292

From intimate private parties to full-scale soirees (up to 4500), California Celebrations will provide the full package which includes five-star chef, Lou Manginelli, florals, decor, and extraordinary locations. Weddings, corporate parties and industry events.

Catering By Field

3380½ S. Robertson Blvd.   (310) 837-4680
Los Angeles, CA 90034

In addition to orchestrating visually pleasing presentations (from instant flower gardens to outdoor twinkling lights), they focus on flavor. Beef tenderloin in Jack Daniels sauce, herb crusted chicken and flourless chocolate torte have become a favorite at numerous sit-down dinners and poolside parties.

Catering by The Ritz-Carlton

One Ritz Carlton Dr.   (949) 240-2000
Dana Point, CA 92629
Web: www.ritzcarlton.com

Bring The Ritz-Carlton hotel's fine cuisine and renowed service into the home, office or a variety of the area's picturesque locations. From party platters, lavish meals prepared and served in the home, to coordination of decorations and entertainment for specialty-themed corporate functions or special events.

The Century Club

10131 Constellation Blvd.   (310) 553-6000
Los Angeles, CA 90067

Exclusive supper club specializing in premieres, wrap parties, and large or small corporate functions. Accommodates up to 1,000 people and features three dance floors, six bars, a spacious, heated outdoor patio, a performance stage with pro sound and light systems, and, of course, valet parking. Outstanding audiovisual design includes the capacity to broadcast from the stage to 25 TV monitors throughout the club. Location-shoot friendly.

Cheers Catering

19431 Business Center Dr.   (818) 772-0233
Northridge, CA 91324

Looking for an unusual place for your next bash? One-of-a-kind locations like beautiful Malibu Lake. Cheers Catering loves to cater with the out-of-the-ordinary, from hors d'oeuvres to vegetarian dinners. Full party planning available.

Clean Cuisine/Immaculate Consumption

1621 W. 25th St.   (310) 832-0509
San Pedro, CA 90732

Two different food delivery services. Clean Cuisine is based on the Pritikin diet, low in fat and calories, but chef June Pagan assures they are high in flavor. A typical day might include fruit muesli, cannelini bean soup, pepperonata salad and seafood skewer over lemon rice. Meals are available six days a week. Immaculate Consumption is for the expectant mother concerned with a well-balanced diet focusing on the special nutritional needs of pregnancy. No salt or sugars are used and foods are calcium and potassium rich, averaging about 2400 calories per day.

Corn Maiden Foods, Inc.
10301 Washington Blvd.   (310) 202-6180
Culver City, CA 90232   (310) 338-3383
Web: www.cornmaiden.com

Handmade tamales from traditional (pork with red chile) to gourmet (Belgian chocolate with raspberry). Full line of Southwest and Mexican foods, salsas, sauces, corn products, cookbooks and more.

de ja Food Catering
24811 N. San Fernando Rd., Unit B-C   (661) 254-4115
Santa Clarita, CA 91321

Full service catering providing quality service for any size gathering in the SoCal area. More than ten years experience with events including film, video and TV productions, business functions, holiday parties, weddings, anniversaries, birthdays and theme dinners. Wide selection of menu items are tailored to meet any dietary and budget constraints. An experience worth repeating.

Drago
2628 Wilshire Blvd.   (310) 828-1585
Santa Monica, CA 90403

Special event planning and catering for parties of two to infinity! Equivalent high caliber cuisine and service to their renowned restaurant. Truffle dinners are their specialty. Ask for the special events department. They've got the hookup for locations, rentals, decor. They'll even book the entertainment. "The whole deal."

Empress Pavilion — Chinese

988 N. Hill St.   (213) 617-9898
Los Angeles, CA 90012
Lunch: Mon - Sun, Dinner: Mon - Sun
All Major Credit Cards, Reservations: Yes

The award winning cuisine that everyone loves from this famous and popular Chinatown restaurant is now available at your event location. Popular dim such as spring rolls and shrimp dumplings make any party a resounding success. Just ask any of the thousands of people at the "Studio 54", "Return to Paradise", or "Stuff" magazine premieres who waited in line to sample our food. One week's notice is all that is needed to provide the same epicurean perfection enjoyed at Los Angeles' premier Chinese dim sum/seafood restaurant. Bring the Empress Pavilion to your next event.

Feast Catering

8739 La Tierra Blvd.   (310) 568-8600
Los Angeles, CA 90045

Direct from London, the gourmet capital of the world where emerging ethnic and product diversity has expanded its culinary acumen to the ends of the earth, is chef Marcus Baird who's goal is to give you what you want at a reasonable price. Impress the big wigs at a corporate luncheon with sate beef & chicken skewers, steamed jasmine rice, green beans with ginger sauce, and banana-kiwi spring rolls. Win over the rock stars at the next music video shoot with chicken parmesan, roasted root vegetables, classic Caesar salad with homemade croutons, and tiramisu. Made to order and fresh, 48 hours notice is required.

Joan's On Third

8350 W. Third St.   (323) 655-2285
Los Angeles, CA 90048

From intimate sit-down dinners of ten to premieres of 2000, complete event planning from rentals to valet parking. Custom designed menus with delectable designs. Corporate luncheons prepared in individual box lunches. Moveable feasts in individual containers (grilled maple rosemary flank steak, chicken Milanese or pesto crusted salmon) for your next party or the Hollywood Bowl.

John Connolly Catering Inc.

11510 W. Pico Blvd.   (310) 479-6653
Los Angeles, CA 90064
Web: www.connollysrestaurant.com

Since 1994, no event too small or too large. From corporate lunches to major studio premieres and even dinner for eight. Need a themed party? No problem. Versatile and eclectic specialists in international buffets with gorgeous presentation and gourmet delights. Will create a truly memorable event for your next soiree. Need a perfect location? Casually elegant and atmospherically flexible Connolly's Restaurant available, too.

Junior's Restaurant Catering

2379 Westwood Blvd.   (800) 475-3354
Los Angeles, CA 90064
Web: www.jrsdeli.com

Keeping the motion picture industry fed and happy since 1959, with full menus and custom orders of drop-off, hot and cold ready-to-eat meals. Accommodates any size event, including wrap parties. French hours on location not a problem. Will deliver anywhere. Features fresh-baked deserts from on-site baking facility. Specializes in elaborate cakes and will duplicate emblems and logos or any other decorating requirements. Generous quality, total convenience, ultimate satisfaction.

Knitting Factory

7021 Hollywood Blvd.   (323) 463-0204
Los Angeles, CA 90028

Knitting Factory can meet all your catering needs. They offer many options of pastas, salads, chicken, meat, fish and desserts. Fusion Chef Mike Borassi is available to prepare a variety of special requess including Kosher, Vegan or Vegetarian options. Sample menus availabe upon request.

Let's Have A Cart Party

426 S. Wetherly Dr.   (310) 786-1719
Beverly Hills, CA 90211

On-site fresh food catering with antique style food carts. Their options include everything from gourmet pizza and salad bar to popcorn and hot dog carts.

More Than A Mouthful

743 S. Lucerne Blvd.   (323) 937-6345
Los Angeles, CA 90005
Web: www.mtam.com

Located in the historic Wilshire Ebell, a private women's club, elegance and romance are primary ingredients in their recipe for success. All chefs are alumni of the Culinary Institute of America. Specializing in wedding receptions and custom design for every aspect of your menu, floral design, photography and decor.

Pacific Park on the Santa Monica Pier

7401 W. 88th Pl.   (310) 649-0906
Los Angeles, CA 90045

With a reputation for award winning cuisine and personalized service they allow their clients to simply relax and enjoy the festivities. Menus and pricing customized to each clients tastes and budget.

Real Food Daily

414 N. La Cienega Blvd.   (310) 289-9910
Los Angeles, CA 90048   (310) 451-7544
Lunch: Mon - Sun, Dinner: Mon - Sun
Web: realfood.com
All Major Credit Cards, Reservations: No

Gourmet, purely vegetarian whole foods with a strong emphasis on certified organic produce. Owner/chef Ann Gentry and her culinary team create daily specials of various international cooking styles and a traditional macrobiotic menu. NO fats, sugars, preservatives, animal or dairy products are used. Catering for all types of events. From intimate dinner parties to wrap parties to all-out grand scale weddings. (Original location at 514 Santa Monica Blvd., SM).

Reel Food Productions

9626 Venice Blvd.   (310) 558-0848
Culver City, CA 90232

Full service catering with an emphasis on customized menus. Specialty food, high end cuisine, home cooking, special diets, vegetarian, macro biotic and exotic foods. Catering services for your home party, wedding, corporate event or movie set available.

Skewers Catering

8939 Santa Monica Blvd.   (310) 271-0555
West Hollywood, CA 90069
Mon - Sun, , Mon - Sun,
All Major Credit Cards, Reservations: Yes

Full catering services specializing in a wide range of grilled skewers from around the world such as teriyaki, Thai and Mediterranean chicken, swordfish, salmon, Cajun shrimp, filet mignon and lamb. Impressive array of appetizers and salads to accent your entree selections. Can structure the event menu around your tastes and dietary needs. (Also at 617 S. Central Ave. Downtown.)

The Stinking Rose, A Garlic Restaurant

55 N. La Cienega Blvd.   (310) 652-7673
Beverly Hills, CA 90211
Web: www.thestinkingrose.com

Bring your event, from an intimate gathering to an extravaganza of 500-the entire Sinking Rose can be yours. Four separate, themed dining rooms-from the Chianti Cafe to Dracula's Grotto. On-site event coordinator will help with all occasions, from wrap parties to location shoots.

● Who Knew We Cater!

323 36th St., Ste. B   (310) 798-9767
Manhattan Beach, CA 90266   (800) 294-6563
Web: www.2whoknew.com

All-inclusive party planning and catering company featuring an endless array of cuisine from around the globe prepared by award-winning chefs, making this an industry favorite. Specializes in complete event arrangements, whether it's a sit-down premiere for thousands, a shoot for a small crew, a chartered yacht, a corporate enclave, an intimate dinner party, or even a wedding on the beach. Pro staff allows you to "Be the star of your own event."

Why Cook?

     (310) 441-9964

Have a craving for a fancy meal but too busy or tired to put on the ritz? Multi-restaurant delivery service brings gourmet dining to your door. In need of Le Pizze Dolce Vita from Farfalla? How 'bout Atlantic's Alaskan Halibut with Snow Pea Puree & Port Wine Balsamic Sauce? These and many other upscale eateries sure don't deliver but Why Cook? will. It's your pipeline to dine fine. Shoes optional.

● Wolfgang Puck Cafe Catering

100 N. Crescent Dr.   (310) 432-1500
Beverly Hills, CA 90210

Creative menus and fresh event ideas with experienced chefs who draw upon Wolfgang's signature recipes. Catering consultants ensure every aspect of your event is spectacular. Ideal for special events including holiday parties, lunch, dinner, premieres (on or off premises), wrap parties, location catering, anniversaries, receptions and company picnics.

Akbar

4356 Sunset Blvd.   (323) 665-6810
Los Angeles, CA 90029

A Silver Lake neighborhood hangout where reasonably priced drinks keep an eclectic crowd coming back. Best jukebox in town plays tunes from Count Basie to The Sex Pistols, not to mention favorite local artists. Happy hour starts at 6pm.

Atlas Supper Club

3760 Wilshire Blvd.   (213) 380-8400
Los Angeles, CA 90010
Web: www.clubatlas.com

In the classic tradition of a 1920s supper club, Atlas features live music from jazz to cabaret. Patronized by entertainment industry elite, expect to compete for dance floor room on Salsa nights each Saturday. Cover varies, call for details and show times.

Bar Marmont

8171 Sunset Blvd.   (323) 650-0575
West Hollywood, CA 90069

Upscale bar attracting industry types from CEOs to mailroom assistants. Count on a scene. Dine in the table area or just become one with a red velvet couch and an $8 beer.

Boardner's

1652 N. Cherokee Ave.   (323) 462-9621
Hollywood, CA 90028

Hollywood hangout for leather clad bikers and rockers. Surprisingly laid back and attitude-free. Drinks are reasonably priced, CD jukebox is diverse and better than average. Go alone and strike up a conversation or show up with your posse and own the joint. It's all good. Outdoor patio and fountain area available for smokers. Check out Bar Sinister in the adjacent goth-ambient room on Saturdays where the elixirs of choice are black martinis and vampyre wine.

C Bar

8442 Wilshire Blvd.   (323) 782-8157
Beverly Hills, CA 90211   (323) 782-8158

This hip Hollywood gathering spot serves caviar and cocktails á la Manhattan chic. Electroplated chairs line the bar where bartenders pour endless streams of martinis, cosmopolitans and sidecars. Nibble on a gravlax roll or sample beluga caviar. For that special occasion there's Louis Roederer Cristal on the menu.

Cat Club

8911 Sunset Blvd.   (310) 657-0888
West Hollywood, CA 90069

Making the Sunset Strip a more notorious hang (and well it should), this is a rock star magnet by virtue of the royalty of its lineage: ex-Stray Cat Slim Jim Phantom and notable music biz partners in crime hold title to this groovy joint. No pretense. No cover. All cool. Even the lone pool table upstairs is a public service. Back patio to light one up and Americana cuisine to chow down. Parking around back.

● The Century Club

10131 Constellation Blvd.   (310) 553-6000
Los Angeles, CA 90067
Web: www.centuryclub.com

Upscale nightclub in the heart of Century City. Large facilities featuring three dance floors, six bars, a stage and a palatial outdoor patio. Different DJs spin music on each dance floor, providing an unparalleled choice of grooves to dance to. Live Salsa (Fridays) and "Fashion Show" featuring techno music (Saturdays).

The Dresden Room

1760 N. Vermont Ave.   (323) 665-4294
Los Angeles, CA 90027

Order a bloody rare steak and a strong highball before taking in lounge-style covers from husband and wife singing duo Marty and Elayne, who've been providing the live vibe six nights a week. Packed with a casual crowd of mixed ages, hep cats and "swingers."

El Carmen

8138 W. Third St.   (323) 852-1552
Los Angeles, CA 90048

Taqueria and cantina featuring more than 200 varieties of tequilas. A lick of salt, a little lime, a jukebox dime and you're good to go. Mexican art and campy wrestler motifs decorate the walls, but everyone comes for the scene brought to you by the owners of Bar Marmont.

Fais Do Do

5257 W. Adams Blvd.   (323) 931-4636
Los Angeles, CA 90016

Originally built as a bank during the turn of the century, this palatial high ceilinged singular room is now filled with diverse regulars hanging out to listen to local blues and jazz acts. Cajun/soul food, too. Cover is usually five bucks. All ages welcome.

Flint's

3321 Pico Blvd.   (310) 453-1331
Santa Monica, CA 90405

Elegant '40s-style roadhouse with all the suave the era conjures. Lobster Thermadore and prime steaks on the menu say it all. Sip a Flintini, one of 14 specialty cocktails of the house, and recline in the luxurious sofa lounge or take in the cool night air on the patio. Cigar Night the first Monday each month enhances the club's sexy persona. Tuesdays feature live jazz. No cover.

Formosa Café

7156 Santa Monica Blvd.   (323) 850-9050
Los Angeles, CA 90046

Full Chinese restaurant and bar. Go strictly for the decor; autographed 8x10s of Hollywood hotshots and Elvis Presley. Built in 1929, the Formosa is a staple of architectural history featuring a dark and intimate atmosphere attracting an eclectic crowd. Get there early to stake your claim at the bar or a table or be left to fend off oncoming traffic in the ever-narrowing walkway. Outdoor patio diverts stampedes and smokers.

Garden of Eden

7080 Hollywood Blvd.   (323) 465-3336
Hollywood, CA 90028

Nightclub fusing various ethnic influenced designs, with an emphasis on Moroccan. An exotic, yet sophisticated atmosphere accentuated by antique wood carvings, plush seating, a unique dance floor and an outdoor smoking patio. VIP mezzanine overlooks the entire club. Ideal location for fully catered parties.

Gotham Hall

1431 Third Street Promenade   (310) 394-8865
Santa Monica, CA 90401
Web: www.gothamhall.com

This Santa Monica hangout has a great atmosphere with private rooms, dance club, pool tables, fantastic food and more. Whether it's just the two of you looking for a place to play pool or a group of up to 1,000 looking for a place to have a party, Gotham Hall has it all.

HMS Bounty

3357 Wilshire Blvd.   (213) 385-7275
Los Angeles, CA 90010

An LA institution for over 37 years. Its nautical theme has lured an entire procession of entertainment royalty including Elizabeth Taylor. Booths bear brass nameplates of the famous derriéres that have warmed the seats. Still the place to be for actors, writers and the like to make the scene, knock back a few and order a hearty meal of steak, chops or eggs any time. Martinis are the house specialty and the jukebox is pure nostalgia.

Kane

5574 Melrose Ave.   (323) 466-6263
Los Angeles, CA 90038

'60s Vegas Rat Pack mixes with '70s Superfly funk. Wed-Sat features go-go girls. Martinis and cosmopolitans are the refreshments of choice in this decidedly decked-out dive. Naturally. Open nightly.

Lava Lounge

1533 N. La Brea Blvd.   (323) 876-6612
Los Angeles, CA 90038

A favorite among celebs who aren't afraid to rub elbows (literally) with locals. This tiki enclave features live entertainment including surf, blues, and disco plus soul/funk trip-hop DJs in a more-than-cozy spot within a Hollywood mini-mall. Live blues on Mondays. Karaoke and sushi on Sundays. Be sure to sample one of the many tropical intoxicants: sinful but sweet.

Lola's

945 N. Fairfax Ave.   (213) 736-5652
Los Angeles, CA 90046

This club that feels like a living room and doubles as a restaurant (serving "food you can eat") 'til 2am, is notorious for its exponentially expanding martini list. There are concoctions on the menu that haven't even been invented yet. Adam's Apple, anyone? (Appropriately green.) Or perhaps a Mrs. Miller's melon martini? The new yardstick of fame isn't a star on the Boulevard but a drink named for you.

Martini Lounge

5657 Melrose Ave.   (323) 467-4068
Hollywood, CA 90038

Olives anyone? Multilevel club with outdoor patio and live music. DJs spin swing, rock, pop, punk and Latino during down time between bands. Sip white chocolate, sour apple or cinnamon martinis at a bar constructed from an airplane wing while 100 antique lights set the mood. Check out the kinky shoe collection while hanging at the front bar.

Molly Malone's Irish Pub

575 S. Fairfax Ave.   (323) 935-1577
Los Angeles, CA 90036

You can bet your lucky charms you'll find Irish barflies ready to chat wistfully 'bout "the old country." Neighborhood regulars pack this friendly little bar featuring live music nightly ranging from Irish folk to rock 'n' roll. Order a Harp Lager on tap and be thankful you found an empty seat. Camp out if you want in on St. Pat's Day.

North

8029 W. Sunset Blvd.   (323) 654-1313
Los Angeles, CA 90046   (805) 963-3564

Hollywood celebs and pretenders congregate in this bar hidden next to Greenblatt's Deli. Dominant redwood paneling and angled, translucent bay windows create a surreal lodge-like vibe. Large circular booths for the lucky, while the majority are left standing. Popularity has its price, n'est-ce pas? So bring a megaphone to be heard over fellow barflies' boisterous babble. Eat, drink and dress well.

SKYBAR

8440 Sunset Blvd.   (323) 848-6025
Los Angeles, CA 90046

There's a whole new meaning to the term 'pool party' at this casual chic watering hole to the upscale and deep pocketed. Sip something exotic amid candles and crowds as you take in the vast expanse of city lights far below. Reservations recommended.

Spaceland

717 Silver Lake Blvd.   (323) 833-2843
Los Angeles, CA 90026   (323) 661-4380
Web: www.clubspaceland.com

Art school attire only for this alternative club in Silverlake. If the music's too experimental, find some tranquility in the cosmic lounge with pool table, respectable CD jukebox, old satellite dishes hanging from the ceiling and a sit-down Ms. Pac Man game. Arrive way early for a fighting chance to get in the door because fashionably equals SOL.

The Stinking Rose, A Garlic Restaurant

55 N. La Cienega Blvd.   (310) 652-7673
Beverly Hills, CA 90211
Web: www.thestinkingrose.com

This long, whimsical, full-service bar is open 365 days a year 'til 1:00am. The cozy lounge with velvet couches and a romantic fireplace is the perfect place to sip a cocktail and listen to the splendid variety of music from jazz, blues, R & B to contemporary sounds. Cigar friendly (on the patio). Happy hour 5-7pm weekdays includes appetizers and reduced drink prices.

The Three Clubs Cocktail Lounge

1123 N. Vine St.   (323) 462-6441
Los Angeles, CA 90038

So inside it doesn't even have an address. Deceiving landmark signage designates "Bargain Clown Mart" though sometimes this consummate old-school lounge is a circus. Accommodating bartenders make a mean cosmo but the secret specialty is the mudslide. Late equals loud but no one seems to mind because the music plays to please.

Tiki Ti

4427 Sunset Blvd.   (323) 669-9381
Los Angeles, CA 90027
Wed - Sat 6pm - 1am

Scarcely bigger than the itsy bitsy bikini the vibe conjures, there are more than 70 Polynesian drinks served at this kitschy and overpopulated watering hole.

Voda

1449 Second St.   (310) 394-9774
Santa Monica, CA 90401

From a chocolate martini (with or without alcohol) to a comfortable bar stool, indulge your cravings and inclinations at this vodka and caviar bar. Fifty-plus vodkas from 15 countries, colorful cocktails and imaginative edibles, too. No cover charge, whether you eat or not but arrive early or call ahead to this incognito speakeasy because later the big line gives away its location.

VooDoo

4120 W. Olympic Blvd.   (323) 930-9600
Los Angeles, CA 90019   (310) 851-6335
Mon - Sun Hours Vary
Web: www.voodoola.com

Phenomenal nightclub in the tradition of Old Hollywood with a hip Polynesian, Tiki twist. Blacklit masks adorn the corridor that leads into the grand main room with stunning floor-to-ceiling waterfalls in each corner. The copper dance floor sits beneath a giant Aztec altar (that disguises the DJ booth pumping out a mix of House, '70s and '80s sounds) and matches the copper bar serving "Voodoo Shooters". Plush, upholstered booths line each wall, while cozy loveseats and tables fill the rest of the space. Upstairs eight private skybooths (with four overlooking the dance floor) can accommodate VIP's and private parties in the same luxurious surroundings as down below. Catered platters and customized party menus available. Valet parking.

Whiskey Bar

Sunset Marquis, 1200 N. Alta Loma Rd.   (310) 657-1333
West Hollywood, CA 90069

Draped across velvet sofas and decorating the patio are supermodels hanging from rock stars hanging from actresses hanging out with sports celebs. Classic rock is the soundtrack du nuit in this 86-person capacity coterie where reservations are essential and hotel guests receive primary consideration.

Family Entertainment

Disneyland
P.O. Box 3232   (714) 781-4560
Anaheim, CA 92803
Web: disney.go.com/disneyland

Let Mickey and the gang make you feel like a kid again at this world reknowned park. Relax to the music of the Tiki Room, go on an adventure with Indiana Jones or blast through infinity at Space Mountain. Find out why everyone's screaming, "I'm going to Disneyland!"

Knott's Berry Farm
8039 Beach Blvd.   (714) 220-5200
Buena Park, CA 90620
Web: www.knotts.com

Western-themed Knott's Berry Farm has something for everyone in your family: from Ghostrider - the world's longest wooden roller coaster, to Camp Snoopy - a fun filled, adventure-around-every-corner place just for kids. Catch spectacular views of the park and surrounding city, (if you dare open your eyes!) on the Supreme Scream. While food opportunities abound, ther are two things you MUST eat while at Knott's. Funnel cake and Mrs. Knott's famous fried chicken and biscuits. For the month of October, the park transforms into Knott's Scary Farm. The entire park is cloaked in spooky fun. Regular ticket prices: $40 for adults; $30 for kids and seniors.

Laser Storm
22535 Hawthorne Blvd.   (310) 373-8470
Torrance, CA 90505

Weave your way through the black and neon lighted arena, while dodging lasers in your glow-in-the-dark vest. Live out your deepest sci-fi fantasies. If you've got the skills, you'll blast all your enemies and reign victorious as laser tag champion. Party rooms and video games are all the more reason for a friendly gathering. Ages 3 and up.

Los Angeles Zoo
5333 Zoo Dr.   (323) 644-60▮
Los Angeles, CA 90027   (323) 662-97▮
Web: www.lazoo.org

This 113 acre zoo is situated in Griffith Park and is home 1,200 animals representing 350 species. Check out the continually expanding Great Ape Forest. Admission is $8.25 f▮ adults and $3.25 for children ages 2 to 12.

Mountasia Fun Center
21516 Golden Triangle Rd.   (661) 253-438▮
Santa Clarita, CA 91350   (877) 826-43▮
Mon - Sun Hours Vary

Two 18-hole miniature golf courses enveloped by a gia▮ waterfall. State-of-the-art roller/inline skating rink, bump▮ boats, go-carts (single and double seated), batting cages, 1▮ game arcade, and M4 motion simulator ride plus more th▮ 100 video and redemption games. Fuel up with a peppero▮ pie at Perky's Pizza.

Pacific Park on the Santa Monica Pier
380 Santa Monica Pier   (310) 260-87▮
Santa Monica, CA 90401
Web: www.pacpark.com

This two acre amusement park on the historic Santa Moni▮ Pier offers 18 midway games, action simulator attractions, ▮ oceanfront food plaza and 12 rides including a solar powere▮ ferris wheel. The park and its seaside "Party Cabana" can ▮ rented for special events.

Raging Waters

111 Raging Waters Dr.   (909) 802-2200
San Dimas, CA 91773
Web: www.ragingwaters.com

Nestled in a lush, park-like setting, this large water park is centrally located where the 210, 10, and 57 freeways meet. The park had 35 rides and attractions, including the Beaches at the Wave Cove and the High Extreme.

Soak City U.S.A.

8039 Beach Blvd.   (714) 220-5200
Buena Park, CA 90620
Web: www.soakcityusa.com

Soak City can be found directly across the street from Knott's Berry Farm and is a fun place to go when the temperature rises. There are over 14 tube and body slides, aptly named Typhoon, Heavy Swell and Rincon. And who can bypass the vertigo and sheer terror of the speed slides Riptide and Pipeline? Tidal Wave Bay has all the tubular waves. The Gremmie Lagoon is the perfect spot for your wee surfer dudes and dudettes. At the end of it, take a relaxing ride on the drifting Sunset River. Regular ticket prices: $19.95 for adults; $13.95 for kids 3-11.

Universal Studios Hollywood

100 Universal City Plaza   (818) 622-3801
Universal City, CA 91608
Web: www.universalstudios.com/unicity2

Experience a real life Hollywood adventure as you tour this film studio and theme park. See how special effects are made, visit your favorite movie's street scenes or ride the movies themselves on one of their adventure rides. Finish with a stroll down City Walk, a fun filled road overlooking Los Angeles.

Wild Rivers

8770 Irvine Center Dr.   (949) 768-9453
Irvine, CA 92618
Web: www.wildrivers.com

Whether you're traveling from L.A. to see the sights in San Diego or vice versa, Wild Rivers is right on your way. With over 40 water rides and attractions, it's the perfect place for a break during your family's travel day.

Live Music

Dragonfly
6510 Santa Monica Blvd. (323) 466-6111
Hollywood, CA 90038
Web: www.dragonfly.com

Large nightclub with four full bars and a center stage featuring cutting edge alternative bands. On nights with no live acts DJs spin funk, retro, hip-hop, house and disco.

The Gig
7302 Melrose Ave. (323) 936-4440
Los Angeles, CA 90046

Check out L.A.'s hottest up-and-coming acts at this venue in the heart of Melrose. Plush couches, a full bar and plenty of young hipsters make this a cozy place to listen to tunes and see the Hollywood scene. Call for show times and bookings.

Knitting Factory
7021 Hollywood Blvd. (323) 463-0204
Los Angeles, CA 90028
Web: www.knittingfactory.com

This "Smart Club," a new age, fully-equipped, arts facility, offers live music networked to its clubs across the globe. Toast a friend in Berlin while listening to a live feed from New York.

The Mint
6010 W. Pico Blvd. (323) 954-9630
Los Angeles, CA 90035 (323) 954-8241

Small club. Respectable names. Lean against the bar sipping a dark, rich Guinness while taking in The Fabulous Thunderbirds (Harry Dean Stanton's band) or any other legendary barroom blues outfit that happens to be in town. Nouveau legendaries who've graced the stage include The Wallflowers, Mary Cutrafello and Janeane Garofalo in one of the club's quirky comedy nights. A mosaic of black vinyl discs decorate the ceiling if you can divert your attention from the stage action long enough to look up.

Rocco
2930 Beverly Glen Circle (310) 475-980
Los Angeles, CA 90077
Web: www.roccoinla.com

Dedicated to displaying the best jazz musicians in Los Angeles this restaurant/bar has a relaxed, comfortable atmosphere complemented by a menu of delicious northern Italian cuisine

Temple Bar
1026 Wilshire Blvd. (310) 393-661
Santa Monica, CA 90401
Web: www.templebarlive.com

Giant portraits of musicians adorn the walls of this psychadelic Santa Monica club featuring a variety of musical acts. Sip a martini from their menu while dining on blackened shrimp tacos and taking in their Sunday night regulars, The Rhythm Room All-Stars, a percussion ensemble. Call or check the website for acts.

Vesuvius
650 N. La Cienega Blvd. (310) 967-000
West Hollywood, CA 90069

Nightlife erupts in sound and vision with two rooms (one VIP) of entertainment and dancing. Themes vary and include live bands playing swing, R&B or other genres plus DJs. Outdoor tropical patio sets the scene for romance and conversation. Available for private parties and location shoots. Call for band schedule Tues.-Sat.

The Viper Room
8852 Sunset Blvd. (310) 358-188
West Hollywood, CA 90069

Showcasing new music for a somewhat industry audience. Be on the lookout for "unannounced" gigs like The Foo Fighters, Marilyn Manson or Stone Temple Pilots. Thursday nights cater to the martini crowd, while other evenings feature live music and DJs.

rie Atlas Presents

(323) 466-7258

triking an exquisite balance between menu lanning/execution and visual design, whether an intimate arty for friends or the social event of the season. Casual chic. ofty elegance. Either way, it will be a gracious event with eamless coordination of every element, thinking beyond tandard thoughts, doing the undoable. Astutely determines eeds, creates a mood, an atmosphere with imaginative nenus, blends of colours, textures, flavours in food, props, heme. Will take care of every thing. Or just one thing. Will plan, lesign, coordinate, cater and make it all happen. Whatever the ccasion calls for. Exceeds requirements always with ensational form following ingenious function.

V Party Rentals, Inc.

4330 San Fernando Rd.   (661) 259-2151
Jewhall, CA 91321   (818) 362-8389
Veb: www.avparty.com

ull service party and event rental company, specializing in veddings, corporate events and parties. They service all of Los Ingeles County.

Beautiful Bartenders

(310) 600-1077

Web: www.beautifulbartenders.com

A unique service agency staffed by experienced professionals which provides more than just a simple cocktail. They will go the extra distance to ensure your event is a success. From intimate parties to all out grand galas their unmatched service will be a hit with your guests. Beauty isn't everything, but it does make the party more fun.

Black Tie Event Productions, LLC

5741 Buckingham Pkwy., Ste. D   (310) 337-9900
Culver City, CA 90230
Web: www.blacktie-event.com

Offering in-house fine food catering, ABC licensed bar catering, event staffing and full service production for all special events.

Blash Carnival Enterprises

11101 Calabash St.   (909) 357-7130
Fontana, CA 92337   (800) 464-3929
Web: www.jablash.com

Largest selection of carnival rides in Southern California. If it's not available in their huge inventory, they'll find it for you! Everything fun from kiddy rides to huge spectacular rides, game booths complete with prizes to candy and food wagons. Memorable way to celebrate the next big occasion in your life.

Brian McMillan's Party Animals
4103 Holly Knoll Dr.   (323) 665-9500
Los Angeles, CA 90024
Web: www.hollywoodanimals.com

Make your party wild! Have live exotic animal actors entertain at your party. Elephants (rides), camels (rides)- tigers and lions and bears oh my ! Cubs, monkeys, chimps orangutans, reptile petting zoos and more. Thirty years experience supervising animals for entertainment. Licensed and insured.

California Speedway
9300 Cherry Ave.   (909) 429-5000
Fontana, CA 92335
Web: www.californiaspeedway.com

Ideal multifunctional location for filming movies and commercials or staging product introductions. The two-mile, high-banked super speedway is surrounded by 529 acres of open space in a secure, park-like setting just 52 miles from Hollywood. A self-contained, no-hassle location with on-site catering, security, medical and emergency staff.

The Century Club
10131 Constellation Blvd.   (310) 553-6000
Los Angeles, CA 90067

Fine dining supper club available for catering and special events. Premieres, wrap parties, concerts, banquets, film and video shoots. Accommodates up to 1,000 people and features three dance floors, a performance stage, heated outdoor patio and a state-of-the-art sound and lighting system.

● **Christiansen Amusements, Inc.**
P.O. Box 997   (800) 300-6114
Escondido, CA 92033
Web: www.amusements.com

Serving California since 1924 with carnival rides and games for rentals, props, parties, special events, TV, film, and video shoots. Pledges safety, quality, experience and dependability. Top-rated liability insurance. Need a ride or game? They'l provide it and be ready on time.

Classic Party Rentals
8476 Steller Dr.   (310) 202-0011
Culver City, CA 90232

Tables, linens, tenting, lighting, china and crystal chafers are available for rental. Wide selection of seating from black plastic to Chavaris (the Rolls Royce of chairs). Will go anywhere from the beach to private homes. Showroom at location for your selections.

Creative Inflatables
1638 Adelia   (626) 579-4454
South El Monte, CA 91733

Decorate your party in style with their custom made inflatable props ranging in size from 8' to 100'. Other available decor includes tents, inflatable rides, wind/tubes dancers and inflatable billboards.

● **Digital Perfect**

18737 Ventura Blvd   818- 654-2500
Tarzana, CA 91356

Get all of your event photography needs taken care of with one phone call. They provide the proof sheets. You pick your favorites.

Duke's Malibu   **California**

21150 Pacific Coast Hwy.   (310) 317-0777
Malibu, CA 90265
Lunch: Mon - Sun, Dinner: Mon - Sun, Brunch: Sat - Sun
Web: www.hulapie.com
All Major Credit Cards, Reservations: Yes

Offering the largest oceanfront banquet facility in LA with many configurations to choose from. Its expansive room for larger events can be closed off for more intimate gatherings such as luncheons or birthday parties. The entire restaurant can be rented out for full-scale wrap parties, fundraisers, weddings and more. Duke's can accommodate up to 250 guests for sit-down affairs and will help you customize as much or as little as you desire.

● **El Capitan Theatre & Entertainment Centre**

6840 Hollywood Blvd.   (818) 295-4259
Los Angeles, CA 90028

Location! Location! Location! Your party, premiere, corporate meeting or other monumental event will be as significant and elegant as the historically relevant 1926 theatre which presides at the apex of the Hollywood Entertainment District. Impeccably restored to its Old Hollywood glory but with state-of-the-art audio and visual technology such as Dolby and digital sound capabilities. The 1000-seat theatre and adjoining 1600-capacity, seven-room Entertainment Centre with professional kitchen and bar have seemingly boundless function capabilities, boasting a ballroom, cabaret/nightclub, office, storage and conference space.

Empress Pavilion   **Chinese**

988 N. Hill St.   (213) 617-9898
Los Angeles, CA 90012
Lunch: Mon - Sun, Dinner: Mon - Sun
All Major Credit Cards, Reservations: Yes

The award winning cuisine that everyone loves from this famous and popular Chinatown restaurant is now available at your event location or its spacious 600-seat dining room. Either Way, the staff will attend to every detail. One week's notice is all that is needed to provide the same epicurean perfection enjoyed at Los Angeles' premier Chinese dim sum/seafood restaurant. To name a few, spring rolls and shrimp dumplings are some of the dim sum that has made our restaurant famous. Just ask any of the thousands of people at the "Studio 54", "Return to Paradise" or "Stuff" magazine premieres who waited in line to sample our food. Let the Empress Pavilion help plan your event.

● Fortune Entertainment

1817 W. Verdugo Ave.	(818) 843-0303
Burbank, CA 91506	(213) 687-0338

Sets a new standard for full-service entertainment. Provides everything under the sun for your next event including: party/wedding planning; variety entertainment from handwriting analysts and murder mysteries to mimes and celebrity look-alikes; bands, DJs and karaoke; professional sound and lighting; celebrity negotiations for your event from Rich Little and Phyllis Diller to Captain & Tennile and Johnny Cash; balloon decoration; photography and video services. Fortune can provide all the "extras," such as limos, valet service, and security. Long list of prestigious clients.

● Fox Studios Food Services & Special Events

10201 W. Pico Blvd.	(310) 369-3663
Los Angeles, CA 90035	

One-stop event coordination through this studio's professional staff. Sound stages, screening rooms, unique exteriors and other exciting customized options for breakfasts, lunches, or dinners.

Good Time Promotions

	(562) 697-4454
	(714) 730-5757

Providing all the equipment you need to make your party a good time. Rental possibilities include carnival games and rides, antique fun-food carts, interactive and arcade games, money booths and portable racecars.

● Gotham Hall

1431 Third Street Promenade	(310) 394-8865
Santa Monica, CA 90401	
Web: www.gothamhall.com	

This Santa Monica hangout has a great atmosphere with private rooms, dance club, pool tables, fantastic food and more. Whether it's just the two of you looking for a place to play pool or a group of up to 1,000 looking for a place to have a party, Gotham Hall has it all. Contact special events director Renee Mizrahi at extension 2 for all your party planning needs.

Hollywood Tentworks

15352 Oxford St. (818) 994-2846
Van Nuys, CA 91411

Having your special occasion outdoors? Let Hollywood Tentworks provide you with all your structural needs. Everything from tents, canopies, tables and chairs to heating, cooling, lights and dance floors.

Knitting Factory

7021 Hollywood Blvd. (323) 463-0204
Los Angeles, CA 90028

This internationally famous New York nightclub has spread its wings to Hollywood. They feature two performance spaces, four bars, a full restaurant and complete party planning services.

Lenetta Kidd Productions

(818) 986-8136

Planning events throughout SoCal for more than ten years. Featuring food, decor, live entertainment and event location. Design a menu around your needs, from hors d'ouevres and canapés through dessert. Select a gourmet menu of French, Italian or Spanish cuisine, or customize your own menu from a broad variety of special themes. Musical entertainment in virtually every genre available including swing, big band, R&B, funk, disco, pop, rock and Latin. Perfect resource for your next meeting, reception, wedding, photo shoot or wrap party.

● Leonard Neil Productions

(310) 453-1137
Web: www.leonardneilproductions.com

When one is looking for quality and integrity in the field of special events, Leonard Neil Productions is at the top of the list. For over two decades LNP has produced innovative theme concepts, unique variety acts, exciting dance bands, original shows and big name celebrity talent, for the social and corporate markets world wide. High speed modem customers can now take advantage of their streaming media to expedite proposals.

Like Nothing You've Ever Seen or Heard

YNAMIC THEMED EVENTS

THEME AND SHOW BANDS

azilian New Year's Party -
egent Beverly Wilshire

A Show Band - A Dance Band
Exciting Arrangements, Costume Changes,
Choreography & Audience Interaction

CELEBRITIES

Summer   Tony Bennett   Bill Cosby   Smokey Robinson

Four Tops   Earth, Wind & Fire

Some of the many stars available through
Leonard Neil Productions

SERVICES

- Variety Acts
- Site Location
- Catering
- Themed Decor
- Celebrity Shows
- Dance & Show Bands
- Video
- Sound & Lighting Systems
- Special Effects
- Original Shows

LEONARD NEIL PRODUCTIONS

Los Angeles • (310) 453-1137 • Fax (310) 315-0089
Las Vegas • (702) 313-9842 • Fax (702) 313-9847
Toll Free • (888) 453-1137

e-mail: leonard@leonardneilproductions.com • web: www.leonardneilproductions.com

Marconi Automotive Museum

1302 Industrial Dr.   (714) 258-3001
Tustin, CA 92780
Web: www.marconifnd.org

Host your next event or party at Orange County's only exotic car museum, featuring rare and vintage racing cars, motor bikes, automotive art and trophy collections. Atmosphere transforms well. State-of-the-art screening facilities. In-house special events staff will assist with every detail. Open to the public by appointment. This nonprofit benefits children's charities within the community.

● Pacific Park

380 Santa Monica Pier   310-260-8744
Santa Monica, 90401

Use this amusement park's seaside "Party Cabana" for your celebration and enjoy all the pier's amenities. Guests can mix and mingle then ride the famous solar powered ferris wheel.

● Paramount Pictures Special Events

5555 Melrose Ave.   (323) 956-8398
Hollywood, CA 90038
Web: www.paramount.com

Who better than a film studio, experienced in staging the most auspicious events imaginable, to plan yours? With 62 acres of glamourous ambiance and historical magic, your party is an automatic hit. A selection of sites will capture the perfect mood and theme. Go high tech at the "B" Tank, dramatic at the Bronson Gate, urban chic on New York Street or utterly romantic in Valentino Park. You'll find a perfect location to complement your artistic vision, while the award-winning staff will take care of talent, props, lighting, decor, and special effects, as well as gourmet cuisine and unique requests. Just pick and choose...and show up for the time of your life.

Party Headquarters!

Games • Rides • Gifts • Prizes • Food & Beverage Carts
Carnival Equipment • 40' Ferris Wheel & Carousel
Video Games • Virtual Reality Games • Sports Games
Slot Car Track • Outdoor Staging & Sound Systems

Xavier International
1 (800) 691-2020
(626) 452-0212
fax (626) 452-0123

Party Planners West, Inc.
4141 Glencoe Ave.   (310) 305-1000
Marina del Rey, CA 90292

With over 20 years of experience in full-services event planning, Party Planners West, Inc. had become synonymous with event professionalism. From movie premiers to sporting events, PPW is constantly creating innovative and unique ways to showcase affairs. Client references available on request.

Premier West Entertainment
3760 Cahuenga Blvd. West, Studio 103   (818) 219-0669
Universal City, CA 91604   (818) 981-1401

Full-service entertainment management. Corporate parties, trade shows and weddings welcome. Offering the finest in dance bands, disc jockeys, cocktail music, string ensembles, karaoke, mariachi and specialty acts. Photographers, lighting and audio design available. Right next to Universal Studios.

● Renditions
2501 Ontario St.   (818) 973-7101
Burbank, CA 91504

A full service event management company that provides custom designed environments for all your party needs. Complete support from planning to coordination and execution.

Robert Kass Event Works
9021 Melrose Ave., Suite 209   (310) 276-0081
West Hollywood, CA 90069

With an impressive list of clients, turns a party into a major event for corporations, the entertainment industry and charities, providing full production planning. Creates a vision for a concept and implements all services and provisions to support that concept, including visual design, property and decor selections, location choice and subsequent contract negotiations plus all necessary permits and security coordination, invitation design and distribution, talent, sound and lighting, publicity, and on-site event management. Food and beverage catering, parking and every other detail, making the impossible an extraordinary reality.

Ryan Scott Locations
2260 Sunset Plaza   (323) 650-5911
Los Angeles, CA 90069
Web: www.fortressproductions.com

Located high atop the Hollywood Hills in a magnificent glass, steel and concrete mansion, this is a prime location for special events, parties, film, video and photo shoots. Spectacular panoramic views are the perfect setting whil experiencing the massive EAW Avalon sound systems, HighEnd Intelligent lighting, and an amazing 16 million color laser system!

● VooDoo
4120 W. Olympic Blvd.   (323) 930-9600
Los Angeles, CA 90019
Mon - Sun Hours Vary
Web: www.voodoola.com

Phenomenal nightclub in the tradition of Old Hollywood with a hip Polynesian, Tiki twist. Blacklit masks adorn the corridor that leads into the grand main room with stunning floor-to-ceiling waterfalls in each corner. The copper dance floor sits beneath a giant Aztec altar (that disguises the DJ booth) and matches the copper bar. Plush, upholstered booths line each wall, while cozy loveseats and tables fill the rest of the space. Entire club can be rented out for larger events (capacity-1200). Upstairs eight private skybooths (with four overlooking the dance floor) can accommodate smaller private parties in the same luxurious surroundings as down below. Catered platters and customized party menus available.

Warner Bros. Studios Special Events
4000 Warner Blvd.   (818) 954-2652
Burbank, CA 91522
Web: www.wbspecialevents.com

The fantasy, magic and wonder that has appeared in thousands of your best-loved motion pictures and television shows can be the location for your next special event. Their service special event team will create an unforgettable experience on the studio lot using all the movie-making resources Warner Bros. has to offer.

Who Knew we cater/Private Yacht Charters
    (310) 884-0996
Web: www.2whoknew.com

Nothing says 'special occasion' quite like a party aboard a private luxury yacht. Themed events, weddings, corporate meetings and seminars are put together for you from start to finish and handled with flawless professionalism and meticulous attention to every detail. The result is a smooth, polished and most impressive celebration. Personalized service includes a customized gourmet menu, entertainment selections such as bands and DJs, comedy and magic shows, elaborate set designs, even special effects like fireworks displays. Available for boat parades and scattering services, as well.

● Xavier International
2300 E. Central Ave., Unit K   (626) 452-0212
Duarte, CA 91010   (800) 691-2020

Your party headquarters! Let them provide you with games, rides, gifts, prizes, carnival equipment, 40' ferris wheel & carousel, video games, sport games, slot car track, outdoor staging & sound systems.

WORLD'S GREATEST PARTIES
@ GOTHAM HALL

Gotham Hall is here
to make your party
experience your best yet.
Award Winning Cuisine,
Atmosphere and Party
Coordination are
a Phone Call Away.

Event Capacity
up to 1000
Private Rooms Available

Please Visit
our Website
@ www.Gothamhall.com

Swing & Salsa

Alpine Village Inn
833 W. Torrance Blvd.   (310) 327-4384
Torrance, CA 90502
Web: www.alpinevillage.net

Put a little oomp-pa-pa in your jitterbug every Monday at this unlikely but viable swing venue where big band verve gets a German accent with authentic eats from Blue Danube country and other European locales. Plenty of room for Lindy hoppers on two huge dance floors. Fine service at two full bars. Free lessons some nights. Call for schedule. No cover.

Atlas Supper Club
3760 Wilshire Blvd.   (213) 380-8400
Los Angeles, CA 90010
Web: www.clubatlas.com

Saturday nights sizzle with Salsa! The best Afro-Cuban-Latin jazz in the classic ambiance of a '20s supper club. Live bands heat up the stage, including Poncho Sanchez and Five Degrees of Soul. Fridays come alive with D.J.'s spinning an eclectic mix of world music. Call for details on show times.

The Borderline
99 Rolling Oaks Dr.   (805) 446-4435
Thousand Oaks, CA 91361

Salsa la noche away Mondays but come Tuesdays, The Borderline belongs to die-hard 20-somethings for East Coast Swing Night. Wednesdays 30-somethings take over for West Coast Swing (the official state dance of California) and two-steppin'. Learn or improve your moves with free hour-long dance classes starting at 6pm with different dances taught nightly. The fabulous Flyin' Lindy Hoppers provide instruction on Tuesdays. Call for complete schedule. Live entertainment Fridays. Sundays it's a family affair all the way with a free buffet.

Cafe Danssa
11533 W. Pico Blvd.   (310) 478-7866
Los Angeles, CA 90064
Fri - Sat 10pm - 2am

Everybody samba! And if you don't know how, a free Friday night lesson (with cover) at 9:30pm may acclimate you quite nicely before the live music kicks in after 10pm. An authentic Brazilian band on Saturday, too. Let your feet do the talking (or just listen to the natives). Indigenous eats available.

Cava
8384 W. Third St., (Beverly Plaza Hotel)   (323) 658-8898
Los Angeles, CA 90048

Transport yourself to Spain for the evening as you dine on tapas and then tango it off on the dance floor. Sizzling Flamenco show Wednesdays. Live bands Thursdays thruough Saturdays; lessons Thursdays only.

The Century Club
10131 Constellation Blvd.   (310) 553-6000
Los Angeles, CA 90067

A dash of spice in the heart of Century City. Enjoy fine food and live salsa music Friday evenings or dance under the stars on the heated patio while DJs spin hot Latin sounds.

Club Monte Carlo
333 S. Boylston Ave.   (213) 989-7979
Los Angeles, CA 90017   (213) 353-9800
Web: www.downtownsoho.com

Friday nights are muy caliente at this upscale 60,000 sq. ft. dance club and restaurant featuring the best in salsa and merengue music. DJ and occasional live bands of a decidedly tropical nature spice things up. Full bar and menu prepared by CIA Chef A. Little. Dinner (reservations a must) begin at 7pm, Salsa lessons start at 8pm and the club opens at 9pm.

Coconut Club At The Beverly Hilton
9876 Wilshire Blvd.   (310) 285-1358
Beverly Hills, CA 90210
Fri - Sat 7:30pm - 2am

Old Hollywood glamour is alive and well at Merv Griffin's trés swank Coconut Club Saturday nights with renowned big band swing orchestras. Zoot suits optional but a good time is mandatory. Call for schedule.

Conga Room
5364 Wilshire Blvd.   (323) 938-1696
Los Angeles, CA 90036
Web: www.congaroom.com

Havana hits the Miracle Mile con mucho flavor! Illustrious performers, vibrant interior and a scorching dance scene. An array of diverse celebrities make this spot one of the most happening scenes in town. Live bands on selected nights. Dance lessons every Thursday and includes cover charge for the evening. Prix-fixe dinner menu.

The Danceman in Hollywood
817 N. Highland Ave.   (310) 479-1138
Los Angeles, CA 90038   (323) 467-0825

Don't envy the Lindy Hoppers or Jitterbuggers. Be one. Or glide across the floor in a polished fox-trot. Throw caution to the wind and let passion move your feet to the Tango. Sparks will fly when you Salsa. Dancing isn't just for other people anymore with these comprehensive courses. Danceman Swing Lounge every Friday offers the chance to polish your moves, regardless of your dance of choice. Call for schedule and fees.

The Derby
4500 Los Feliz Blvd.   (323) 663-8979
Los Angeles, CA 90027
Web: www.the-derby.com

Get ready go-daddy-o! To the Derby, that is, the reigning king of the LA swingers scene. So shine up those wing tips, knot your loudest tie, put on your swankiest lid and get ready to jive like a hep cat. Don't know how? Well, get off your keister for some free West Coast Swing instruction or stop by Mondays to learn the Lindy Hop. Private parties for up to 750.

El Floridita
1253 N. Vine St.   (323) 871-8612
Los Angeles, CA 90038
Web: www.calendarlive.com/elfloridita

Break out those cha-cha heels! El Floridita is the closest LA will ever come to a pre-socialist Cuban supper/dance club. Reservations are a must as cuba libre drinking fills the club to capacity nightly. Live salsa bands Mondays, Wednesdays, Fridays and Saturdays. Wednesdays, work up an appetite for sumptuous native cuisine with free dance lessons from 8pm-9pm. Cover charge if you don't plan to eat. Sundays feature richly textured Flamenco music.

LA Dance Experience
1941 Westwood Blvd.   (310) 475-1878
Los Angeles, CA 90025

Six-week lessons will have ya flashing your Crazy Legs and flaunting a pocket watch chain just like a regular big bad voodoo daddy. East or West Coast swing, Lindy hop and ballroom classes available, but if it's español that makes your hips hip, there's always tango, salsa and Argentine dance lessons available. There's even the chance to practice what you prance with dance parties, too. Call for upcoming class schedule, registration and fees.

The Mayan
1038 S. Hill St.   (213) 746-4287
Los Angeles, CA 90015

Friday and Saturday nights, live salsa so hot it promises to pop the cork off champagne bottles. Huge dance floor at this downtown locale packed with a diverse mix of scenesters. Dance lessons from 8-9pm are free with cover.

Nicholby's
404 E. Main St.   (805) 653-2320
Ventura, CA 93001
Web: www.nicholbysvta.com

Wednesdays swing for initiates and the dexterous alike with plenty of room on the massive parquet dance floor for everyone. Beginning lessons 7:30pm; advanced 8:15pm followed by live music. And what would the swing experience be without a perfect martini? If it's salsa that moves you, Tuesdays have got it goin' on starting at 7:30pm with lessons and live bands.

Pa Paz
1716 N. Cahuenga Blvd.   (323) 461-8190
Los Angeles, CA 90028

Hollywood heats its heels with salsa and rock en español Thursdays and Saturdays. Massive dance floor fills up fast and stays that way as DJs mix inarguable powers of persuasion. Located conveniently behind Sharkey's Mexican Grill to satiate that inevitable taquito jones. Free dance lessons Thursdays 8:30pm-9:45pm and no cover.

Pasión Supper Club And Restaurant
12215 Ventura Blvd.   (818) 752-7333
Studio City, CA 91604   (818) 752-7336
Web: www.pasion-club.com

Dine and baile the night away. Tuesday Tango, Wednesday Swing, or Thursday Salsa. Fridays and Saturdays showcase Latin and salsa bands, and a dazzling tango or flamenco floor show. Don Uncle Fito's (or Fred's) fedora for Sunday Swing. Lessons (gratis!) prior to floor show.

Regent Beverly Wilshire Hotel

9500 Wilshire Blvd.   (310) 275-5200
Beverly Hills, CA 90212
Web: www.fourseasons.com

Conjure the magic and elegance of ballroom dancing Friday and Saturday evenings. With dinner reservations on your dance card, you'll receive a full fledged invite to waltz around the hotel's grand dance floor, only mere feet from your table in The Dining Room. Three-piece live band offers a refined blend of fox trot, East Coast swing, and big band. Friday 8-11pm; Saturday 8pm to midnight.

Rhino Room

7979 Center Ave.   (714) 892-3316
Huntington Beach, CA 92647

Charge the dance floor to live big band swing every Wednesday. Whether you're perfecting smooth moves or Lindy hopping for the first time, a pro instructor offers lessons at 8:30 and 9:30pm.

Roca and Bolero at Café America

1933 S. Broadway   (323) 957-4648
Los Angeles, CA 90007   (323) 255-1390
Web: www.rocanetwork.com

Salsa served up and down where you'll enjoy two clubs in one every Saturday. Primo bands and pro dancers with lessons at 8:30 taught by Los Rumberos. First floor features Spanish pop, rock en español and house. Cool down on the patio and be social.

Rudolfo's

2500 Riverside Dr.   (323) 669-1226
Los Angeles, CA 90039

Forget that generic Gap commercial. At Rudolfo's, salsa is served muy caliente and mucho of it. Dance lessons available. Call for event-packed schedule.

The Tantra Bar at St. Mark's

23 Windward Ave.   (310) 452-2222
Venice, CA 90291

Salsa on Tuesday nights with live band. Lessons begin at 8:00 sharp and "musica" at 9:30. Since you'll be burning the calories off, make reservations for dinner while you're at it.

Art brillant

The world famous Rodeo Drive in Beverly Hills is the location of our spacious, elegant gallery. We bring you the leading edge of artistic trends in the world of art.

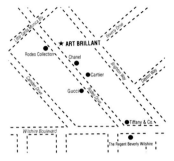

FILMING OR EVENT LEASING AVAILABLE

428 N. Rodeo Drive
Beverly Hills, CA 90210

Tel: (310) 246-0471
www.artbrillant.com

Elegant stairways viewed from the lobby.

Gorgeous atmosphere

Beautiful antique furniture displayed on the seco

Culture

Art Galleries

Art Brilliant
428 N. Rodeo Dr.   (310) 246-9400
Beverly Hills, CA 90210
Web: www.artbrilliantrodeo.com

This stunning 5460 square foot Beverly Hills gallery features a magnificent collection of artwork by international artists. Located on Rodeo Drive, the gallery itself is a must see with a double spiral staircase and a luminous crystal chandelier. A great location for parties.

China Art Objects Galleries
933 Chung King Rd.   (213) 613-0384
Los Angeles, CA 90012
Wed - Sat Noon - 6pm

Contemporary art project swims against the tide of conventional galleries with a focus on emerging artists exhibiting works in an unlikely city locale. In addition to cutting edge art presented in the context of a Chinese-modern design interior, the space hosts live music performances, record release parties and celebrity roasts.

Daniel Saxon Gallery
552 Norwich Dr.   (310) 657-6033
West Hollywood, CA 90048
Tue - Sat 11am - 5pm

The only national gallery devoted exclusively to paintings, drawings, prints & sculpture by Chicanos...Gronk, John Valadez, Carlos Almaraz, Einar & Jamex De La Torre and Patssi Valdez.

Delirium Tremens
1553 Echo Park Ave.   (213) 861-6802
Los Angeles, CA 90026
Fri - Sun 1pm - 5pm & by appointment

Expanding the definition of the term 'art gallery' with performances, performance artists, and lectures, this small space that attracts a big draw showcases illustrations, installations and fine art, often by artists making their debuts. Discovering new talent is a point of pride. Never a cover charge, artists receptions the first Saturday of each month. Even dogs are welcome at this artistic gathering of the vibe.

DiRT Gallery
7906 Santa Monica Blvd., Ste. 218   (323) 822-9359
West Hollywood, CA 90046
Thu - Sat Noon - 5pm

Bohemian offbeat gallery located in the Campbell building, a 1930s converted hotel (check out the shower gallery). Interesting shows highlighting emerging artists. Affordable prices.

Form Zero
2433 Main St.   (310) 450-0222
Santa Monica, CA 90405
Mon - Sat 10:30am - 7pm, Sun 11:30am - 6pm
Web: www.formzero.com

An architectural gallery which sponsors four major exhibitions a year and author signings throughout the year. Outstanding retail bookstore and publishing press focusing on 20th century architecture. Well-versed staff and comprehensive website.

Fototeka
1549 Echo Park Ave.   (213) 250-4686
Los Angeles, CA 90026
Fri - Sun 1pm - 5pm

Photography gallery focusing on high caliber emerging artists. Neighborly space, part of a trio of galleries in Echo Park. Openings bring out a melange of art lovers. Most pieces under $600.

Galerie Morpheus
9250 Wilshire Blvd.   (310) 859-2557
Beverly Hills, CA 90212
Mon - Fri 10am - 6pm, Sat 11am - 4pm

Gallery shows original works, sculptures and lithographs. Publishes fantastic realism books by H.R. Giger, Jacek Yerka, De Es and Sebastian Kruger.

Gallery of Functional Art
Bergamot Station, 2525 Michigan Ave. E3   (310) 829-6990
Santa Monica, CA 90404
Tue - Sat 11am - 7pm, Sun Noon - 5pm
Web: www.galleryoffuctionalart.com

One of a kind limited edition furniture, lighting, ceramics and jewelry. Artists include Joel Stearns, Pippa Garner John Bok, Floyd Gompf, David Rudolph, Paul Freundt and others.

La Luz De Jesus Gallery
4633 Hollywood Blvd.   (323) 666-7667
Los Angeles, CA 90027
Mon - Wed 11am - 7pm, Thu - Sat 11am - 9pm,
Sun 12pm - 6pm
Web: www.laluzdejesus.com

One of the best scenes for underground and offbeat art. Gala openings are the first Friday of every month and are always jam-packed to the rafters with cutting-edge art lovers.

MAK Center For Art & Architecture, Schindler House
835 N. Kings Rd.   (323) 651-1510
West Hollywood, CA 90069
Wed - Sun 11am - 6pm

Vienna's MAK sponsors 2-4 shows annually at the Schindler house, which completed restoration and can now be viewed in its finest form. These are long-term architectural and art shows featuring works with a spatial dimension.

Merry Karnowsky Gallery
170 S. La Brea Ave.   (323) 933-4408
Los Angeles, CA 90036
Tue - Sat Noon - 6pm
Web: www.mkgallery.com

Located in a preserved art deco building, ascend the spiral marble staircase to second floor gallery. Contemporary underground artwork with an emphasis on new surrealism. Artists include Todd Schorr, Kent Williams, Kathy Staico Schorr, Becca and Toshio Saeki, Camille Rose Garcia, Shepard Fairey, Dean Karr, Dave McKean, Alex Gross and others.

Ojala
1547 Echo Park Ave.   (213) 250-4155
Los Angeles, CA 90026
Fri - Sun 1pm - 5pm

Tiny space in a trio of eastside galleries showing contemporary furniture and fine arts. One-of-a-kind pieces at reasonable prices with the same quality as those higher priced galleries with better addresses.

Peter Fetterman Gallery
Bergamot Station   (310) 453-6463
2525 Michigan Ave., Ste. A7
Santa Monica, CA 90404
Tue - Sat 11am - 6pm
Web: www.peterfetterman.com

A favorite gallery among cinematographers and directors, Fetterman Gallery stocks the largest inventory of blue-chip photography on the West Coast. Cozy study-like space with personal assistance. Artists include Berenice Abbott, Henri Cartier Bresson, Alfred Eisenstadt, Andre Kertesz, Weegee and many others.

Self Help Graphics
3802 Cesar Chavez Ave.   (323) 264-1259
Los Angeles, CA 90063
Tue - Sat 10am - 4pm
Web: www.selfhelpgraphics.com

An institution in the Latino arts community, Self Help hosts workshops, tertulias (artist/community dialogues) and performances of all genres. On selected nights, local and internationally acclaimed Latino artists present original works. Don't forget to pay homage to the ten foot high fiberglass Virgen de Guadalupe whose base is covered with neighborhood flowers and whose presence has blessed the site for over 20 years.

Track 16
Bergamot Station, 2525 Michigan Ave., C1   (310) 264-4678
Santa Monica, CA 90404
Tue - Sat 11am - 6pm
Web: www.track16.com

Track 16 describes itself as "an eclectic space that organizes exhibitions of contemporary art, and 20th century Americana and applied arts. "One of the largest spaces at Bergamot, it is open and airy and allows the art work enough room to be appreciated. Openings are always a cool scene.

Zero One
7025 Melrose Ave.   (323) 965-9459
Los Angeles, CA 90038
Tue - Sat 11am - 6pm
Web: www.01gallery.com

Zero One shows the hippest contemporary art of the 21st century. Arrive on time to openings or you won't get in. Featured artists include Chaz Bojorquez, Gahan Wilson, Mear, Marcy Watton, Ausgang, Raul Gonzalez, Van Arno and Ron English.

Auctions & Flea Markets

A.N. Abell

2613 Yates Ave.   (800) 404-2235
Los Angeles, CA 90040   (323) 724-8102

Previews on Wednesday and auctions every Thursday at this venerable auction house. An all-day event with every kind of item imaginable found here. Auction begins with smaller household items and heightens into the prize antiques. There are always finds for the savvy buyer, even novices.

Butterfield & Butterfield

7601 Sunset Blvd.   (323) 850-7500
Los Angeles, CA 90046
Web: www.butterfields.com

Estate auctions held monthly. Specializing in entertainment memorabilia, arts and crafts, and art nouveau. The most fun is their free appraisal clinic held every first and third Tuesday of the month from 9:30am-12:30pm. You can bring up to five items - first come, first served. Insurance appraisals available.

Chait Gallery Auctions

9330 Civic Center Dr.   (310) 285-0182
Beverly Hills, CA 90210
Web: www.chait.com

Auctions held once a month, usually the third Sunday. Exclusively Asian art and antiques including Chinese, Korean Japanese, Indonesian and Mongolian. Call to set up appointment for appraisals. Specializes in antiques, but carries some modern decorative items.

Christie's

360 N. Camden Dr.   (310) 385-2600
Beverly Hills, CA 90210
Web: www.christies.com

Christie's specialists are available to appraise your signed jewelry and watches, paintings, motor cars and other fine collections. Please call for a confidential appointment. Auctions held throughout the year.

Culver City Antique Market

Culver Blvd. & Overland Ave.   (323) 933-2511
Culver City, CA 90230
8am - 3pm

By Veterans Memorial Park, the bargain hunters will hunt the third Sunday of every month. Peruse the offerings of many vendors for that claw foot bathtub or one-of-a-kind smoking jacket. Unusual finds galore. Free, convenient parking.

Fairfax High School Flea Market

Fairfax Ave. & Melrose Ave.   (323) 655-7678
Los Angeles, CA 90046

Every Sunday, local hipsters gather to search out bargains or just mingle with the friendly crowds. Lots of regulars show their wares from week to week. Antiques, clothes and artistic crafts.

Glendale Community College Swap Meet

1500 N. Verdugo Rd.   (818) 240-1000
Glendale, CA 91208
8am - 3pm

Enjoy a hilltop view overlooking the city while browsing through booths of antique vendors on the third Sunday of the month from 8am to 3pm. Free admission.

Golden West College Flea Market

15744 Goldenwest St.   (714) 898-7927
Huntington Beach, CA 92647
Sat 8am - 3pm, Sun 8am - 3pm

Garage sale treasures and swap meet merchandise for sale every Saturday and Sunday, rain or shine. Saturdays have more used merchandise than Sundays. Free admission.

Northridge Antique Market

Devonshire and Lindley Ave. (562) 633-3836
Northridge, CA 91325
5am - 3pm

Held every fourth Sunday and fifth Sunday when it occurs (4 X a year). Fifth Sunday hosts twice as many dealers. Friendly atmosphere for vendors and customers. European and American antiques, china, linens and more. $5/early birds, $3/general admission.

Orrils

1910 W. Adams Blvd. (310) 277-7373
Los Angeles, CA 90018
Tue 9:30am - 4:30pm

Auctions every Tuesday for the last 51 years. Home furnishings - modern and antique. Make your friends green with envy with your 1940s steel cabinet that you got for 100 bucks. Gavel banging from 9:30am-4:30pm; bring a lunch. Cash deposit required; balance can be paid by check or credit card.

Outdoor Antique And Collectible Market

Lakewood Blvd. and Conant St. (323) 655-5703
Long Beach, CA 90808
5:30am - 3pm

Over 800 dealers in all types of antiques and collectibles ranging from art to xylophones and everything in between. Held the third Sunday of the month. Early birds/$10, General/$4.50.

Pasadena City College Flea Market

1570 E. Colorado Blvd (626) 585-7906
Pasadena, CA 91106
8am - 3pm
Web: www.paccd.cc.ca.us

Free admission and free parking at this market which takes place the first Sunday of the month except in January (second Sunday). 480 dealers with an additional 70 vendors devoted exclusively to music-related items. Sure to have that rare LP you're looking for. Campus clubs sell snacks from tamales to cookies.

Rose Bowl

1001 Rose Bowl Dr. (323) 560-7469
Pasadena, CA 91103
6am - 3pm

Grandmammy of flea markets held the second Sunday of the month, rain or shine. Over 2200 vendors peddle their wares which runs the gamut from antiques to new merchandise to arts and crafts. $15/VIP admission, $10/early bird 7:30-9, $6/general admission.

Santa Monica Outdoor And Antique Collectible Market

Airport Ave. Off Bundy Dr. (323) 933-2511
Santa Monica Airport (South Side)
Santa Monica, CA 90405
6am - 3pm

The only flea market in the country that you can actually fly into (and people do!) meets the fourth Sunday and and fifth Sunday of every month. High-end antiques and collectibles featured by 200 vendors. Fresh grilled portabello mushrooms and fries draw the crowds -- and their dogs. The only market of its kind where canines are welcome. Early birds/$6. General admission/$4.

Sotheby's

9665 Wilshire Blvd. (310) 274-0340
Beverly Hills, CA 90212
Mon - Fri 9am - 5pm
Web: www.sothebys.com

Previews held five days prior to auction. Try and snag a catalogue which often become collector's items themselves. Auctions include jewelry, wine, movie memorabilia, fine and decorative art. There are bargains to be had.

Booksellers

Atlantis Books
144 S. San Fernando Blvd.   (818) 845-6467
Burbank, CA 91502
Mon - Sun 10am - 6pm
Web: www.abebooks.com/home/atlantis/

An X-Phile's dream come true, this alternative bookstore maintains a large selection of books, videotapes (over 1000), pamphlets and religious texts on UFOs, paranormal activities, secret government, secret societies, radical politics and the occult. Hey, stop following me!

Beyond Baroque Literary/Arts Foundation
681 Venice Blvd.   (310) 822-3006
Venice, CA 90291
Hours Vary

LA's leading literary/arts center hosts storytelling, performance art and poetry readings on a regular basis. Writing workshops have produced legendary alums Wanda Coleman, Tom Waits, and Exene Cervenkova run year-round, many of which are free.

Bodhi Tree Bookstore
8585 Melrose Ave.   (310) 659-1733
West Hollywood, CA 90069
Mon - Sun 10am - 11pm

Books to illuminate the senses and soul from all disciplines with the sweet aroma of burning Tibetan incense. New age music, books and greeting cards. Don't miss their used bookstore just around the corner for significant bargains.

The Cook's Library
8373 W. Third St.   (323) 655-3141
Los Angeles, CA 90048
Mon 1pm - 5pm, Tue - Sat 11am - 6pm

Need to whip up a romantic soufflé at the last minute? With over 4500 titles, choose from their large American regional section or many imports from England and France (in French). Cookbooks for kids, too.

Cookbooks By Janet Jarvits
321 N. San Fernando Blvd.   (818) 848-4630
Burbank, CA 91502
Mon - Fri 11am - 7pm, Sat 10am - 6pm, Sun 12pm - 6pm
Web: www.cookbkjj.com

Wanna whip up an Apple Brown Betty but can't find Mom's Betty Crocker Cookbook? Look no further, Janet Jarvits will have it and if she doesn't, she'll do a global search and get it for you. Hard-to-find cookbooks that date back to the 1800's and junior league cookbooks from all over America.

Counterpoint Books And Records
5911 Franklin Ave.   (323) 957-7965
Los Angeles, CA 90028
Mon - Thu 11am - 11pm, Fri - Sat 11am - Midnight,
Sun 1pm - 8pm

Looking for a pre-20/20 Hugh Downs singing folk ditties on blue vinyl? You just may find it at Counterpoint. Besides vinyl from all eras, they carry CDs, videos and affordable used books in a wide range of subjects including science fiction, poetry and film.

Daily Planet Bookstore
5931 1/2 Franklin Ave.   (323) 957-0061
Los Angeles, CA 90028
Mon - Fri 11am - Midnight, Sat - Sun 9am - Midnight

Avant-garde bookstore with individually selected titles on fiction, poetry, film, meditation and children's titles. Art openings, book signings and quaint neighborhood atmosphere make this store a long time favorite among locals.

Dangerous Visions
13563 Ventura Blvd.   (818) 986-6963
Sherman Oaks, CA 91423
Tue - Sun 10am - 7pm
Web: www.readsf.com

Your one stop shop for H.P. Lovecraft, Harlan Ellison and Philip K. Dick. Sci-fi horror, fantasy, mystery and suspense works. New, used and out-of-print both in hard and soft cover. Rare pulp magazines in stock. In-store events and book signings.

The Gamble House Bookstore / USC

4 Westmoreland Pl.   (626) 449-4178
Pasadena, CA 91103
Tue - Sat 10am - 5pm, Sun 11:30am - 5pm
Web: www.thegamblehouse.com

Set on the site of the historical Gamble house on a private street in Pasadena, this charming bookstore specializes in the arts and crafts movement worldwide. Books, magazines, periodicals both in-print and out-of-print. Hand-lettered small press books created in the tradition of the arts and crafts movements. Reproduction pieces. All profits benefit the Gamble House.

Hennessey And Ingalls

1254 Third Street Promenade   (310) 458-9074
Santa Monica, CA 90401
Mon - Sun 10am - 8pm
Web: www.hennesseyingalls.com

A breath of fresh air amidst the chaos of the Third Street Promenade. Every imaginable art, architecture, photography and design book under the sun. Rows and rows, stacks and stacks of new and out-of-print books.

Meltdown

7529 Sunset Blvd.   (323) 851-7283
Los Angeles, CA 90046   (323) 851-7223
Sun - Mon Noon - 7pm, Tue - Sat Noon - 9pm
Web: www.meltcomics.com

Comics and collectibles with an emphasis on esoteric and independent titles and winner of the Will Eisner award. New and used titles with a strong foreign language import section. Toys, figures, trading cards and signings.

Other Times Books

10617 W. Pico Blvd.   (310) 475-2547
Los Angeles, CA 90064
Tue - Sat Noon - 6pm

Movie buffs alert! This shop carries out-of-print books with a gigantic performing arts section and oversized picture film books. Cool used jazz section, literature and the humanities. Many contemporary first editions.

Skylight Books

1818 N. Vermont Ave.   (323) 660-1175
Los Angeles, CA 90027
Mon - Sun 10am - 10pm
Web: www.skylightbooks.com

Independently owned in the eternally young and hip section of Los Feliz, Skylight Books hosts readings from emerging new writers to bona fide Hollywood celebs. Locals catch up on the latest hardcovers under a huge indoor ficus tree. Catering to eclectic tastes, no displays of Barbara Cartland here.

Traveler's Bookcase

8375 W. Third St.   (323) 655-0575
Los Angeles, CA 90048
Mon - Sat 10am - 6pm, Sun 11am - 5pm
Web: www.travelbooks.com

Whether you're planning that second honeymoon or a simple three-day getaway, go to the experts at this cozy Third Street shop. 14,000 travel titles from all over the planet (Bali, Yemen, Thailand, Mozambique and, of course, regional California books). Well-journeyed staff will point you in the right direction. Works with production companies and has the largest selection of color location photographs in town.

Cultural Tourism

Archititours

(323) 294-5825
(888) 627-2448

Web: www.architours.com

Their mission is to bridge the gap between design professionals and the public. Groups spend six hours with an individual artist or architect and go through an entire project. Itineraries customized to group needs.

Bob's Big Boy

4211 Riverside Dr.   (818) 843-9334
Burbank, CA 91505

The only Boy in town without a bedtime. Opened in 1949, it's the oldest remaining Big Boy in America. Informal car shows Friday nights.

Chinese Historical Society Tour

(323) 222-0856

A walking tour through Chinatown; explore the architecture and history of this vibrant neighborhood. Tour length varies from one-to-two-hours depending upon group interest. Tours usually start in front of Phoenix Bakery on Broadway, include the Union Station area in the area. Call for appointments.

Desert Adventures Jeep Eco-Tours

67555 E. Palm Canyon Dr., Ste. A-104   (760) 324-5337
Cathedral City, CA 92234
Web: www.redjeep.com

Jeep adventures through the desert from September-June. Two, three or four hour eco-tours explore colorful vistas with histories of a bygone era. Visit Native Americans sites, retrace trails of the first explorers. Pass through three life zones in the desert. Learn about native medicinal plants.

Downey McDonald's

10207 Lakewood Blvd.   (562) 622-9248
Downey, CA 90240

Built in 1953, the world's oldest operating McDonald's retains its golden arches and original speedy character sign with moving lights. Get a large fries or visit the gift shop and museum. Open 7:30am-10:00pm seven days a week.

El Pueblo De Los Angeles

125 Paseo de la Plaza   (213) 628-3562
Los Angeles, CA 90012

Imagine a time when LA was nothing but a small desert village. Located in downtown Los Angeles, El Pueblo is the first settlement of Los Angeles and is preserved as a state historical park. It reflects the cultural influence of Hispanic, Black, Chinese, French, Italian and Anglo settlers who migrated there as early as 1781. One hour tours depart from 10am-12pm on the hour Wed-Sat.

Fashion District Tour

110 E. Ninth St., Ste. 6625   (213) 488-1153
Los Angeles, CA 90079
Web: www.fashiondistrict.org

LA's Fashion District can go head to head against NY's anytime. Tour will provide insider-shopping tips. Trolley picks up at Olympic Blvd. between Los Angeles and Main Streets the last Saturday of every month. Departures at 10am, 11am, and 12 noon.

Frito Lay

22801 Hwy. 58   (661) 328-6060
Bakersfield, CA 93312   (661) 328-6000
Web: www.fritolay.com

Ever contemplate how a Frito becomes a Frito or what a Cheeto is made of? This is where the answers are. Eat hot chips right off the line and view firsthand the inner workings of the plant where America's favorite munchies are processed and packaged. A tour guide will walk you through the fascinating steps involved. Pay attention; a quiz will be given and prizes awarded. Complementary bags of fresh product for everyone. Tuesdays only. Reservations required.

Googie Tours

(323) 980-3480

To hear owner and guide John English, we should have listed these tours in our Museum Section. To John, Googie, otherwise known as 1950s modern roadside architecture (motels, bowling alleys, cocktail lounges and coffee shops) is worthy to be called art. Ask about Route 66 tours.

Hollywood Roosevelt Hotel

7000 Hollywood Blvd.   (323) 466-7000
Los Angeles, CA 90028   (800) 950-7667
Web: www.hollywoodroosevelt.com

1928 Hollywood landmark was home to the first Academy Awards and carries on its industry tradition as a film-friendly location where shoots check in almost as often as guests. Spectacular Spanish art deco, a chandelier-laced lobby and freshly refurbished rooms. Two floors of cabanas with private patios or balconies and poolside Tropicana Bar form a magical oasis. Views of the Hollywood Hills and downtown LA. Home to the world famous Cinegrill and lesser known but equally fabulous Teddy's.

LA Bike Tours, LLC

(323) 658-5890
Web: www.labiketours.com

This company replaces tour buses with mountain bikes for the adventurous traveler visiting Los Angeles. Take one of their approximately 9 mile, 3 hour tours through Hollywood or Beverly Hills. If you feel up to it go for the 30 mile Getty Center Tour (a shorter option is available). Bicycle rentals are included.

LA NightHawks Tours

(310) 392-1500
Web: www.la.nighthawks.com

On-the-town deluxe tours in stretch limos to the coolest rock clubs, the bluesiest R&B joints, the most dazzling discos, or up close and personal with exotic hunks or gorgeous ladies. Daytime tours (for groups of 12 or more) of the musical history of L.A. VIP treatment all the way.

Los Angeles Conservancy Tours

523 W. Sixth St., Ste. 1216   (213) 623-2489
Los Angeles, CA 90014

From jazzy art deco to the stately marble columns of the Biltmore Hotel, discover LA's architecture every Saturday morning through one of the Conservancy's eleven walking tours of downtown LA. Call for reservations.

Mural Conservancy Of Los Angeles

(818) 487-0416
Web: www.lamurals.org

Widely acknowledged as one of the mural capitals of the world, LA's murals reflect the cultural diversity of this megapolis. Both famous and anonymous artists have created these numerous LA landmarks. Mural tours each month.

Original Pantry

877 S. Figueroa St.   (213) 972-9279
Los Angeles, CA 90017

Since 1924, this landmark owned by Richard Riordan (who sold the air rights so no one will ever tear it down). Americana at its best: meaty BBQ ribs, sirloin tips, hamburger loaf, chicken fried steak and mac'n'cheese.

SPARC: Social & Public Art Resource Center

685 Venice Blvd.   (310) 822-9560
Venice, CA 90291
Web: www.sparcmurals.org

For over 25 years, the experts on murals and public art in Los Angeles. Tours are offered here six months out of the year, each with a different theme based on cultural and ethnic backgrounds. Sponsors of over 500 citywide murals. Looking for a muralist? This is the place to go. On-site gallery boasts over 60,000 slides, the largest collection of slides of public art in the world.

Warner Bros. Studios VIP Tour

4000 Warner Blvd.   (818) 972-8687
Burbank, CA 91522
Web: www.studio-tour.com

The only studio tour where you can enjoy an in-depth personalized look, inside the movie magic machine, at one of Hollywood's busiest and most historic motion picture and television studios. Guests are escorted through the studio streets via carts visiting their film museum, exterior sets, sound stages, technical and craft shops. No two tours are exactly alike as they vary with daily on-lot production schedules. Children under the age of eight are not allowed. Reservations are recommended for this 2-hour tour.

Wildlife Waystation

14831 Little Tujunga Canyon Rd.   (818) 899-5201
Angeles Nat'l Forest, CA 91342
Web: www.waystation.org

Enter big cat country where this nonprofit wild animal sanctuary rescues and provides a home for approximately 1200 primates, felines, pachyderms and many others on 160 rugged acres. Residence to five Siberian tigers (only 200 remain in the wild), one weighing in at 750 lbs., and other endangered species. Open first and third Sundays so plan ahead. Immerse in the animal kingdom with an exciting Sunset or Starlight Safari offered June through September. Call for schedule and book reservations well in advance.

Gardens

Arboretum Of Los Angeles County
301 N. Baldwin Ave. (626) 821-3222
Arcadia, CA 91007
Mon - Sun 9am - 4:30pm

127 acres of varied gardens in a tranquil setting. Herb garden with herbs mentioned in Shakespeare. Historic architecture, roaring waterfall and roaming peacocks, ducks and geese. Australian gardens contain the largest plantings of eucalyptus outside of Australia.

Descanso Gardens
1418 Descanso Dr. (818) 952-4385
La Cañada Flintridge, CA 91011
Mon - Sun 9am - 4:30pm

Built in the '30s, 160 acres of topiary, maze, Japanese and children's gardens with an international Rosarium containing 5,000 species of antique, modern and native varieties. Maintains the largest planting of camellias in the world (100,000).

Huntington Botanical Gardens
1151 Oxford Rd. (626) 405-2100
Pasadena, CA 91108
Tue - Fri Noon - 4:30pm, Sat - Sun 10:30am - 4:30pm
Web: www.huntington.org

An oasis within the city and complete outing for the entire day. Landscapes include Japanese, desert, rose, camellia, palm, subtropical, jungle, lily and more. One mansion houses "The Blue Boy" and "Pinkie" as part of its collection of American and British art. Included in over 600,000 books and three million manuscripts in the library is a Gutenberg Bible (c. 1455). Tea is served in the rose garden (Call ahead for reservations).

Living Desert Wildlife & Botanical Park
47-900 Portola Ave. (760) 346-5694
Palm Desert, CA 92260
Mon - Sun 9am - 5pm
Web: www.livingdesert.org

Zoological and botanical garden with four hundred acres of developed desert. 400 animals representing 130 species can be viewed in enclosures while some (e.g. jackrabbits) run wild. All this plus wilderness hiking trails.

Quail Botanical Gardens
230 Quail Gardens Dr. (760) 436-3036
Encinitas, CA 92023
Mon - Sun 9am - 5pm
Web: www.qbgardens.com

Herb, walled, subtropical fruit (mango, fig, banana) and California native gardens on thirty acres. Three-story waterfall with exotic rain forest exhibit, stream, pond, overlook and a special collection of palms, bamboo and cyads. Picnics welcome.

Rancho Santa Ana Botanic Garden
1500 N. College Ave. (909) 625-8767
Claremont, CA 91711
Mon - Sun 8am - 5pm
Web: www.rsabg.org

Eighty-six acres of exclusively native California flora. Excellent book selection and California plant garden shop. Guided wildflower tours in spring. Education classes, lectures, and field trips offered. Don't miss their enormous plant sale the first weekend of November.

Santa Barbara Botanic Garden
1212 Mission Canyon Rd. (805) 682-4726
Santa Barbara, CA 93105
Mon - Fri 9am - 5pm, Sat - Sun 9am - 6pm
Web: www.sbbg.org

Wind your way up the hills of Santa Barbara to sixty-five acres of native plants. Enjoy the redwood forest, historic dam and panoramic views of the neighboring Channel Islands. Five and a half miles of walking paths. Friendly gift shop. Call for tour and admission fee information.

Theodore Payne Foundation
10459 Tuxford St. (818) 768-1802
Sun Valley, CA 91352
Wed - Sat 8:30am - 4:30pm, Sun 11am - 4:30pm

California native plant nursery encourages Californians to grow native plants not only for their beauty but for their drought tolerance. Good selection, reasonable prices and friendly staff. Tours and classes offered. Membership packages available.

U. C. Riverside Botanic Gardens
900 University Ave. (909) 787-4650
Riverside, CA 92521
Mon - Sun 8am - 5pm

Forty acres of gardens with five miles of walking trails. Plants from around the world and a huge herb garden with medicinal, culinary and dye herbs. Wildlife preserve with over 200 species of birds. Geodesic dome houses tropical plants. Wheel chair access.

Museums

Aquarium Of The Pacific
100 Aquarium Way   (562) 590-3100
Long Beach, CA 90802
Mon - Sun 9am - 6pm
Web: www.aquariumofpacific.org

12,000 ocean inhabitants from 550 different species occupy the exotic galleries and the painstakingly reproduced habitats of the aquarium. From as far as Russia and as near as Catalina Island, brilliantly-colored fish and playful pinnipeds welcome you to their new home. Group tours, gift shop and cafe.

Autry Museum of Western Heritage
4700 Western Heritage Way   (323) 667-2000
Los Angeles, CA 90027
Tue - Sun 10am - 5pm
Web: www.autry-museum.org

For 10 years, the Autry museum has paid homage to the glamorous American West, from prehistoric roots to gold rush days and the romantic notions created by Hollywood. Visitors encounter treasures of an unexpected range from cowboy chaps, spurs, and saddles to the paintings of Albert Bierstadt and from the armor of Spanish conquistadors to a chenille kiddie bedspread bearing the hallowed Hopalong Cassidy name.

Cabrillo Beach Marine Aquarium
3720 Stephen White Dr.   (310) 548-7562
San Pedro, CA 90731
Mon - Fri Noon - 5pm, Sat - Sun 10am - 5pm
Web: www.cabrilloaq.org

A museum/aquarium devoted to promoting awareness and knowledge of the rich marine life of Southern California. Designed By Frank Gehry, the aquarium offers a range of classes, tours and public programs including seasonal whale watching trips. Guided tours of the tide pools in the Point Fermin Refuge.

California African American Museum
Exposition Park, 600 State Dr.   (213) 744-7432
Los Angeles, CA 90037
Tue - Sun 10am - 5pm
Web: www.caam.ca.gov

The mission statement of the museum is to collect, preserve and interpret the contributions of African Americans to world history and culture. Exhibits reflect this statement and vary from local to national to international artists.

California Surf Museum
223 N. Coast Hwy.   (760) 721-6876
Oceanside, CA 92054
Thu - Mon 10am - 4pm
Web: www.surfmuseum.org

Paddle out to the Surf Museum and catch sight of some gnarly surfing artifacts. From turn of the century wooden boards through foam boards. View the Tom Blake (first surfing) trophy from 1928 alongside the first waterproof camera. Free admission dude.

Exotic World
29053 Wild Rd.   (760) 243-5261
Helendale, CA 92342
Mon - Sun 10am - 4pm

Tourists from all over the world visit the burlesque hall of fame, located just off famed Route 66 between Barstow and Victorville smack in the middle of the desert. See Sally Rand's original hand fan or Gypsy Rose Lee's sequined bodices from "For The Boys". Gowns belonging to Tempest Storm and Lily St. Cyr are preserved here beside Jayne Mansfield's ottoman. Suitable for all ages. Free admission.

The Getty Center
1200 Getty Center Dr.   (310) 440-7300
Los Angeles, CA 90049
Tue - Sun Hours Vary
Web: www.getty.edu

Reach LA's largest cappuccino bar via a swooping tram, then wander the stunning courtyards, gardens, restaurants and atriums. The well-endowed Getty does house priceless classical art, if you have time to poke around its actual galleries, but the real attraction is the Westside vistas from ocean to downtown. Preview how clogged the 405 will be as you head down to reality. Like a blockbuster movie where FX dominates character arcs, this is the art museum LA deserves.

Griffith Observatory Planetarium & Laserium
2800 E. Observatory Rd.   (323) 664-1191
Los Angeles, CA 90027   (818) 901-9405
Tue - Sun 12:30pm - 10pm
Web: www.griffithobs.org

Renowned planetarium atop the Hollywood Hills. Exhibits, lectures and cool, retro Laserium light shows with '70s and '80s rock (Pink Floyd et al). For the Laserium, call (818) 901-9405. For a quarter you can peer through one of many large telescopes overlooking the city's endless lights. From dusk to 9:45pm. Call for schedule. $4/adults, $3/seniors, $2/kids.

Japanese American National Museum

369 E. First St.　　　　　　　　　(213) 625-0414
Los Angeles, CA 90012
Tue - Sun 10am - 5pm, Thu 10am - 7:30pm
Web: www.janm.org

The museum has been housed in a former Buddhist temple since 1992. Brand new is their sister museum triple in size. Designed by Gyo Obaga, it will incorporate elements of the original structure and reflect the old building in the new glass. It will preserve and tell the story of Japanese-Americans through any remaining resources including two-dimensional works, photos and home movies. The new national resource center will feature computers, audiovisual materials and a live history section.

Laguna Art Museum

307 Cliff Dr.　　　　　　　　　　(949) 494-8971
Laguna Beach, CA 92651
Tue - Sun 11am - 5pm
Web: www.lagunaartmuseum.org

Founded in 1918, the Laguna Art Museum is the oldest cultural institution in Orange county. Changing exhibitions feature historical, contemporary, and pop culture-related art. A 5000-piece permanent collection emphasizes the art of California.

Los Angeles County Museum Of Art (LACMA)

5905 Wilshire Blvd.　　　　　　　(323) 857-6000
Los Angeles, CA 90036
Mon - Sun Hours Vary, Wed Closed
Web: www.lacma.org

Beyond the famous glass brick exterior, you'll find an impressive permanent collection, cutting-edge contemporary exhibitions and a Zen pavilion for Japanese art. Free jazz in the courtyard (rain or shine) on Friday nights, year-round. Check out the Art Rental and Sales Gallery which features local talent.

Museum Of Contemporary Art (MOCA)

250 S. Grand Ave.　　　　　　　(213) 626-6222
Los Angeles, CA 90012
Tue - Sun 11am - 5pm, Thu 11am - 8pm
Web: www.moca.org

MOCA's extensive art collection spanning from 1940 to the present includes abstract expressionism, pop art by Roy Lichtenstein, Claes Oldenburg and Robert Rauschenberg. Works of minimalist, post-minimalist and neo-expressionist paintings, sculpture, photography and drawings are presented from the '60s-'80s.

Museum Of Jurassic Technology

9341 Venice Blvd.　　　　　　　(310) 836-6131
Culver City, CA 90232
Thu 2pm - 8pm, Fri - Sun Noon - 6pm
Web: www.mjt.org

Museum with a really funky attitude; exhibits, unlike anything you've ever seen, combine natural and manmade objects into weird and creative images, where nothing is quite what it seems. Example curiosities: Human horns and mice on toast.

Museum of Television & Radio

465 N. Beverly Dr.　　　　　　　(310) 786-1000
Beverly Hills, CA 90210
Wed - Sun Noon - 5pm, Thu Noon - 9pm
Web: www.mtr.org

Designed by Getty architect Richard Meier, this handsome structure contains over 100,000 radio and TV programs, not to mention rare "I Love Lucy" episodes, with a comprehensive self-guided research facility. Attend screenings, seminars and lectures or watch a live radio broadcast.

● Museum Of Tolerance

9786 W. Pico Blvd.　　　　　　　(310) 553-8403
Los Angeles, CA 90035　　　　　(800) 900-9036
Mon - Thu 10am - 4pm, Fri 10am - 1pm, Sun 11am - 5pm
Web: www.wiesenthal.com/mot/

A must-see destination which helps visitors understand and experience discrimination. Learn about 250 hate groups on a wall-sized computer-generated map of America. The Holocaust exhibit is a reenactment of a decade's worth of events leading up to the ultimate example of man's inhumanity to man. Holocaust survivors speak daily.

Norton Simon Museum Of Art

411 W. Colorado Blvd.　　　　　(626) 449-6840
Pasadena, CA 91105
Wed - Mon Noon - 6pm, Fri Noon - 9pm
Web: www.nortonsimon.org

Noteworthy collection of European art from the Renaissance through the 20th century, tapestries and dramatic Indian/Southeast Asian sculpture.

Pacific Asia Museum

46 N. Los Robles Ave.　　　　　(626) 449-2742
Pasadena, CA 91101
Wed - Sun 10am - 5pm
Web: www.westmuse.org/pacasiamuseum

Housed in a Chinese imperial palace replica, this museum features costumes, ceramics, textiles, 18th century Japanese paintings, and Southeast Asian ceramics. Art from India, the Philippines, Afghanistan, Japan, China, Korea. Enjoy a calming break in the Chinese garden complete with koi pond.

Page Museum at the La Brea Tar Pits

5801 Wilshire Blvd.   (323) 934-7243
Los Angeles, CA 90036   (323) 857-6311
Mon - Fri 9:30am - 5pm, Sat - Sun 10pm - 5pm
Web: www.tarpits.org

Did you know that the La Brea tar pits are really asphalt pits? Best place in LA to find fossilized woolly mammoth and the La Brea Woman - a 9000 year old gal. Bring the kids.

Shambala Preserve/The Roar Foundation

6867 Soledad Canyon Rd.   (661) 268-0380
Acton, CA 93510
By Appt Only
Web: www.shambala.org

Founded by actress Tippi Hedren, the Shambala Preserve is home to 60 big cats including lions, tigers, black leopards, snow leopards, mountain lions, servals and a Florida Panther. Also an African elephant, assorted species of duck, and a beautiful Liger (1/2 lion, 1/2 tiger). Open one weekend a month. Advance reservation only. $35/person, 18+over.

UCLA Hammer Museum

10899 Wilshire Blvd.   (310) 443-7000
Los Angeles, CA 90024   (310) 443-7020
Tue - Sat 11am - 7pm, Sun 11am - 5pm
Web: www.hammer.ucla.edu

Permanent collections of masterworks by renowned artists including Van Gogh and Monet. Home to the Grunwald collection of 35,000 works on paper (dating from the Renaissance to the present) by Daumier, Lautrec, Durer and Degas.

UCR/California Museum Of Photography

3824 Main St.   (909) 787-4787
Riverside, CA 92521
Tue - Sun 11am - 5pm
Web: www.cmp.ucr.edu

Houses a unique and remarkable camera collection, the largest archives of stereographic images, daguerreotypes and the Keystone-Mast collection of 350,000 prints with original glass negatives. Heavyweight permanent collection includes Ansel Adams, Manuel Alvarez Bravo, Edward Weston, and Bernice Abbott.

health, sports & fitness

Health, Sports & Fitness

Aerial Sports

Air Adventures Skydiving Inc.
Brown Field Airport, 1590 Continental St.   (619) 661-6671
San Diego, CA 92173

Choose from three exhilarating jumps: static line from 3000 feet (solo with a line that releases your chute), tandem harness with your instructor or, best of all, free fall from 13,000 feet with two instructors on each side holding on to you like training wheels. Take the plunge with confidence; this is a USPA member facility. By appointment only.

American Flyers
2501 Airport Ave.   (800) 233-0808
Santa Monica, CA 90405
Web: www.americanflyers.net

In business for 59 years, the oldest and largest flight training school in the world employs fully certified instructors to teach intro to career levels. Fly their Cessna 172's (four seat airplane).

Biplane, Air Combat & Warbird Adventures
2160 Palomar Airport Rd.   (760) 438-7680
Carlsbad, CA 92008
Web: www.barnstorming.com

Relive the glory days of aviation. Open Cockpit Biplane Rides for 2 people can be "gentle as a featherbed, or more thrilling than a roller coaster". Or, thrill to the yankin' and bankin' of mock air combat where you do most of the flying...no pilot's license required, just guts. Or even take the controls of an authentic WWII warbird as an instructor talks to you through loops and rolls.

Bravo Helicopters & Wing
3401 Airport Drive   (310) 325-9565
Torrance, CA 90505   (800) 773-5946
Web: www.bravoair.com

Achieve a panoramic perspective with a helicopter sightseeing tour package, limo included, or a dinner flight for a special occasion. Fly & Golf, Fantasy, and Catalina Island Paradise are among the many soaring journeys available. Fleet of more than 30 aircraft and deluxe charters means the sky's the limit for your adventure. Offers special event and party facilities to prolong the adrenaline rush of flight. Variety of programs include executive and talent luxury transportation via copter or jet. Specializes in aerial location scouting and innovative production work to enhance any film or video concept. Helicopter and plane flight training available for all ratings and licenses.

Bungee America
(310) 322-8892
Web: www.bungeeamerica.com

Jump from the "Bridge To Nowhere" in the Angeles National Forest in Asuza. This arc-shaped concrete bridge, built in 1936, is accessed via a four-mile hike (two hours each way) from the ranger station. You'll cross ten creeks, so feet can get wet along the way. Once on the bridge, take a swan dive, backwards plunge, front or back flip, or the Supreme Three jump package which includes an ankle harness jump. Spectators welcome. Group discounts. Saturday and Sunday by reservation only.

California City Skydive Center
2251 Airport Way   (800) 258-6744
California City, CA 93505   (760) 373-2733
Web: www.calcityskydive.com

Go for the thrill of your life. Choose how to make your first jump: tandem (harnessed with an expert), 30 minute training; static line (your parachute pulls as you leave the plane), four hour training; after intense seven hour course, jump for 50 seconds of freefall bliss or terror (depending on your reaction to taking wing).

Flyaway Indoor Skydiving
200 Convention Center Drive   (877) 545-8093
Las Vegas, NV 89109   (702) 731-4768
Mon - Sat 10am - 7pm, Sun 10am - 5pm
Web: www.flyawayindoorskydiving.com

Too chicken for the real deal? You can still experience the feeling of skydiving at a fraction of the cost. One of only five in the world, this vertical wind tunnel facility simulates the free fall sensation of skydiving. Fly in a column of air 12 feet across and 22 feet high moving at airspeeds up to 115 mph! Safety procedures and preliminary instruction provided. Allow about an hour for each flight. Observation gallery for spectators. Weight restrictions apply. $35 or ask about double-fly specials.

Heli U.S.A. Helicopter Adventures
16303 Waterman Dr.   (310) 641-9494
Van Nuys, CA 91406

Board your helicopter at Van Nuys Airport. Choose a flight soaring over downtown skyscrapers. See the beauty, feel the romance and sense the adventure.

King Aviation Center

Van Nuys Airport, 16644 Rosco Blvd.   (818) 988-5152
Van Nuys, CA 91406   (800) 273-4686
Web: www.kingaviation.com

Helicopter and airplane rentals, tours and flight academy. Their popular "Tour Over LA," rides accommodate up to three passengers over downtown Los Angeles, the Hollywood sign, and Long Beach. Flight school offers courses to attain private, commercial, instructor's, and ATP licenses. Robinson R22's and Bells helicopters; Cessna, Grob and Katana airplanes.

Long Beach Flying Club & Flight Academy

2631 E. Spring St.   (562) 290-0321
Long Beach, CA 90806
Mon - Sun 9am - 4:30pm

Flight training, rentals and sightseeing charters. Rent anything from a Cessna to a Piper. Sightseeing lasts one hour, flying over Catalina, the Hollywood sign, Hollywood Bowl or the Queen Mary. Call for reservations.

Mammoth Balloon Adventures

(760) 934-7188
Web: www.mammothweb.com

Sunrise flights with an FAA certified balloonist who has more than 15 years experience. Float above the clouds on a four-hour brunch flight. Four-passenger capacity on this unique, outdoor adventure perfect for anniversaries, weddings, graduations, vacations, holidays or even marriage proposals. All flights take place near Long Valley and the largest volcanic crater in Southern California. Liftoff begins at sunrise with touchdown at 11 am. Best views are enjoyed June through October. $200 per person or fly standby for half-price.

Sky Sailing

31930 Highway 79   (760) 782-0404
Warner Springs, CA 92086
Web: www.skysailing.com

Sit back and experience the eye-popping sights with your loved one or take the controls and experience flying firsthand. Gliders tour Lake Henshaw, the Palomar Mountains, Indian reservations and more.

Skydiving Adventures

4420 Waldon Weaver Rd.   (800) 526-9682
Hemet, CA 92545   (909) 925-8197
Web: www.skydivehemet.com

Did you know it's five times safer to jump from a plane than ride in car? Specializing in training, this U.S. Parachute Association member offers two programs of progressive ground school and supervision to prepare you for a same-day assisted or accelerated free fall while putting the process in perspective to give you confidence to do the deed. Low pressure, big thrills. Optional still photo and video package of event. Experienced in commercials and photo shoots, too, either to fake the jump or facilitate the real deal.

A Skysurfer Balloon Company, Inc.

1221 Camino Del Mar   (800) 660-6809
Del Mar, CA 92014
By Appt Only

Experience a champagne flight over the Del Mar coast at sunset or float across Temecula wine country while the sun's rays kiss misty hilltops. Open seven days a week. Call for reservations. Balloons hold 8-14 people.

Windsports Hang Gliding

16145 Victory Blvd.   (818) 988-0111
Van Nuys, CA 91406
Web: www.windsports.com

Since 1974, Windsports has taught over 20,000 hang gliding lessons. Learn this exhilarating sport at 3500 feet in the San Gabriel Mountains of Sylmar. High altitude tandem (student and instructor) for $149, including preflight ground school. Low altitude launching from a 25-foot hill, 10 flights for $99. Low altitude or high, the sky's your limit.

Auto/Motorcycle Racing

California Superbike School

141 Allen Ave.   (818) 841-7661
Glendale, CA 91201   (800) 530-3350
Web: www.superbikeschool.com

Motorcycle school meets at Willow Springs in Rosamond and a dozen tracks across the US plus England and Australia. Sessions last all day, rain or shine. Level I school focuses on basic cornering skills, while Levels II & III introduce advanced techniques. Bring your own bike, or rentals are available. Strap on your leathers and make a day of it!

Danny McKeever's Fast Lane Racing School

P.O. Box 2315   (888) 948-4888
Rosamond, CA 93560
Web: www.raceschool.com

Have the need for speed? Thrive on adrenaline rushes? Come to the one, two or three day racing school at Willow Springs Raceway and you'll train with instructors who teach the celebrities for the Toyota Grand Prix of Long Beach. Bring your own vehicle or use one of their race-prepared Toyota Celica cars.

Dodge Skip Barber Racing School

29 Brook St., P.O. Box 1629   (800) 221-1131
Lakeville, CT 60390
Web: www.skipbarber.com

Bring your driver's license and the ability to drive a stick. Learn the art of trailbraking, heel and toe downshifting and grab the opportunity of open-wheel Formula Dodge racing with 90 minutes of seat time. Discover where the limits of adhesion are and create your own road rules. Look for the school's Willow Spring's or Laguna Seca locations.

Drivetech Racing School

7242 Scout Ave., Unit B   (800) 678-8864
Bell Gardens, CA 90201   (562) 806-0306
Web: www.drivetech.com

Ladies and Gentlemen, start your engines! NASCAR race cars burn rubber with real horsepower (400 to be exact). All the performance equipment you'd expect, like Goodyear racing slicks. Drive at California Speedway and other exciting tracks.

Jim Hall Kart Racing Schools

1555-G Morse Ave.   (805) 654-1329
Ventura, CA 93003
Web: www.jhrkartracing.com

Sun, Sand and Speed. Whether you're looking for a first-time thrill in their 60-mph sprint karts or to hone your skills in a 90-mph shifter, they have a class for you on the California coast. Half-day to multi-day programs. Safety gear provided. Corporate/team building opportunities. The nation's longest running, most famous school. Wrap parties welcome. Reservations required.

Motorcycle Training Center

P.O. Box 16478   (818) 932-0433
Encino, CA 91316
Web: www.ccriderlosangeles.com

Contracted by the California Highway Patrol's Motorcycle Safety Program, you will learn skills that would dazzle Ponch. Training center offers day courses that allow novices to get DMV certified, and experienced cyclists to lower their insurance rates. Two other locations in Reseda and Wilmington.

Team Hammer Advanced Riding School

P.O. Box 183   (909) 245-6414
Wildomar, CA 92595
Web: www.teamhammer.com

Many pros have learned from endurance champion Michael Martin, head teacher of the school. You too, can challenge the speed of light. No previous racetrack experience required. Rental leathers must be reserved in advance (boots and gloves not available). Classes taught at Willow Springs in Rosamond, CA (10 different tracks nationally).

Bowling

All-Star Lanes

4459 Eagle Rock Blvd.　　　　　(323) 254-2579
Los Angeles, CA 90041

22-lane alley is home of the Red Dragon, a Chinese restaurant. Tuesday, Wednesday, Thursday and Friday are karaoke nights. Saturday night hosts live bands.

AMF Bahama Lanes

3545 E. Foothill Blvd.　　　　　(626) 351-8858
Pasadena, CA 91107

Classic among local alleys with some of the most boisterous bowlers around. Wednesday, Friday and Saturday are Extreme Bowl, black light bowling at its best. On Thrifty Tuesday, fork over $4 admission, then pay only 50 cents per game. There's a cocktail lounge, and Bahama's old school coffee shop is worth the trip alone.

AMF Mar Vista Lanes

12125 Venice Blvd.　　　　　(310) 391-5288
Los Angeles, CA 90066
Web: www.amf.com

Need a break from heaving endless gutter balls? Try out their karaoke station (Sunday nights) or grab a hefty fajita burrito from Pepy's Galley, their coffee shop, which remains standing-room only with the regulars.

AMF Rocket Lanes

9171 De Soto Ave.　　　　　(818) 341-0070
Chatsworth, CA 91311

Fridays and Saturday nights this haven for teens and adults turns off the fluorescent lights in favor of strobe lights, a disco ball, and music for "Extreme Bowling." Tired of the pins' pressure? Try out their arcade, featuring the latest blood'n'gore, action-packed video games.

Brunswick West Covina Lanes

1060 San Bernardino Rd.　　　　　(626) 339-1286
Covina, CA 91790

Like a mirage rising out of the valley floor, this Egyptian/Tiki/Aztec palace of terrazzo and volcanic rock is more than just a bowling alley; it features a cocktail lounge, coffee shop, day-care center and beauty salon. "Cosmic Bowling," on Friday and Saturday evenings is "outasite," with loud music, flashing overhead lights and glow-in-the-dark balls and pins.

Gable House Bowling Alley

22501 Hawthorne Blvd.　　　　　(310) 378-2265
Torrance, CA 90505

"Rock and Glow" nights are sure to bring out the Roy Munson in your game. DJ spins '70s tunes while glow-in-the-dark balls roll down the blacklit lanes (Fridays, Saturdays and Sundays midnight to 3am).

Hollywood Star Lanes

5227 Santa Monica Blvd.　　　　　(323) 665-4111
Los Angeles, CA 90029

Weekends are packed with tattooed long-haired clubsters and serious corporate league types decked out in sponsored uniforms. Sick of technology? These lanes offer old-fashioned manual scoring. Full bar and snack shop prepares diner-style Korean, Mexican and American food.

Pickwick Bowl

921 W. Riverside Dr.　　　　　(818) 842-7188
Burbank, CA 91506
Web: www.pickwickcenter.com

The proud proprietors of Pickwick present Electric Fog each and every Saturday night beginning at 7pm, complete with fog, strobe lights, glow-in-the-dark pins, and, of course, rock'n'roll blasting from the jukebox. Fridays come for the rock sans the fog. Make a real night of it and cool off after working up a sweat on the lanes at the adjacent Pickwick Ice Center.

Wagon Wheel Bowl

2801 Wagon Wheel Rd.　　　　　(805) 485-4915
Oxnard, CA 93030

Where bowling is a lifestyle and not a mere background for campy snapshots, the Wagon Wheel Bowl boasts over thirty lanes, automatic scoring and coffee shop. Friday and Saturday night treat yourself to "Glow Rock'n'Bowl," complete with fog, lights, and a live deejay. Too tired to make the drive back to La-La Land? Check into the Wagon Wheel Hotel with rooms starting at $37.95.

Climbing

Crux Climbing Center
1160 Laurel Ln.   (805) 544-2789
San Luis Obispo, CA 93401

State-of-the-art rock climbing gym offers more than 1,000 challenging routes on fifteen 35-foot high walls. All levels welcome. Iron climbs, family climbs and more. Bring the kids, just call ahead to make arrangements.

Joshua Tree Rock Climbing School
P.O. Box 29   (800) 890-4745
Joshua Tree, CA 92252
Web: www.desertgold.com

Joshua Tree is a fantastic place to visit but you really haven't experienced its full majestic splendor until you've climbed it. Friendly school offers lessons year round. Classes limited to five students, mostly adults.

JPL Hiking Club
    (818) 354-8341
Web: www.jplerc.org/hiking/

Offering day and weekend journeys for beginner and intermediate rock climbers to Joshua Tree, led by a climber with 25 years experience. Not into the hard stuff? You don't have to be a member (but it's inexpensive and worthwhile to join!) to enjoy tons of other outdoor activities like walking tours, week-long cross country skiing and boating trips the club plans throughout the year. Even wine-tasting and beach combing are on the agenda. Meet new people, make new friends, do fun stuff. You gotta love an organization with a traditional happy hour on trips. The website is a wealth of current info.

● Quantum Rock
P.O. Box 4032   (310) 378-2171
Palos Verdes Peninsula, CA 90274
Web: www.quantumrock.com

The mountain comes to you, along with all the gear, a qualified staff and a safety system so you and your guests can climb with confidence. This 24-foot-high mobile climbing wall is so realistic, you'd swear it was blasted from a granite formation in Yosemite for deposit in the location of your choice. No experience? No problem. This fun, safe and challenging rock climbing adventure is designed with four different skill levels, creating positive energy and a sense of accomplishment among participants. Ideal for small groups, corporate events and as an effective promotional tool. Artificial and bare feet welcome.

The Rock Gym
2599 Willow St.   (562) 981-3200
Signal Hill, CA 90806

Even Peter Parker would be a bit intimidated by the tallest and largest climbing gym in Southern California. Featuring over 10,000 square feet of innovative climbing surfaces, a 30-foot high ceiling with a huge arch and horizontal roof. 7,000 square feet of leadable climbing. Go Spidey, go!

Rockreation
11866 LaGrange Ave.   (310) 207-7199
Los Angeles, CA 90025   (310) 207-9755
Mon - Sun Hours Vary
Web: www.rockreation.com

Look out below! Westside location offers 220 climbing combinations with lead, top rope and bouldering routes in 10,000 square feet of space. Yoga stretching, private coaching and teen times available. Long-term memberships available.

Uprising Rock Climbing Center

1500 S. Gene Autry Trail (888) 258-2683
Palm Springs, CA 92264 (760) 320-6630
Web: www.uprising.com

Go climb a rock. And the country's only outdoor rock climbing center is the place to do it. With its dramatic setting and safe, controlled environment, they specialize in beginner instruction. Learn the ropes (literally), fancy footwork, technique and safety. All equipment is supplied; just show up in comfortable clothes and you're good to go. Shade and micro-misting are bonuses with this all-over workout. Also an excellent resource for experienced climbers. Outdoor guided trips, team-builders and corporate packages available.

Vertical Adventures

P.O. Box 7548 (949) 854-6250
Newport Beach, CA 92658 (800) 514-8785
Web: www.vertical-adventures.com

Since 1981, offering year-round programs with low student to instructor ratios. Courses are held at Joshua Tree and Idyllwild. One day courses from beginner up to intermediate leading fundamentals. Multi-day seminars allow you to maximize your learning capacity. Guided climbing is available to individuals or small groups with individualized programs for every level. Advanced courses include rescue basics, the "Yosemite Method", sportclimbing, technical training and stunt coordination. The corporate ladder is available to companies and is a great way to build teamwork, trust and camaraderie.

Dance Instruction

Academy 331

530 N. La Cienega Blvd.　　　　　(310) 652-0353
Los Angeles, CA 90048

Long time dance studio has been offering ballet, tap and jazz to scores of youngsters and adults. These days hard-core street hip-hop is a favorite taught by Gee Gee Ibarra. Kids pay by the month, adults by the class (or series).

Alva's Dance and Theatrical Supply

1417 W. Eighth St.　　　　　(310) 519-1314
San Pedro, CA 90732
Web: www.alvas.com

You want to turn that spare room into an authentic dance studio or fitness space. This is the place that has those cool ballet barres you've always liked at the gym. And padded sub flooring, lightweight unbreakable mylar mirrors and all the hardware. Pro equipment is their specialty, recommending and providing equipment to individuals and businesses. 3,000 sq. ft. retail dance wear shop features clothes and shoes for all styles and levels of dance, with instructional videos and music titles. Three studios offer instruction in ballet, tap, jazz, yoga, cardio kickboxing, and tai chi.

Art Of The Dance Academy

11144 Weddington St.　　　　　(818) 760-8675
North Hollywood, CA 91601

Performing arts camp in summer featuring two musicals. Dance academy runs year round for 18 months-adult. "Mommy & Me", tap, jazz, pointe, and boys-only classes offered and special Nutcracker piece performed yearly. Choreographer in residence, Maureen Kennedy.

Belly Dance By Europa@Hollywood Dance Center

817 N. Highland Ave.　　　　　(323) 467-0825
Los Angeles, CA 90038

"If you can walk you can belly dance," says instructor Europa, a dancer in Arabic nightclubs since 1972. She teaches Egyptian style, which is more ethnic than cabaret. Classes meet Thursday evenings from 8:30-9:30. Ongoing, beginners welcome. Monthly discounts available. Dress comfortably and bring a scarf to fit around your hips.

Dance Studio No. 1

1803 Pontius Ave.　　　　　(310) 446-4443
Los Angeles, CA 90025

Originally in Sweden, this multi-faceted studio with a European sensibility is a prestigious Royal Academy of Dance school where students may take the exam, or learn ballet, tap, jazz, expressercise and more for the fun of it. Small classes assure individual attention. Private dance and singing classes upon request. Summer mini camps available. Adult belly dance, Flamenco, salsa and others.

EDGE Performing Arts Center

1020 N. Cole Ave., Fourth Fl.　　　　　(323) 962-7733
Los Angeles, CA 90038

Professional training facility is open to the public and offers instruction six days a week in jazz, ballet, hip-hop, movement for actors, salsa and more. Take a single class or buy a card.

Graham's School of Dance

　　　　　(310) 652-7212

Offers affordable private and small group belly dancing. Natural movement ensures anyone can do it (even guys!). Former elementary school teacher provides instruction at all levels, including basic intro to elements of this oldest dance, plus veil work, turns, finger cymbals, choreography and improvisational solo performances. Classes are fun, inspiring and creative, and each student receives personal attention. Open to all ages and genders. Mondays, Thursdays 7pm; Fridays, 4pm. Will start new classes upon request.

LA Dance Experience

1941 Westwood Blvd.　　　　　(310) 475-1878
Los Angeles, CA 90025

Six-week lessons will have ya flashing your Crazy Legs and flaunting a pocket watch chain just like a regular big bad voodoo daddy. East or West Coast swing, Lindy hop and ballroom classes available, but if it's español to make your hips hip, there's always tango, salsa and Argentine dance lessons available. There's even the chance to practice what you prance with dance parties, too. Call for upcoming class schedule, registration and fees.

SwordPlay Fencing Studio

64 E. Magnolia Blvd.   (818) 566-1777
Burbank, CA 91502
Web: www.swordplaystudios.com

Gain the reflexes, timing, and muscle tone of a boxer while achieving the strategic abilities of a chess master. Group and private lessons for foil, epée and saber. Monthly tournaments held for all levels. Offers martial arts, stretching and stage combat. Instructors include two former Russian Olympians. Plan your next pirate party here.

Westside Fencing

8737 Washington Blvd.   (310) 204-2688
Culver City, CA 90232

Looking for that unique workout? Study the art of stage combat with sabers, rapiers, daggers and the occasional bullwhip. You have nothing to lose, the first time is free! The owner knows EVERYTHING about fencing and will gladly share his knowledge on which movies have good fencing.

Body Maxx

8474 W. Third St.   (323) 655-8365
Los Angeles, CA 90048   (323) 851-6139
Web: www.bodymaxx.com

Membership or private training. Elegant environment with total privacy. All types of Cybex, Body Master and full line of free weights. Professional trainers whose goals are to design bodies to be efficient and elegant. Will match your workout needs to your personality.

Body & Soul Workout

     (310) 659-2211

A fitness sanctuary where the mind and body are encouraged, their connection reinforced. Offering seven varieties of Yoga and premiere spinning classes. Its ambiance and amenities rival fine hotel resorts: waterfalls and gentle lighting, towels and bath products, aromatherapy machines and an oxygenation system. It's enough to make you look forward to your next workout. And to work out more often.

Boulevard Health Club

120 N. Robertson Blvd.   (310) 659-5002
Los Angeles, CA 90048

If you blink, you'll miss it. But isn't it nice to work out at a club that's your own little secret? The 900-member facility thrives on referrals. Someone told Janet Jackson about it. And Jerry Seinfeld. The high school student and the retired teacher. Non-intimidating atmosphere is conducive to life-changing goals. Never overcrowded. Always clean. Plenty of equipment to go around. Martial arts, yoga, cardio classes.

The Center for Physical Health - Movement Forward

10780 Santa Monica Blvd., Ste. 470   (310) 475-6038
Los Angeles, CA 90025
Web: www.physicalhealth.com

Specializing in fitness training, Pilates-based conditioning, Gyrotonic Expansion System, physical and massage therapy, and a variety of other methods to rehabilitate injuries and restore range of motion caused by musculoskeletal, nerve and circulatory damage. On-staff clinical specialists evaluate individual needs and design personal wellness programs. One-on-one sessions and educational classes also available.

Century Sports Club & Day Spa

4120 W. Olympic Blvd.   (323) 954-1020
Los Angeles, CA 90019
Mon - Fri 6am - 10pm, Sat - Sun 7am - 10pm

Diverse facilities include: spacious single-sex traditional spas, free weights, Nautilus machines, aerobics room and lap pool. Services include massage (acupressure/Shiatsu or oil), body scrubs and skin care (moisturizing, seaweed, modeling masks). A state-of-the-art bi-level driving range complete with automatic ball dispenser and cooling mist is open to the public. Continental restaurant with hip, stylish nightclub. VIP luxury suites overlook the dance floor.

Crunch

8000 W. Sunset Blvd.   (323) 654-4550
Los Angeles, CA 90046
Web: www.crunchfitness.com

Designed by I.M. Pei architect Frank Denner, 30,000 square feet of space including workout area, giant galvanized steel sculptures, DJ booth, black rubber flooring and unique shower rooms. There's "gospel aerobics" with a church choir, "hip-hop" with a live DJ, and an Afro-Brazilian Cardio class.

Gold's Gym Venice

360 Hampton Dr.   (310) 392-6004
Venice, CA 90291
Web: www.goldsgym.com

Mecca of bodybuilding contains 35,000 square feet of workout area. Aerobics, yoga, boxing, spinning and kickboxing classes. Private training available. All ages and body shapes workout here.

Kennedy & Strom Fitness

(310) 657-6834
Web: www.ksfitness.com

You can't show up for a 7am Step class. And you can't buy a membership. But what you get with these private fitness trainers is a lifestyle program of health, nutrition, physical and mental well-being. Based in the state-of-the-art fitness center they designed in a prestigious hotel, they also specialize in location training and insane client schedules. Clients include Julia Roberts, Winona Ryder, Jennifer Lopez, Kevin Costner, and pretty much anyone else who has a killer body.

Los Angeles Athletic Club

431 W. Seventh St.   (213) 625-2211
Los Angeles, CA 91030
Web: www.laac.com

Founded in 1880, this LA landmark was the first private downtown club. Extensive athletic facilities include pool, spa, yoga, spinning, aerobics, basketball and squash courts, nautilus and free weights. Unique classes such as disco cycle and rockin' cycle.

Madonna Grimes Fitness & Dance Theatre Company

980 N. La Cienega Blvd.   (310) 659-4739
West Hollywood, CA 90069
Web: www.madonnafitness.com

Imagine a facility where you can take classes from Madonna Grimes AND Karen Voight-this is the place. Two beautiful studios with an outdoor feel, surrounding a courtyard with hardwood floors and mirrored walls. Madonna Grimes teaches Body Sculpt and Street Dance, while Karen Voight teaches Hi-Lo. Pay by the class or buy a series card.

Malibu Fitness

29575 Pacific Coast Hwy.   (310) 457-5220
Malibu, CA 90265

This open-air fitness center boasts inspirational scenery surrounding its state-of-the-art equipment and friendly, attentive service. Features a full complement of fitness programs from Pilates-based bodywork to therapeutic Swedish ball classes to Spinning and aerobics. If gymnastics is your thing, join the class from Pepperdine. Staff trainers are certified with safety and well-being top priorities.

Navy SEALS Fitness

(562) 436-9775
Web: www.sealevents.com

Get in gear and get a hard body. Former Navy SEAL has designed a personal training outdoor fitness program that's fun, challenging and effective. A few weeks of basic training is followed by a five-day maintenance regime. Running, swimming, cross training, weight training plus sound nutritional advice. Move it, move it, move it at 6am daily, Santa Monica Pier. $15 per class or by the month for $250 for a series of 20. Three-week sprint course offered.

Performing Arts Physical Therapy & Pilates Studio

8704 Santa Monica Blvd. Ste. 300   (310) 659-1077
West Hollywood, CA 90069
Mon - Fri 7am - 8pm, Sat 9am - 5pm
Web: www.pilatestherapy.com

Fully-equipped physical therapy and Pilates exercise center offering classes to those wishing to explore this alternative fitness discipline as well as certification to aspiring instructors. Pilates method focuses on increased strength and flexibility, using spring resistance to develop lean toned bodies, long popular with dancers and actors.

VETERANS SPORTSCOMPLEX
FILM & VIDEO SHOOTS, CARSON, CA
310.830.9991

HOME OF THE LA CLIPPERS 12,000 SQ. FT. GYMNASIUM
Also featuring: Olympic Gymnastics Wing, Racquetball Courts, 3,600 Sq. Ft. Fitness Center, Locker Rooms and Parking Lot.

Featured in the Cable Guy and numerous Nike commercials.

Spectrum Clubs
2250 Park Place   (310) 643-6878
El Segundo, CA 90245

65,000 square feet of workout space including a basketball court, spinning, aerobics, pool, kickboxing and yoga. Facility houses a restaurant, bar area, day spa, pro-shop and physical therapy services.

The Sports Center Gym
6711 Forest Lawn Dr.   (323) 851-9376
Los Angeles, CA 90068   (323) 851-6000

Limited membership at this exclusive entertainment industry gym. Renowned kickboxing program. Private by-appointment-only personal training studio for maximum privacy and efficiency. New additions include spinning studio and group exercise studio (aeroboxing, yoga, body sculpting and Pilates mat classes). Outdoor Jacuzzi and three-lane heated lap pool. Full-court basketball. Showers with all toiletries provided. Can come in and work with personal trainer or take a class without being a member.

Sports Club LA
1835 Sepulveda Blvd.   (310) 473-1447
Los Angeles, CA 90025

An oasis within the city, boasting 100,000 sq. feet of state-of-the art fitness equipment, a hair salon, day spa, childcare facility, Olympic pool with sun deck and two restaurants. Over 140 aerobics classes a week in 30 different varieties. Sports Club's own personal trainers on site.

A Tighter U
10854 Washington Blvd.   (310) 202-6344
Culver City, CA 90230
Web: www.atighteru.com

The most private fitness studio in the city offers one-on-one training and a complete program of diet, aerobics and weights. Having trained Olympic hopefuls and pro baseball players, they know how to whip you into shape for that next audition. Each piece of equipment is furnished with its own television.

● Veterans SportsComplex
22400 Moneta Ave.   (310) 830-9991
Carson, CA 90745
Web: www.ci.carson.ca.us/sportscomplex.htm

Practice like a pro on the same NBA-size basketball court where the Clippers and visiting teams work their moves. With a gym so large, feature films and WNBA and pro volleyball commercials shoot there. But it is about way more than hoops and nets. Multipurpose room is great for group excercise classes to get you started and take you further. Step, cardio kickboxing, judo and yoga classes available. Boasts four air conditioned racquetball courts and fitness center with large inventory of free weights and state-of-the-art cardio and weight machines with on-site trainers. Adjacent to a scenic park with two baseball diamonds, picnic areas and meeting facilities. Members get free access to city pools.

Westside YMCA

11311 LaGrange Ave.   (310) 477-1511
Los Angeles, CA 90025

So much for so little, indoor heated pool with water aerobics. Outdoor walking/running track, basketball court, weights, cardio equipment. Racquetball and handball courts. Child care available. Locker room facilities include steam, sauna and Jacuzzi.

Workout Warehouse/The Speed Center

648-650 N. La Peer   (310) 358-1838
West Hollywood, CA 90069   (888) 295-2798
Web: www.thespeedcenter.com

Personal training gym on the Workout Warehouse side. Use their trainers or bring your own. Free weights, strength equipment, stairclimbers, elliptical climbers and more. Fully stocked locker rooms. Next door at The Speed Center, mount a stationary bike for the workout of your life. Offering free workshop for novices and spin classes for beginner, intermediate and advanced. Pay by the class or buy a series.

Horseback Riding

Baldwin Lake Stables

E. Shay Rd.   (909) 585-6482
Big Bear City, CA 92314

Horseback riding year-round, even in the snow, with views of the surrounding mountains and Baldwin Lake. Choose from one, two, three or four hour guided trail rides. Pony rides for children six years and under, petting zoo, sunset rides, overnight camp rides with views across Big Bear Valley.

Circle Bar B Stables

1800 Refugio Rd.   (805) 968-3901
Santa Barbara, CA 93117
Web: www.circlebarb.com

Start off through back canyons, ford through streams, pass waterfalls, circle around mountains to Lookout Point and view valleys, the ocean and Channel Islands for 90 minute rides. Trotting and loping offered for experienced riders. Lunch ride leaves at 9 am and gets back at 1pm, with lunch under a eucalyptus grove with incredible views stretching to Santa Barbara.

Circle K Stables

914 S. Mariposa St.   (818) 843-9890
Burbank, CA 91506
Mon - Sun 7:30am - 7pm

Absorb the stunning scenery of Griffith Park through open riding provided by Circle K. Guided rides available by request and are mandatory if owners think you need one. BBQ rides are a pleasant way to end the day.

The Connemara Ranch

5904 Bonsall Dr.   (310) 457-5838
Malibu, CA 90265

Award-winning stable features scenic trails which reward riders with river and ocean views. Led by Talley Willmont, the well-groomed horses lead you past native flora and huge sycamore & oak trees. Be sure to bring an apple or carrot for your new four-legged pal. At Zuma Beach, by appointment only.

L.A. Equestrian Center

480 Riverside Dr.   (818) 840-8401
Burbank, CA 91506   (818) 840-9063

On the north side of Griffith Park, in the depths of the prestigious LA Equestrian Center, lies one of the better horse rental stables around. Famous for their 90 minute guided sunset barbecues rides. All levels are welcome. Hourly rentals $20.

Long Horn Trading Post

914 S. Mariposa St.   (818) 558-7821
Burbank, CA 91506
Mon - Sun 8am - 7pm

Perhaps the most eclectic and unusual of riding shops. Joe carries vintage boots, vintage blankets, cowboy lamps, turquoise jewelry, cowboy memorabilia, New Mexican furniture, Native American art, and French pastry (to go with the cappuccino). Make sure to check out the working 1940s Coke machine.

Smoke Tree Stables

2500 Toledo Ave.   (760) 327-1372
Palm Springs, CA 92264

Choose from one or two hour guided rides daily. Hour rides go through a dry river bed and two hour rides clip clop through Andreas Canyon, a natural oasis.

Sunset Ranch

3400 N. Beachwood Dr.   (323) 469-5450
Los Angeles, CA 90068

Moonlit horse rides offered every Friday night, sign-up begins at 5pm, the ride starts at 6pm and returns at 11pm. These rides offer magnificent views of the city. Large groups must call for appointments on alternate nights.

Two Winds Ranch

4801 W. Potrero Rd.   (805) 498-9222
Newbury Park, CA 91320
Thu - Sun 9am - 4pm

Rent horses by the hour, take the kids for pony rides or the whole office on a hay ride. Try the Western barbecues with country music under the stars and scenic views of Mt. Boney and the Santa Monica Mountains.

Massage

Trevor Bailey

(310) 915-4117

Named one of the best massage therapists in Los Angeles by Allure magazine. Practices a combination of Swedish, Deep Tissue and Shiatsu massage. Also available for on site Chair Massage. Clients include Minnie Driver, Joanne Whalley, Megan Mullally and Natalie Imbruglia.

Karen Becker/Massage Therapy

9845 Santa Monica Blvd.   (818) 543-1739
Beverly Hills, CA 90212   (818) 246-7773

Karen's services include Manual Lymph Drainage, Deep Tissue/Sports Massage, Acupressure/Shiatsu, Structural Integration, Foot Reflexology, Aromatherapy, Scalp Massage, Facelift Contour, Pregnancy Massage, Cellulite Treatment, Aura Cleansing, Yoga/Body Balance Sessions, TMJ Release and On-Location Chair Massage.

Brooks Massage Therapy

7619-21 Beverly Blvd.   (323) 932-9738
Los Angeles, CA 90036
Mon - Sat 10am - 10pm, Sun 10am - 9pm

Celebrating 45 years of business, Brooks is constantly upgrading their establishment, which provides professional therapeutic massage service. On staff, fully licensed chiropractor and on-location film set and studio massage services available. SAG/AFTRA insurance accepted. Half-hour massage $35, full hour is $65, both include unlimited use of single-sex dry rock sauna with eucalyptus and steam room facilities.

Century Sports Club & Day Spa

4120 W. Olympic Blvd.   (323) 954-1020
Los Angeles, CA 90019
Mon - Fri 6am - 10pm, Sat - Sun 7am - 10pm

Diverse facilities include: spacious single-sex traditional spas, free weights, Nautilus machines, aerobics room and lap pool. Services include massage (acupressure/Shiatsu or oil), body scrubs and skin care (moisturizing, seaweed, modeling masks). A state-of-the-art bi-level driving range complete with automatic ball dispenser and cooling mist is open to the public. Continental restaurant with hip, stylish nightclub. VIP luxury suites overlook the dance floor.

Paige Cline

(213) 991-7612

Relax and discover serenity in the privacy and comfort of your own home with a luxurious massage tailored to your needs. A combination of Swedish, deep tissue, Shiatsu, reflexology and acupressure will be used to find and melt away your tension and stress. Please call ahead for weekend bookings as appointments fill up in advance.

Anna Dekker

(310) 581-5302
(310) 587-6646

The "Dutch Touch" will bring Swedish, deep-tissue, shiatsu and acupressure into your home via The Netherlands. Relaxing classical meditation music and aromatherapy. Available seven days a week.

Diane Hubner's Body Energizers

(310) 306-3333
(800) 330-2956

Couples can choose a romantic interlude location for aromatherapy massage, custom-designed meal by a chef and delivered by tuxedoed server, live music of their choice and finished with an essential oil bubble bath. How about a European day spa at home? Your choice of meals, physical, nutritional and behavioral consultations, full body massage, aromatherapy steam bath are just a few choices.

Tracy Gassel

(310) 960-1873

Relax and rejuvenate in your own home. Specializing in Swedish, deep tissue, acupressure, reflexology and aromatherapy. On-set massage (chair or table). Certified and licensed IMA member. Available seven days a week.

Mitch Gries

7721 Hollywood Blvd., Ste. 3   (323) 851-3508
Los Angeles, CA 90046   (323) 864-7050

Over 22 years experience as a certified neuromuscular therapist and licensed massage therapist. Also trained to use the Ida Rolf method of structural integration. Will accept most union insurance. Specializing in dance and athletic injuries. House calls seven days a week.

Jane Stefani Kasdan

(310) 574-8867
(800) 497-8277

Kasdan has enjoyed an active massage and teaching practice since 1982. She began her studies of movement & the human body with the Alexander Technique in 1972 while a performing concert musician. Her massage therapy is tailor made for the individual. She also has expertise in pregancy massage, deep tissue therapies, energy and polarity work, and facial massage.

Sasha Lauren

(323) 549-0961
(310) 636-6902

Sasha's clientele include professional and Olympic athletes as well as many film actors and directors. Her expert, soothing sessions penetrate as deeply as necessary to alleviate tension and pain. Also a licensed hypnotherapist, she teaches relaxation and meditation techniques. Available for outcalls.

Magic Hands

(310) 394-7909

In addition to Swedish and sports massage, shiatsu and reflexology, on-site massage therapists specialize in reiki (relaxation through chakra stimulation), and osteopathic-based techniques cranio-sacral manipulation (literally creates head space via micro-shifting skull bones to improve communication between brain and spine) and zero balancing (an energy-moving science in which energy fields of bones organize themselves through use of hands as fulcrums in noninvasive/clothes-on stress-zapper). All therapists will come to you or perform services in their healing environment.

Quiet On The Set Massage Therapy

(818) 726-9453

It's the middle of your workday and you're wound like a spring. A massage would be just the thing, but sneaking out for two hours and fighting traffic would be stress inducing and counter productive. In walks a licensed, certified massage therapist and puts you back together with a Swedish, deep tissue, acupressure, sports or aromatherapy massage, either seated or full body. Soon you're human again. The luxury of convenience is yours with this essential service.

Michael Simon, CMT

7814 Willoughby Ave. (323) 655-5454
Los Angeles, CA 90046 (213) 707-9762

Will gladly come to your home or give you a massage in his home studio. Forget your troubles with Swedish, deep-tissue, sports or aromatherapy massage. Seven days a week. Can put together complete packages with other therapies.

Samantha Wood/Namaste Restoration Massage

(310) 252-9042

Samantha specializes in prenatal and labor massage. Other modalities offered include deep tissue, medical massage for rehabilitation, energy work, lomi lomi (Hawaiian technique), shiatsu, Swedish and also offers polarity work. Trained in Hawaii.

Albert Wyss

(323) 465-3542

Trained and certified at the National Holistic Institute and practicing for over 13 years. Your place or his, Albert combines a combination of styles: Swedish, shiatsu, sports and deep tissue.

Running

Culver City Western Hemisphere Marathon

(310) 253-6667
(888) 844-8474

Begun by the Helms bakery in 1948, this is America's second oldest consecutively run marathon. Seven age divisions and separate men's and women's trophies. With about 700 participants, full marathon, 1/2 marathon, 5K run and bicycle tour starting at staggered times. The course is undergoing a major change and will be recertified.

Foothill Flyers Running Club

2522 Paxson Ln. (626) 447-4565
Arcadia, CA 91007

Arcadians stay in shape with the Foothill Flyers' weekly runs each Wednesday at 6pm. Walks and runs of varying paces last approximately an hour. Use the weekends for races and trail runs, and participate in social events. Meet in the back parking lot of REI (Corner of Santa Anita Ave. and Santa Clara St.)

Frontrunners Of Greater Los Angeles

(323) 460-2554

Promoting gay and lesbian camaraderie and a means of exercise, the Frontrunners meet Tuesdays in Silverlake; Wednesdays at Palisades Park; Thursdays in either West Hollywood or Pasadena; Saturday mornings at Griffith Park; Sundays vary. Catch brunch or dinner with the bunch after each run. Annual sponsor of the Gay & Lesbian Pride Run/Walk in West Hollywood.

LA Leggers

(310) 577-8000

Web: home.earthlink.net/~laleggers

The largest SoCal marathon training program. Join this 32-week program based on Olympian Jeff Galloway's technique of incorporating walking breaks to prevent wear and tear on your body. Meets Saturday mornings at the Santa Monica Senior Center (1450 Ocean Ave). Seminars held after each run. Walkers welcome. Social events such as a Malibu camp-out.

LA Roadrunners

11110 W. Ohio Ave., Ste. 100   (310) 444-5544
Los Angeles, CA 90025
Web: www.laroadrunners.com

The LA Roadrunners is a 28 week program that includes your entry into the Los Angeles Marathon, Official LA Roadrunner t-shirt, and seminars. The cost is $95. The training program is designed for all levels from beginner to advance, runners and walkers. The running coach is Pat Connelly and the walking coach is Bob Hickey. The Official training begins in August.

Los Feliz Flyers

P.O. Box 251065   (626) 794-3307
Glendale, CA 91225   (626) 449-1579

Sick of the sofa? Long distance running club led by a USATF coach is sure to get you moving. Meets four times a week, at different locations that offer a change of pace. Tuesday meet at the Sport Shoe (3216 Los Feliz Blvd.) and trek through Griffith Park. Wednesday meet at Cal Tech's track, and Friday do timed runs at the Rose Bowl. Sunday mornings are long runs, as the Flyers forge through the San Gabriel Mts.

Off 'n' Running Tours' Running & Walking Club

1129 Cardiff Ave.   (310) 246-1418
Los Angeles, CA 90035

Meet every Saturday and Sunday at 8am in different Westside locations. Normal runs/walks are four to six miles in length. Marathon runners take advantage of the lengthier courses. Fruit, bagel, and water provided. Try the guided tours for up to eight people. Scenic routes have included runs on Rodeo Dr., Sunset Blvd., past the Playboy Mansion and Spelling Estate.

Orange County Track Club

760 Alta Vista Way   (949) 497-3692
Laguna Beach, CA 92651
Web: www.octrackclub.org

Tuesday is the main run night at Orange Coast College, with a 3-mile coached track workout. Weekend runs are longer with varied locales, such as Chino Hills and El Moro. Monthly newsletter advises members on local races, monthly meetings, potluck dinners and discussion groups.

A Running Experience Club

3747 Fanwood Ave.   (562) 421-6563
Long Beach, CA 90808

Free five-mile fun runs each Wednesday at 6:30pm for all levels at Limerick's Irish Pub. Sundays at 8am, runners meet at the corner of Bay Shore and Ocean for a seven-mile loop. Courses are on city streets and runners stay cool with the ocean breeze. Club social events and competitions happening all the time. Call for more info.

A Snail's Pace Running Club

8780 Warner Ave.   (714) 842-2337
Fountain Valley, CA 92708   (949) 707-1460
Web: www.asnailspace.net

Beginners to advanced are among the nearly 300 members of two Snail's Pace clubs. Meet Mondays and Wednesdays at 6pm to run around Mile Square Park. Monthly group meetings held second Wednesday, after the run. Other locations at 24741 Alicia Parkway in Laguna Hills, and 1040 E. Imperial Hwy. in Brea.

Starting Line

114-A Washington Blvd.   (310) 827-3035
Marina Del Rey, CA 90292

Small specialty running store in business for over 15 years with experts at fitting folks for forward motion activities. Will match your foot to the right shoe and let you test it on the in-store treadmill. Once a month sports injury clinic with podiatrist and chiropractor. Fun runs meet Wednesdays and Thursdays at 6:30pm for 3-6 miles.

Amadeus Spa

799 E. Green St.   (626) 578-3404
Pasadena, CA 91101
Mon - Sun Hours Vary
Web: www.amadeusspa.com

Grown over the years but maintaining that "family feeling." The Amadeus goal is to provide a sanctuary for the guest with seaweed body masques, solar bronzing and hydrotherapy pedicures.

Aqua Spa

1422 Second St.   (310) 899-6222
Santa Monica, CA 90401

Aqua spa is located in a 15,000 square foot facility, which includes a cafe and conference center, saunas, steam rooms, showers and hot, tepid and cold pools surrounded by fountains and wall murals. They offer massage, ayurvedic and hot stone therapies, Vichy scrubs and wraps, facials, microdermabrasion, and hand and foot care treatments.

Ashram

(818) 222-6900
Web: www.theashram.com

Located in the Santa Monica mountains 30 minutes outside of Los Angeles this spa offers an intense one week program of extensive physical activities, strict diet, yoga and meditation. Their tough love attitude helps take off the pounds and makes you leave feeling invigorated.

Beverly Hot Springs

308 N. Oxford Ave.   (323) 734-7000
Los Angeles, CA 90004
Mon - Sun 9am - 9pm

105 degree mineral water flows from their own natural artesian well. For $40 you have unlimited use of the pools. Go from cold (40 degrees) to hot while sampling the various saunas and steam rooms in between. It's akin to having a double espresso with a shot of tequila and, if you're hooked, Beverly Hot Springs offers annual memberships, salt rubs and extra services.

Brooks Massage Therapy

7619-21 Beverly Blvd.   (323) 932-9738
Los Angeles, CA 90036   (323) 932-8854
Mon - Sat 10am - 10pm, Sun 10am - 9pm

Celebrating 45 years of business, Brooks is constantly upgrading their establishment, which provides professional therapeutic massage service. On staff, fully licensed chiropractor and on-location film set and studio massage services available. SAG/AFTRA insurance accepted. Half-hour massage $35, full hour is $65, both include unlimited use of single sex dry rock sauna with eucalyptus and steam room facilities.

Burke-Williams

1460 Fourth St.   (310) 587-3366
Santa Monica, CA 90401
Mon - Sun 9am - 10pm

Burke-Williams is a prime industry hot spot. Head-to-toe spa indulgence available, not to mention fabulous bathrooms. Second location at Sunset and Crescent Heights, is equivalent in size and exquisite service.

● Century Sports Club & Day Spa

4120 W. Olympic Blvd.   (323) 954-1020
Los Angeles, CA 90019
Mon - Fri 6am - 10pm, Sat - Sun 7am - 10pm
Web: www.centuryspa.com

Diverse facilities include: spacious single-sex traditional spas, free weights, Nautilus machines, aerobics room and lap pool. Services include massage (acupressure/Shiatsu or oil), body scrubs and skin care (moisturizing, seaweed, modeling masks). A state-of-the-art bi-level driving range complete with automatic ball dispenser and cooling mist is open to the public. Continental restaurant with hip, stylish nightclub. VIP luxury suites overlook the dance floor.

Du Bunne Day Spa & Massage Center

23725 Arlington Ave.   (310) 326-9062
Torrance, CA 90501
Mon - Sun Hours Vary
Web: dubunne.com

Down to earth spa offers a wide variety of pampering at reasonable prices. Choose from an herbal linen wrap, ayurvedic treatment or Jacuzzi pedicure. A 5,000 sq. ft. facility with showers, lockers, steam and rain forest room.

Fayces

11373 Washington Blvd.   (310) 313-3223
Culver City, CA 90066
Tue - Fri 11am - 7pm, Sat 9am - 5pm
Web: www.fayces-skincare.com

Experts in facials for corrective skin conditions, acne and skin discoloration. Preventive aging a specialty. Using glycolic and light chemical peels, no harsh machines. Why pay more? Fantastic prices. Custom formulas for home use available.

Finland Baths

13257 Moorpark St.   (818) 784-8966
Sherman Oaks, CA 91423
Mon - Fri 9am - 9pm, Sat - Sun 9am - 6pm

This Finnish spa is at the same location since '48 when Humphrey Bogart was a regular. $60 for one hour of deep tissue massage with sauna or $10 for unlimited use of the sauna (who knows who you may run into).

Georgette Klinger

131 S. Rodeo Dr.   (310) 274-6347
Beverly Hills, CA 90212
Mon - Sun Hours Vary

Georgette Klinger is an innovator of the "facial." Serene professionalism and a hands-on approach with no machines used. Try an oxygenated facial utilizing fresh oxygen products or an alpha-hydroxy facial using fruit-acid based products. Even their basic facials last well over an hour. Kindhearted place for your teen's first facial (even young men). Liposome-based products target fine lines and hydrate the skin. For a full-body experience try the seaweed and revitalizing body facial.

Glen Ivy Hot Springs Spa

25000 Glen Ivy Rd.   (909) 277-3529
Corona, CA 92883   (888) 258-2683
Mon - Sun 9:30am - 6pm
Web: www.glenivy.com

Glen Ivy Hot Springs, in the foothills of the Santa Ana Mountains, is known for its mud baths. $24/weekdays, $29/weekends. Includes use of all pools, sauna, mud bath and spas. Bring your own swimsuit, towel and an old swimsuit as the mud (clay) stains some fabrics. Full line of massage. Must be 16+over.

The Greenhouse

417 Canon Dr.   (310) 274-6417
Beverly Hills, CA 90210   (215) 643-2954
Web: www.thegreenhousespa.com

This day spa offers a balance of modern and ancient healing methods from both Eastern and Western traditions. Use one of their customized nourishing facial therapies or get an advanced laser facial.

The Guest House Day Spa

246 N. Palm Canyon Dr.   (760) 320-3366
Palm Springs, CA 92262   (800) 661-2204
Mon - Sun By Appt Only
Web: www.tropicalspa.com

This tropical day spa is privately yours. Owner Sharon Flannagan presents a unique tropical setting complete with waterfall and the sounds of nature. Try the "Beach Bums," a side by side treatment in your own candlelit room, which is always stocked with champagne.

Hahm Rejuvenation Center

8474 W. Third St., Ste. 204   (323) 966-4141
Los Angeles, CA 90048   (323) 966-4142
Mon - Sun 9am - 9pm
Web: www.hahmrejuvenationcenter.com

Renowned for the services of Suk Hahm, blind since age 12, and who offers an incredible shiatsu experience. Leave there without the pains, knots and ailments you arrived with. He will work on movie sets.

Hair at Fred Segal

420 Broadway   (310) 451-5155
Santa Monica, CA 90401

The agency that represents some of Hollywood's most reputable hair and makeup professionals also runs this Santa Monica salon. Get your hair, makeup, skin, body, nails, waxing and tinting services done by the best.

As relaxing as a good night's sleep...

As cool as shade on a sunny day...

As refreshing as a dip in a swimming pool...

As invigorating as a good workout...

Century Sports Club & Day Spa offers a variety of services to help you relax and feel rejuvenated. Whether you find peace through a massage or by intense cardiovascular workouts, Century is the one place you can do both. Come discover for yourself what others have been raving about.

CENTURY
SPORTS CLUB & DAY SPA

120 W. Olympic Blvd. Los Angeles, CA 90019 Tel: (323) 954-1020 Fax: (323) 954-1243 www.centuryspa.com

Lisa Wilson Skin Care at The Alex Roldan Salon

Wyndham Bel Age Hotel,   (310) 855-1113
1020 N. San Vicente Blvd.
West Hollywood, CA 90069
  By Appt Only

You don't have to be a paying guest in this chichi rooming house for entertainment royalty to receive the royal treatment from expert aesthetician Lisa Wilson. In addition to a variety of elaborate facials and hair removal, herbal body wraps and eyelash and brow tints are also available. Revitalize without paying a king's ransom.

Ritz Carlton Rancho Mirage

68-900 Frank Sinatra Dr.   (760) 321-8282
Rancho Mirage, CA 92270   (760) 321-6928
Mon - Sun 8am - 8pm

The resort sits on the edge of a 900-acre wildlife preserve for Big Horn Sheep and is one of only two places in California offering Pancha Karma massage and other Ayurvedic services. The therapists, trained by an Indian master, also offer a Namaste (an Indian greeting which recognizes the divine in all) package and other mix-and-match treatments. Toast the outer you with a champagne facial.

Skin Science

427 N. Cañon Dr., Ste. 110   (310) 275-7531
Beverly Hills, CA 90210
Tue - Sat 8:30am - 7pm

Serene and tranquil salon offering facials, waxing and micro-dermabrasion, which scrapes off the top layer of skin and promotes the production of collagen. Offered by single treatment or purchase a series of three. Their most popular facial is the glycolic with vitamin C mask lasting over an hour. Full body waxing available.

Skin Sense

8448 W. Third St.   (323) 653-4701
Los Angeles, CA 90048
Mon - Sun Hours Vary

Emphasizes the benefits of aromatherapy in our daily lives and the profound effects it can have. Stress relief is part of all treatments and each one is customized to the individual. Offers a wide array of spa services including "English day spa" treatments.

Skin Spa

17401 Ventura Blvd.   (818) 995-3888
Encino, CA 91316
Tue - Sat 9am - 9pm, Sun 9am - 7pm
Web: www.skinspa.com

Delightful treatments and packages which include tropical rainfalls, Swiss needle showers and a Niagra waterfall room. Most intriguing is the fourhanded body extravaganza with radiant facial, body shampoo, foot reflexology, phytotherapy scalp treatment and the piéce de résistance, the one-hour two-masseuse massage.

Skinworks

8012 W. 3rd St.   (323) 658-7900
Los Angeles, CA 90048   (323) 658-9111

Visit this quaint sanctuary to enjoy one of the many facials, body waxing or massage treatments administered by a member of their trained staff. As a result-oriented salon they use both clinical and more natural and homemade treatments and masks to achieve targeted results. Free consultations offered and complimentary refreshments served.

Spa Hotel and Casino

100 N. Indian Canyon Dr.   (760) 325-1461
Palm Springs, CA 92262   (888) 293-0180
Mon - Sat 8am - 7pm
Web: www.aguacaliente.org

The only spa in Palm Springs with its own pure mineral water, Agua Caliente, bubbling up from the ground. The springs were discovered by the Cahuilla Indians hundreds of years ago. Outside, the water is 106 degrees, but inside it's cooled to various levels. The "Taking of the Waters" in a private sunken tub is but one facet of a rejuvenating experience like Pamper Day, Bridal Romance Escape or Day of Beauty. Wide array of individual massage therapies and body treatments.

Spa Ojai

Ojai Valley Inn & Spa, 905 Country Club Rd. (805) 646-5511
Ojai, CA 93023   (888) 772-6524
Web: www.ojairesort.com

Located at the Ojai Valley Inn, the luxurious settings amidst Spanish revival architecture, enhance the feeling of relaxation and pampering. Choose from an endless menu of healing and rejuvenating services. Skin and body treatments use the finest ingredients to nourish and relax. All types of massage available including Watsu, Shiatsu and Deep Tissue. Traditional soaking baths inspired by the Chumash Indians. Yoga, Tai Chi, Spinning, Pilates and weight training classes. Yamaguchi hair salon offers styling, color, makeup and more. Wear comfortable clothing and make a day of it!

Thibiant Beverly Hills Day Spa

449 N. Cañon Dr.   (310) 278-7565
Beverly Hills, CA 90210   (800) 825-2517
Sun - Wed 10am - Midnight, Thu 10am - 1am, Fri - Sat
10am - 2pm
Web: www.thibiantspa.com

A welcoming sanctuary that offers state of the art treatments and skin care products. Delight in spa body treatments and custom facials developed specifically to support, reinforce and improve the skin's natural functions. Escape for a few hours or indulge in The Ultimate Spa Sanctuary, a seven hour day of beauty. Gift Certificates and Corporate Programs available.

U Salon

1772 S. Robertson Blvd.   (310) 204-4995
Los Angeles, CA 90035
Tue - Fri 8am - 6pm, Sat 8am - 5pm, Sun - Mon 10am - 3pm

Finally. A tony hair salon sans the exorbitance. Owned by famed coiffeur Umberto, the stylists and colorists on staff are half artist, half scientist, ensuring a bungle-free experience. Your tresses will love you for it and your checkbook will be grateful.

Vera's Retreat In The Glen

2980 Beverly Glen Circle   (310) 470-6362
Los Angeles, CA 90077
Tue - Sat Hours Vary
Web: www.verasretreat.com

A soothing and healing retreat from daily stress. Quality facials utilizing Vera's own natural products (free samples given with your facial) while the DNA Eye Lift Facial smoothes delicate eye area. The live cell therapy treatment is designed to reduce fine lines and improve skin tone. But try the Ultimate Pampering Experience three full hours of herbal massage, deluxe European facial and body scrub. Aaaaah.

Yamaguchi Salon & Coastal Day Spa

3295 Telegraph Rd.   (800) 572-5661
Ventura, CA 93003   (805) 658-7909
Mon - Sat Hours Vary

Every client is treated like an honored guest when they step in to de-stress and revitalize. What better way to start the day then with the "Asahi Riser," which includes a full body massage, facial, hand and foot treatment, hairstyle and makeup application, with a light breakfast. Offering many spa packages, facials, wrap treatments and message therapies.

Yoga

Angel City Yoga

12408 Ventura Blvd.   (818) 762-8211
Studio City, CA 91604
Mon - Sun Hours Vary

Over 80 classes a week. Hatha, ashtanga, iyengar, kundalini, sivananda (a gentle meditative yoga which emphasizes proper breathing and stretching). Children's classes and pre- and postnatal yoga. Fully equipped space, just come barefoot.

Diana Beardsley

     (213) 250-0763
By Appt Only

Private instructor offering classes at her place or yours. Group or private instruction. Eclectic approach using Ashtanga, Iyengar and Vinna yoga. The focus is on breath and stress reduction. Beginners start with gentle movements and work up to vigorous styles.

BKS Iyengar Yoga Institute Of LA

8233 W. Third St.   (323) 653-0357
Los Angeles, CA 90048
Hours Vary

Iyengar, a form of hatha yoga with an emphasis on proper alignment and precision posture, for all levels. Uses props including blocks, belts, wall ropes and blankets to assist in achieving optimal results. Prenatal, children and scoliosis classes. Call for schedule and workshops.

Brentwood Yoga

11740 San Vicente Blvd., Ste. 202   (310) 442-6724
Los Angeles, CA 90049
Hours Vary
Web: www.brentwoodyoga.com

Brentwood Yoga is situated in the heart of Brentwood across the street from Whole Foods Market, next to Chin Chin. A variety of styles and levels of yoga classes are offered including Iyengar, Hatha, Gentle and Flow. They have classes 7 days a week, and also have monthly special events and workshops. The yoga studio is designed to soothe your senses from the moment you walk in the door and your first class is complimentary.

The Expanding Light

14618 Tyler Foote Rd.   (800) 346-5350
Nevada City, CA 95959   (530) 478-7518
Web: www.expandinglight.com

Ananda yoga and meditation retreat. Their motto is "you don't have to be young, thin or flexible". Guided yoga and meditations enable you to release life long tensions. Situated in the picturesque foothills of the Northern California Sierra Nevadas. Reservations required.

Golden Bridge

5901 W. Third St.   (323) 936-4172
Los Angeles, CA 90036   (877) 236-9642
Web: www.goldenbridgeyoga.com

Two forms of yoga taught: Kundalini, a spiritual form which includes meditations and aids in reducing stress; and Flow, a type of Ashtanga which is more physical. Specializes in prenatal and postnatal practices and meditations. Also offers a Pilates mat class. Many ongoing workshops and sacred music nights. Family oriented with yoga for kids. Two beautiful studios. Taught by Gurmukh Kaur Khalsa. Pay per class or receive super discounts with a series pass.

Harbin Hot Springs

18424 Harbin Springs Rd.   (707) 987-2477
Middletown, CA 95461
Web: www.harbin.org

Take a self-directed retreat at this 1,160-acre nonprofit, clothing-optional alternative resort. Drop in for the day or make reservations for longer stays. Rustically charming accommodations or dormitory-style for the budget conscious. Hot pools, cold plunges and a wonderful variety of massage treatments, plus workshops, certification programs and daily yoga. This facility originated Watsu (water Shiatsu) and trains instructors at those "higher priced spas.

Larchmont Center For Yoga

230 1/2 N. Larchmont Blvd.   (323) 464-1276
Los Angeles, CA 90004
Mon - Fri 8am - 9pm

Forty hatha yoga classes a week. The oldest yoga studio in LA, housed in an old Masonic temple. Spacious room with beams of light and hardwood floors.

Maha Yoga

13050 San Vincente Blvd., Ste. 202   (310) 899-0047
Los Angeles, CA 90049
Mon - Thu 8am - 9:30pm, Sat - Sun 8:30am - 9pm

Popular westside spot offering various yoga including traditional and contemporary (yoga with music). Power yoga taught by owner Steve Ross. Beautiful interior with hardwood floors, white billowy curtains and soft lighting. Free chanting classes. Lectures by prominent authors and yogis.

Planet Yoga

518 Pier Ave., 2nd Fl.   (310) 376-5354
Hermosa Beach, CA 90254
Mon - Fri 6:30am - 9pm, Sat 9am - 6:30pm, Sun 9am - 5pm
Web: www.planetyoga.com

Classes seven days a week in hatha yoga. Features highly-trained guest speakers and lecturers, weekend workshops, retreats and yoga-teacher training and certification.

Power Yoga Center

522 Santa Monica Blvd.   (310) 281-1170
Santa Monica, CA 90401
Hours Vary

Brian Kest has achieved guru-like status among his devoted show business and lay followers. Practicing one of the most intense forms of yoga, students are admitted to class only by permission, but that doesn't keep them from lining up around the block.

School Of Traditional Yang Style Tai Chi Chuan

8225 Coldwater Canyon   (818) 509-7826
North Hollywood, CA 91605
Mon - Wed 8pm - 9:30pm

Classes are held at Wat Thai Buddhist Temple on Coldwater Canyon. Tai Chi distributes "Chi" or energy flow throughout the body and the mind. Mandana Doust incorporates two cultures to familiarize the students in the West with the traditions of the East.

Yoga Garden

2236 26th St.   (310) 450-0133
Santa Monica, CA 90405
Hours Vary

Iyengar yoga taught either in a beautiful indoor facility with hardwood floors overlooking a garden or, weather permitting, in the garden itself. About 16 classes offered per week either individually or by series. Ask about specialty courses.

Yoga West

1535 S. Robertson Blvd.   (310) 552-4647
Los Angeles, CA 90035
Hours Vary

Yoga West offers kundalini yoga, a powerful form of yoga which incorporates all other styles. Meditations at the end of each class. Special workshops, guest speakers and teacher training offered.

Yoga Works

1426 Montana Ave., 2nd Fl.   (310) 393-5150
Santa Monica, CA 90403
Mon - Sun 7:30am - 7:30pm
Web: www.yogaworks.com

Over 150 classes per week taught in hatha, iyengar and ashtanga yoga. Good shop with books, yoga mats, yoga clothes, videos, CDs. (Also at 2215 Main St. SM).

destinations

Destinations

Bed & Breakfast

Artist's Inn

1038 Magnolia St. (626) 799-5668
South Pasadena, CA 91030 (888) 799-5668
Web: www.artistsinns.com

Choose among four rooms in the 1895 main house or one of five rooms or suites in the 1909 cottage. Both facilities are fully restored with European influences. Room themes are based on a particular artist; O'Keeffe, Van Gogh, Grandma Moses, Gauguin, Degas or period expressionists, impressionists, English or Italian. An artistically delightful experience.

Artist's Loft

(760) 765-0765
Web: www.artistsloft.com

Call well ahead to secure reservations at this environmentally sensitive oasis sheltered by elegant pines and oaks with unsurpassed views of the Cuyamaca Peaks and the Coronado Islands off Mexico. Choose rooms at the main inn or at the adjacent Cabin at Strawberry Hill, featuring a towering ceiling, grand stone fireplace, separate bedroom with study, cedar paneling and a nine-sided bathroom. A new addition is the 1929 craftsman revival style Big Cat Cabin on six acres.

Bella Maggiore Inn

67 S. California St. (805) 652-0277
Ventura, CA 93001 (800) 523-8479

European style inn welcomes you with elaborate fresco carving in front. Inside the 1920s structure, warm rose and creme tones invite you to relax by the fire or the antique Steinway piano. Choose a room with a fireplace and spa tub, or go all out with a two-room suite. Complimentary full breakfast served in their open-air cafe surrounded by trees, birds and a fountain. Choose from steak and eggs to cinnamon cream cheese stuffed French toast (lunch and dinner also available). Afternoon wine and hors d'oeuvres are a perfect treat after a long day of shopping at the nearby antique stores. Or spend a day at the beach, only two blocks away. Don't forget to say hello to the historical ghost!

The Blue Whale Inn

6736 Moonstone Beach Dr. (800) 753-9000
Cambria, CA 93428 (805) 927-4647
Web: www.bluewhaleinn.com

Six ocean-view mini-suites complete with private entrances, gas fireplaces and canopy beds. Full gourmet breakfast and afternoon refreshments. Close to Hearst Castle and the quaint seaside village of Cambria. Wine-tasting in Paso Robles only 30 minutes away.

Channel Road Inn

219 W. Channel Rd. (310) 459-1920
Santa Monica, CA 90402
Web: www.channelroadinn.com

Colonial/Revival style inn designed by Frank Kegley in 1910. Fourteen rooms with antique four poster beds, plush down comforters and dreamy ocean views. Room Three features dark cherry wood furniture, an extra large bathroom jacuzzi tub for two and a fireplace. Romantic retreat tucked away, yet close by.

Cheshire Cat Inn

36 W. Valerio St. (805) 569-1610
Santa Barbara, CA 93101
Web: www.cheshirecat.com

Sophisticated Victorian inn featuring Laura Ashley wall coverings. "White Rabbit" is a spacious split-level room with a king size brass bed above the sitting room. Deck overlooks gardens and mountains. Larger and more private cottages available.

Country Inn By the Sea

128 Castillo St. (805) 963-4471
Santa Barbara, CA 93101 (800) 455-4647

Comfort and service are key elements to Country Inn's success. Four-poster beds, pine furnishings and huge floral duvets make for quaint accommodations. Guest lounge is complete with a library and sitting area where you can enjoy seasonal fruit, chocolate chip cookies and continental breakfast pastries that are devilishly delicious. Pool, spa, and redwood sauna. Located in the West Beach area; many restaurants, shops and the ocean in walking distance, if you can peel yourself away from this cozy inn.

Doryman's Oceanfront Inn

2102 W. Ocean Front   (949) 675-7300
Newport Beach, CA 92663
Web: www.dorymans.com

Sky lighted hallway leads to one of ten lavishly decorated rooms, complete with fireplace, sunken marble tubs, Victorian wallpaper, and one-way windows for privacy, much needed on Newport Beach's bustling pier. Six guest quarters offer ocean views. Breakfast in bed or on the terrace but the first floor is where you'll find 21 Ocean Front, a popular seafood restaurant.

Garden Street Inn

1212 Garden St.   (805) 545-9802
San Luis Obispo, CA 93401   (800) 488-2045
Web: www.gardenstreetinn.com

1887 Italianate/Queen Anne home exquisitely decorated with many antiques and upright pianos. "Edelweiss" room exudes an Austrian motif with mellow blues and creams, a claw foot tub and perhaps the prettiest fireplace of the inn. Breakfast served at individual tables in the stained glass windowed dining room.

Gold Mountain Manor Historic Bed And Breakfast

1117 Anita, P.O. Box 2027   (909) 585-6997
Big Bear City, CA 92314   (800) 509-2604
Web: www.goldmountainmanor.com

6000 sq. foot log mansion built in 1928 on an acre forested with pine and cedar trees. Manor is wrapped with an old fashioned veranda. Six guest rooms decorated with antiques, Mission style furniture, maple floors, beamed ceilings. Den contains a pool table, surround-sound movie system and library; guest kitchen stocked with homemade sweets and breads; parlor features a quartz rock fireplace.

Inn At Playa del Rey

435 Culver Blvd.   (310) 574-1920
Playa Del Rey, CA 90293
Web: www.innatplayadelrey.com

Sister inn to Channel Road Inn, and overlooking the main channel of Marina del Rey and a 200-acre bird sanctuary. Room 304 features see-thru fireplace, oversized Jacuzzi, sailboat and harbor views during the day, twinkling lights from the Marina village at night.

Inn On Summer Hill

2520 Lillie Ave.   (800) 845-5566
Summerland, CA 93067
Web: www.innonsummerhill.com

Each of 16 rooms offers an unparalleled ocean view, canopy bed, duvet, Jacuzzi, gas fireplace, and are decorated in traditional New England style. Ask about their famous bread pudding, one of their evening desserts served in the romantic candlelit dining room. Located five minutes south of Santa Barbara.

Julian White House Bed & Breakfast

P.O. Box 824-3014 Blue Jay Dr.   (760) 765-1764
Julian, CA 92036   (800) 948-4687
Web: www.julian-whitehouse-bnb.com

Stroll by the mammoth white pillars through the front entrance and you'll suddenly be swept back in time to a Colonial plantation filled with that good ol' Southern hospitality. Four large guest rooms, three feature Victorian motifs such as a French claw-footed slipper bathtub and a white Victorian iron queen bed. The French Quarter Room is New Orleans-themed complete with feather masks and Mardi Gras memorabilia. Ask for a room with a fireplaces and whirlpool. For reservations call 9am to 9pm or website after hours.

Korakia Pensione

257 S. Patencio Rd.   (760) 864-6411
Palm Springs, CA 92262

Once the heart of Palm Springs' literary and art community, it's now called home by young Hollywood. Moroccan style oasis built in 1924. Rooms are sumptuously furnished with antiques, oriental rugs and handmade furnishings. Relax by the pool or try your hand at watercolors in the art studio where Sir Winston Churchill pressed brush to canvas. Closed for the summertime through Labor Day.

Loma Vista Bed & Breakfast

33350 La Serena Way   (909) 676-7047
Temecula, CA 92591

Experience the hilltop view of the Temecula Mountains, vineyards and citrus groves with 13 wineries within a one-mile radius. Originally built as a B&B, Loma Vista's pride and joy is convenience, tranquility and service. Large balconies accompany most rooms.

San Ysidro Ranch

900 San Ysidro Ln.   (805) 969-5046
Santa Barbara, CA 93108

Exclusive rustic retreat ranch nestled in the majestic Santa Ynez Mountains, and surrounded by flower gardens and citrus groves. Twenty-one separate cottages (one with its own private pool). Tennis courts, heated ocean view pool, Ayurvedic spa services, nanny service, children's pool and special children's menu. Privileged pet program allows your pooch to select gourmet meals ranging from N.Y. Steak to Veggie Biscuits.

Seal Beach Inn And Gardens

212 5th St.   (562) 493-2416
Seal Beach, CA 90740   (800) 443-2929
Web: www.sealbeachinn.com

Elegant historic Inn with lush petite gardens and exquisite suites. Beautiful fountains and private pool. Antiques and fine furnishings adorn each room. Lavish breakfast, evening tea and appetizers, fresh flowers and more greet each guest. Just one block from the ocean.

Simpson House

121 E. Arrellaga St.   (805) 963-7067
Santa Barbara, CA 93101   (800) 676-1280
Web: www.simpsonhouseinn.com

The first and only AAA Five Diamond North American Bed and Breakfast Inn. All rooms in this Victorian house are lavishly appointed (including antiques) but the Old Barn guest rooms and Cottages are truly magnificent, offering a "hayloft" with streams of natural light, antique pine floors and Oriental rugs. French doors open onto private decks overlooking the gardens.

Two Angels Inn

78120 Caleo Bay   (888) 226-4546
La Quinta, CA 92253   (760) 564-7332
Web: www.bbonline.com/ca/twoangels

Eleven-room French chateau with Old World ambiance overlooking a man-made lake and surrounded by three mountain ranges. Each room is unique in style, from the St. Andrews Room featuring natural pines and Scottish plaids, to the Safari Room with a symphony of black, gold and bamboo furnishings. Daily "interludes" among guests and proprietors commence each evening, complete with local award-winning wines and hors d'oeuvres. Meditation library holds daily soft yoga class. Many prestigious golf courses and tennis courts nearby.

Catalina

Armstrong's Fish Market & Seafood Restaurant

306 Crescent   (310) 510-0113
Avalon, CA 90704

The place for fresh seafood in Avalon. Get your fill of sashimi, clams, oysters, mussels and abalone. Take out and delivery available.

Catalina Adventure Tours

P.O. Box 797   (310) 510-2888
Avalon, CA 90704
Web: www.catalinaadventuretours.com

See what the island has to offer through their tours. Everything from scenic harbor cruises and botanical garden tours to a seal rocks observation or a trip in a yellow submarine.

Catalina Island Banning House Lodge

P.O. Box 5086, Two Harbors   (310) 510-2800
Avalon, CA 90704
Web: www.catalina.com/twoharbors

Overlooking picturesque Isthmus Cove and Catalina Harbor, this historical bed and breakfast offers a quiet retreat, continental buffet and outstanding country atmosphere. Reservations mandatory.

Catalina Island Channel Express

                                      (310) 519-1212
Web: www.catalinaexpress.com

Take a spacious, multi-deck boat to L.A.'s own fantasy island port o' call and enjoy the hour ride from convenient departure points in San Pedro, Long Beach or Dana Point. Call for schedule, directions and reservations 5:30am to 10pm Monday through Friday and 6am to 9pm Saturday and Sunday. Plan on rising early for this high seas adventure. Because getting there is half the fun. Adults $38, seniors $34.50, kids $28.50, infants $2.00.

Catalina Island Museum

P.O. Box 366   (310) 510-2414
Avalon, CA 90704

Open daily from 10:30am to 4pm, this museum features artifacts from 7000 years of the island's history. Excellent books and souvenirs of the island are available.

Catalina Kayak Adventures

120 Pebbly Beach Rd.　　　　　(310) 510-2229
Avalon, CA 90704
Mon - Sun 9am - 6pm
Web: www.catalinakayaks.com

See the island from a local's perspective with a half or full day kayak trip to challenge the body and dazzle the eye. Each adventure comes with an experienced guide, snorkel gear and instruction for a trip within a trip. Picnic lunch provided. For a different kind of water excursion, paddle boats are also available. If the art of the snork is what floats your boat, go snorkeling in the Avalon Marine Preserve for an up-close-and-personal look at ocean life.

Catalina Ocean Rafting

P.O. Box 2075　　　　　　　(310) 510-0211
Avalon, CA 90704　　　　　　(800) 990-7238

Climb aboard one of their inflatable power driven rafts and take an exciting and educational tour of the island. Excursions range from two hours to two days. Whale migration tours available January-March and snorkeling trips available year-round.

Catalina Scuba Luv

P.O. Box 2009　　　　　　　(310) 510-7270
Avalon, CA 90704　　　　　　(800) 262-3483

Divers and snorkelers of all experience levels can enjoy the depths of the island through this 30 year old dive shop. Their diving professionals offer a range of training and diving packages.

Discovery Tours

(800) 626-1496

Tours available by land or by sea. Take a ride through Avalon or head into the island's wilderness. Cruise around the island in one of their glass-bottom boats or semi-submersable ships.

Flip's

128 Catalina Ave.　　　　　　(310) 510-8585
Avalon, CA 90704　　　　　　(310) 510-2277
Web: www.flipsushi.com

By day they charter fishing boats for those with valid California fishing licenses. By night they're a sushi and steak serving comedy club.

Hamilton Cove

P.O. Box 367　　　　　　　　(310) 510-0190
Avalon, CA 90704
Web: www.hamiltoncove.com

This private cove right next door to Avalon offers secluded villas with panoramic ocean veiws. Rentals are ideal for romantic excursions or family retreats.

Harbor Reef Restaurant

(310) 510-4233

This casual South Sea restuarant and saloon lets visitors to the isthmus of Two Harbors sample the fish from the local waters as well as steaks, ribs, chicken and prime rib.

Hotel St. Lauren

P.O. Box 2166　　　　　　　(310) 510-8299
Avalon, CA 90704　　　　　　(800) 645-2471
Web: www.stlauren.com

The charm of a Victorian style hotel with all the important modern comforts. Each of their 42 rooms and suites contain rosewood furniture, ceiling fans, ceramic tile and brass fixture bathrooms.

Island Express Helicopter

1175 Queens Hwy South　　　(310) 510-2525
Long Beach, CA 90802　　　　(800) 228-2566
Web: www.islandexpress.com

Travel to the island in style with their helicopter service. 14 minute flights available daily from Long Beach.

Santa Catalina Island Resorts Services

P.O. Box 811　　　　　　　　(310) 510-7400
Avalon, CA 90704
Web: www.scicio.com/cirs/

Plan any big event or intimate affair through their dedicated staff. Enjoy a day of golf and dine in the Clubhouse at the Catalina Country Club. Sit back with a blended drink and take in the ocean at the Descanso Beach Club, or spend a night of elegance at the Casino Theater and Ballroom.

Snug Harbor Inn

108 Sumner Ave., P.O. Box 2470   (310) 510-8400
Avalon, CA 90704
Web: www.catalina.com/snug_harbor_inn/

Six cozy Cape Cod rooms with ocean view, fireplace, jacuzzi, king-size beds and air conditioning. Special attention is paid to detail with rooms containing fresh cut flowers, complimentary terry cloth slippers and in-room magazines.

Villa Portofino

111 Crescent Ave., P.O. Box 127   (310) 510-0555
Avalon, CA 90704
Web: www.hotelportofino.com

Operated in the tradition of a European seaside resort, this hotel features ocean facing rooms with balconies, tiled bathrooms, cable television and air conditioning. Visit the adjacent ristorante specializing in regional Italian cuisine.

Getaways

Adventure 16

11161 W. Pico   (310) 473-4574
Los Angeles, CA 90064
Web: www.adventure16.com

One of the best stores for outdoor clothing and gear in LA, with inspiration built in to every visit. For those scared of commitment, tent rentals and backpacks available. Instructional classes and Wilderness Outings and rock climbing geared to make you a modern Grizzly Adams. Learn first aid, mapping, photography, and introductory backpacking. (Locations in Tarzana, Costa Mesa, San Diego, Solana Beach.)

Adventure Fitness Training

1527 Yale St., Ste. 6   (310) 581-2556
Santa Monica, CA 90404   (888) 488-4238
Web: www.adventurefitness.com

Swim a mile, run a trail, paddle a lake, and rappel a mountain - all before lunchtime. Led by a former Reconnaissance Marine (the Marines' version of Navy SEALS) AFT is for the hard core enthusiast who demands challenge. Offers butt-kicking Phase I, II, III courses focusing on the mental, emotional and physical. You'll swear you're in boot camp. Day trips and extended vacations can be arranged but 3-day weekend nearby getaways are a specialty. Private adventure training also available. Beginner through advanced welcome.

Backroads

801 Cedar St.   (800) 462-2848
Berkeley, CA 94710-1800   (510) 527-1555
Web: www.backroads.com

Luxury theme trips for the active traveler with a 5-day minimum stay. Bicycle through wine country, spend a day learning to cook in Tuscany, hike through Costa Rica. Rest your head on a feather pillow in your 5-star hotel at the end of the day or lodge like a local. Handling all planning and arranging, U.S. and international trips to more than 90 breathtaking and exotic locales are tailored to personal travel style and preferences.

Canadian Mountain Holidays

Box 1660   (403) 762-7100
Banff, Alberta, Canada T0L 0C0   (800) 661-0252
Web: www.cmhhike.com

Largest and most sophisticated Heli-Ski and Heli-Hike operation in North America. From December to May, Heli-Skiing trips run from 11 locations. From June to December, Heli-Hiking treks from five summer lodges. Luxurious accommodations, meals, guide service, skis, and a guarantee of 100,000 vertical feet of Heli-Skiing. Offers programs for first-time powder skiers.

Carmel Valley Ranch

One Old Ranch Rd.   (831) 625-9500
Carmel, CA 93923
Web: www.grandbay.com

144-suite luxury accommodations on a 17,000 acre estate set in the Monterey Peninsula, six minutes east of Carmel, offering tennis packages including daily 4-hour USPTA clinics and 13 tennis courts. Unlimited court time and use of the ball machines. Golf packages for women beginners on private courses, Pete Dye's 18-hole championship golf course, spa facilities, and horseback riding make this an exciting vacation.

Catalina Island

     (310) 510-2800
Web: www.catalina.com

Idyllic resort village called Two Harbors, located at the isthmus of Catalina Island 22 miles off the coast of Southern California. Passenger service available from San Pedro or Long Beach. Ocean-view hiking with many trails, camping, diving, boating, fishing, year-round special events. Hotel packages available.

Coastwalk

1389 Cooper Rd.   (800) 550-6854
Sebastopol, CA 95472   (707) 829-6689
Web: www.coastwalk.org/coastwalk

Coastwalk is dedicated to protecting the California coast and establishing a coastal trail. 4-6 day hiking and camping trips are offered in all 15 coastal counties. Explore trails, learn about human and natural history, and enjoy the scenery. Day hikes, too.

Dodgers Adult Baseball Camp

P.O. Box 2887   (800) 334-7529
Vero Beach, FL 32961   (561) 569-4900
Web: www.dodgers.com

Be a player and score big in Dodger blue where the major leaguers get down to business. Work out, eat well and train like a pro in the only fully self-contained camp of its kind. Swim, golf and party like a champ in this deluxe resort setting where spring training's in session February and November. You'll get great pointers from former Dodger greats who coach by day and regale with stories from the diamond by night. Play ball!

ECHO

6529 WB Telegraph Ave.   (510) 652-1600
Oakland, CA 94609   (800) 652-3246
Web: www.echotrips.com

For nearly 30 years, expert guides have been leading trips to The Tuolumne, "the Dom Perignon of white water and wilderness." Rafts maneuver over 30 legendary rapids such as Sunderland's Chute, Grey's Grindstone and Clavey Falls. Besides the thrill of rafting, you're surrounded by scenic splendor. Encounter hidden waterfalls and cool swimming holes. Food and rafts provided; bring your own gear.

Harbin Hot Springs

18424 Harbin Springs Rd.   (707) 987-2477
Middletown, CA 95461
Web: www.harbin.org

Take a self-directed retreat at this 1,160-acre nonprofit, clothing-optional alternative resort. Drop in for the day or make reservations for longer stays. Rustically charming accommodations or dormitory-style for the budget conscious. Hot pools, cold plunges and a wonderful variety of massage treatments, plus workshops, certification programs and daily yoga. This facility originated Watsu (water Shiatsu) and trains instructors at those higher priced spas."

High Sierra Goat Packing

     (209) 536-9576
Web: www.goatpack.com

The only mountain guide company in California using goats as pack stock. Three-day to two-week hiking excursions such as the Emigrant Wilderness, with its blue alpine lakes (noted for trout fishing) or glacial polished valleys (so-called since the rock appears to be wet) through regions in the Sierra Mountains. Goats can carry 50-90 lbs. and are sweet and friendly. Trips run from May-October accommodating groups of eight.

Hilton Garden Inn Valencia Six Flags

27710 The Old Rd.   (661) 254-8800
Valencia, CA 91355
Web: www.hilton.com

Closest hotel to two popular amusement parks, Six Flags Magic Mountain and Hurricane Harbor Water Park. Oversized guest rooms are airy and restful, comfortably spacious, with technologically efficient workspaces complete with ergonomic chairs and easy access high speed internet access. It's this attention to detail coupled with standard amenities like coffee makers, microwaves and refrigerators that make it like home -- only better. Because your success doesn't shut down at 6pm, 24-hour complimentary business center is ready to work when you are. Boasts fitness facilities, outdoor heated pool and restaurant, as well.

Holiday Expeditions, Inc.
544 E. 3900 South   (800) 624-6323
Salt Lake City, UT 84107
Web: www.bikeraft.com

Vacation on a real working cattle ranch with optional white water rafting or take a bike or sea kayak trip suitable for the whole family, originating in Utah, Idaho and Colorado, with sea kayaking in Baja, Mexico. Also offering challenging trips for intermediate and advanced athletes. In addition, 4-6 day women-only yoga retreats in the great outdoors are available. Journeys are 4-6 days in length, have women guides exclusively and include meals (special diets welcome), yoga and massage.

Hyatt Valencia
24500 Town Center Dr.   (661) 799-1234
Valencia, CA 91355

The newest California Hyatt and the only full service luxury hotel in the scenic Santa Clarita Valley, offers two exciting packages to relax and recharge. Enjoy deluxe room accommodations with the Spa & Putt package, which includes facials for two at the hotel's Natural Beauty InSPArations plus two rounds of putting on the unique 27-hole putting course designed by Ted Robinson. Or thrill with a Six Flags Magic Mountain adventure featuring two adult passes to the park and the convenience of an overnight stay at the hotel. rooms are equipped with dual phone lines so you can chat and surf, on-command video and plenty of other little things that make a big difference. Get away without going too far. Packages subject to availability.

Idyllwild Inn
P.O. Box 515   (888) 659-2552
Idyllwild, CA 92549
Web: www.idyllwildinn.com

High above Palm Springs is a year-round, peaceful retreat nestled in the San Jacinto mountains. Offering lovely theme rooms and cozy yet spacious cabins with fireplaces and kitchens, some with redwood decks. Clean air, clear streams, scenic trails - very rustic and relaxing. Close to town, restaurants but who needs civility when there's all this tranquility?

La Mancha Resort Village
444 Avenida Caballeros   (760) 323-1773
Palm Springs, CA 92263   (888) 526-6242
Web: www.la-mancha.com

Secluded luxury villas with private cabanas and pools, patios and wet bars in a romantic, tropical paradise. Full spa services including pool side massage. Feast on epicurean delights in your private retreat. Personal trainers on site. Ultra-deluxe facilities with smaller villas for the smaller pocketbook. Discount and golf packages available.

Otter Bar Lodge - Kayak School
P.O. Box 210   (530) 462-4772
Forks Of Salmon, CA 96031
Web: www.otterbar.com

Located in the Klamath National Forest, offering all levels of kayak instruction as one of the finest schools of its kind. In addition to state-of-the-art equipment, amenities include outdoor hot tub, wood-fired sauna, private decks and gourmet meals. Remote but luxurious, hundreds of square feet of glass windows complement the surrounding forest, bringing the outside in. Mountain bikes available.

Outer Edge Expeditions
4830 Mason Rd.   (517) 552-5300
Howell, MI 48843   (800) 322-5235
Web: www.outer-edge.com

Specializing in small group expeditions to remote locations around the globe or customize your adventure to include side trips. Immerse yourself in the culture of your desired destination. Everything from diving or biking in Australia and dogsledding in Canada to caving in Borneo and sailing off Turkey. Most trips are geared towards the active individual. Don't just see the world; be a part of it.

Production Travel & Tours
10554 Riverside Dr.   (818) 760-0327
Toluca Lake, CA 91602
Web: www.adventureplanners.org

Arrive as acclimated as a native to an adventure destination of your choice, debriefed and apprised of every essential nuance. Specializing in adventure and production travel, both domestic and international. Know what to eat and when to swim in the Amazon. Maximize your trip to the Himalayas. Navigate Antarctica with aplomb. They'll even tell you what table at which to sit in a London restaurant to best see and be seen. African excursions are their forte. Like having a private tour guide 24/7 only with the exhilaration of confident independence.

Rancho Bernardo Inn

17550 Bernardo Oaks Dr.   (800) 542-6096
San Diego, CA 92128
Web: www.ranchobernardoinn.com

Seamlessly combines elements of comfort and warmth with elegance and style to create a world class resort. A relaxation and recreation destination, it offers inviting quarters with private patios and balconies, secluded hydro-spas, two heated pools, 18-hole championship golf, a 12-court tennis facility, fitness center, and rolling hills plus a wealth of entertainment in surrounding San Diego. Rooms and suites offer private patios or balconies.

Shirley Meadows Ski Area

P.O. Box Q, 1600 Ranchero Rd.   (760) 376-4186
Wofford Heights, CA 93285
Web: www.shirleymeadows.com

Beginner ski and snowboarding classes are held several times a day. Located in the Sequoia National Forest and catering to beginner and intermediate skiers. All equipment, including snowboards, can be rented on-site. Two double chairs open Friday-Sunday and all holidays from 9am-4pm.

Snow Summit Mountain Resort

P.O. Box 77   (909) 866-5766
Big Bear Lake, CA 92315
Web: www.snowsummit.com

Check great deals and the Guaranride and Guaranski programs. Four hours of snowboard or ski lessons GUARANTEES you'll make it down the mountain by yourself. (If not, you'll get free lessons until you make it). World class freestyle parks complete with half-pipes. Limited ticket sales ensures under crowding. During the summer, some of the best mountain biking around. Killer views from the Scenic Sky Chair.

Tops In Travel

1409 Montana Ave.   (310) 393-3791
Santa Monica, CA 90403
Mon - Fri 9am - 5pm, Sat 11am - 3pm
Web: www.topsintravel.com

Full-service travel agency offering domestic and international packages. Whether it's trekking in Napal, pawing Polar Bears in Canada, or gallivanting on the Galapagos Islands, well-traveled and knowledgeable staff will plan your getaway and give valuable tips.

Two Bunch Palms

67-425 Two Bunch Palms Trail   (760) 329-8791
Palm Springs, CA 92262   (800) 472-4334
Web: www.twobunchpalms.com

The rustic bohemian-style hideaway has remained an exclusive tranquil haven for the entertainment industry for over three decades. With a spectacular natural desert oasis setting, abundant hot mineral springs, great food, phenomenal treatments and a friendly welcoming staff- it continues to offer a truly unique relaxation and rejuvenation experience.

Western Spirit Cycling

478 Mill Creek Dr.   (800) 845-2453
Moab, UT 84532
Web: www.westernspirit.com

Civilized tours in uncivilized terrain. Fully supported 4-6 day mountain biking/camping trips for both experts and beginners, and can recommend the perfect back country adventure for your skill level. Go to Moab, Bryce/Zion National Park, Telluride and more. Will haul all your gear and provide hearty, dietary-accommodating food and cushy camping accommodations. Family, women's, group and customized tours available. March-October.

Whistler-Resort-Association

4010 Whistler Way   (800) 944-7853
Whistler, CAN BC VON 1B4
Web: www.whistler-resort.com

Seven thousand acres of the most challenging ski terrain in North America. Boasting two mile-high mountains and a huge variety of runs, Whistler delivers the most important ingredient, snow and lots of it. Start at the top of an alpine glacier, ski down to your hotel and relax in this attitude-free atmosphere. Wander the modernized cobbled street pedestrian town square.

Who Knew we cater/Private Yacht Charters
(310) 884-0996

Web: www.2whoknew.com

The world is your oyster when you charter a private yacht for the ultimate vacation. For the day. For the weekend. Sail away on an experience of a lifetime on a fully crewed luxury sea vessel, complete with chef service and concierge-level amenities like those found at a five-star hotel - only you have it all to yourself with only the ocean to share it with. Tool around on jet skis, splash in the waves on inflatables or enjoy the use of premium fishing and snorkeling gear. It's the meticulous attention to each detail, every arrangement that will make this a total trip.

Wildland Adventures
3516 Northeast 155th St. (800) 345-4453
Seattle, WA 98155 (206) 365-0686
Web: www.wildland.com

Authentic worldwide explorations to unspoiled habitats in Antarctica, Latin America and Africa. Two-week soft adventures incorporate an ecological approach with native guides providing insight to indigenous cultural and natural history. Trekking, bird-watching, observation and safaris. Dietary concerns, no problem. Guests are matched with destinations according to interests and capacity for exercise.

The World Outside
2840 Wilderness Pl., Ste. F (800) 488-8483
Boulder, CO 80301 (303) 413-0938
Web: www.theworldoutside.com

Providing exhilarating guided tours since 1988, specializing in kayaking, white water rafting, mountain biking, hiking and rock climbing. Single activities like the Rocky Mountain Rambler and multi-sport packages like the Colorado Sampler available. Wilderness destinations also to California, Wyoming, Hawaii, Alaska, New Zealand, Costa Rica and several others. Adventures last 6-14 days and include accommodations at historic inns and B&Bs. Groups limited to 14, backup (vans on biking trips, gear toters while hiking) is provided.

Hotels

Anabelle Hotel
2011 W. Olive Ave. (818) 845-7800
Burbank, CA 91506

Luxury hotel with a less-than-luxury price tag offering standard rooms, suites with full kitchens and junior suites with king and sofa beds, wet bars and microwaves. Features, many of them complimentary, include parking and airport shuttle to Burbank Airport, local phone calls and in-room coffee, work stations with two-line phones and refrigerators, video games and movies. Pool and deck, fitness room, even guest laundry facilities. A pair of rich, terry robes complete your gracious living experience. Close to the studios, shopping and other attractions.

The Argyle
8358 W. Sunset Blvd. (323) 654-7100
W. Hollywood, CA 90069

A national historic landmark, The Argyle (the former St. James Club) was built in the 1920s and completely renovated in the mid-1980s. From spectacular architecture to furnishings that are custom period reproductions by master artisans, the hotel is the ultimate art deco experience offering 15-stories of elegance in the heart of the Sunset Strip.

The Avalon Hotel
9400 W. Olympic Blvd. (310) 277-5221
Beverly Hills, CA 90212

A premiere boutique hotel housed within three '50s Modern buildings, all completely redone. The lobby is attractive in cool tones of blue-green which lead all the way out to the pool. Rooms are warm and luxurious in earthy tones and accentuated by overstuffed beds, triple-sheeted bedding and plump quilts, all adorned with signature throws for romantic cuddling. Turndown service includes six pillows. High-tech business amenities for the industry pro include dual phone lines, fax, cd player, VCR and more. Some rooms have completely outfitted kitchenettes. 24-hour room service, restaurant and meeting rooms.

Best Western Sunset Plaza Hotel
8400 Sunset Blvd. (323) 654-0750
West Hollywood, CA 90069 (800) 421-3652

Cosmopolitan yet affordable, the Sunset Plaza is ideally located amid famous clubs and attractions on the Sunset Strip. Its central West Hollywood address offers minutes away access to attractions such as Hollywood's Walk of Fame, Universal Studios, Farmers Market and Museum Row in Los Angeles' Mid-Wilshire district.

RELAX

FOR RESERVATIONS PLEASE CALL 888 419 7600

MONDRIAN

8440 SUNSET BOULEVARD WEST HOLLYWOOD CA 90069
PHONE 323 650 8999 FAX 323 650 5215
IAN SCHRAGER HOTELS. NEW YORK MIAMI LOS ANGELES LONDON
COMING SOON SAN FRANCISCO SANTA BARBARA

● BestRest Inn

51541 N. Peace Valley Rd.   (661) 248-2700
Lebec, CA 93243

Ideally located hotel for your next film project just off I-5 at the top of the Grapevine, nestled in rolling hills of oak and mountains of pine. Great corporate rates and free continental breakfast. Rooms have computer hookups, refrigerators, cable TV and VCRs. 24-7 restaurant on the premises. Seasonal heated pool and Jacuzzi. Four seasons area which is accessible to Los Padres National Forest, Mt. Pinos, Fort Tejon and Hungry Valley. Pyramid Lake is also close by for boating, skiing and fishing.

Beverly Plaza Hotel

8384 W. Third St.   (323) 658-6600
West Los Angeles, CA 90048   (800) 624-6835

This "Boutique" styled hotel borders Beverly Hills and West Hollywood and prides itself on their attention to details. Amenities include two-line telephones with data port and voice mail, satellite remote television and in room dining including free delivery from Jerry's Deli. While there visit Cava, their celebrated cafe and tapas bar.

The Cadillac Hotel

8 Dudley Ave.   (310) 399-8876
Venice, CA 90291
Web: www.thecadillachotel.com

A pink and turquoise art deco monument known as the most fashionable place to stay in its heyday-a stomping ground for Charlie Chaplin and Cecil B. DeMille. The interior of the hotel has been completely redone from top to bottom. Sitting right on the beach, many of the 38 rooms afford ocean views with some of the best restaurants in the city just five minutes away. European-style service.

Casa Del Mar

1910 Ocean Way   (310) 581-5533
Santa Monica, CA 90405   (800) 898-6999
Web: www.hotelcasadelmar.com

Built in 1929 and now restored to its lavish heyday, there are penthouse suites with views to exceed even the highest expectations, a pool deck for basking, a ballroom for all manner of revelry, and an aptly named restaurant, Oceanfront. With a menu of California-French and enclosed by glass walls facing an endless expanse of sea, it's intimate and spacious all at the same time.

destination:
the anabelle hotel

features and amenities

- two-line telephones, with a data port and voice mail with complimentary local calls
- cable television, in-room movies, nintendo games and free hbo
- in-room safes
- iron, ironing board and hair dryer
- terry cloth bathrobes & complimentary in-room coffee
- large desk & chair

ake yourself comfortable

- six suites with full kitchens & living rooms
- nine suites with wet bars & microwaves
- nightly turn down service
- complimentary shuttle service to Burbank, Glendale, Pasadena Airport
- Olive's Bistro & Lounge serving breakfast, lunch and dinner
- fitness room
- room service from Olives Bistro & Lounge

The ANABELLE
HOTEL

Located midway between Hollywood & Universal City.

11 west olive avenue, burbank, CA 91506 phone 818.845.7800 fax 818.845.0054

The Safari Inn

- TELEPHONES WITH A DATA PORT AND VOICE MAIL
- CABLE TELEVISION, IN-ROOM MOVIES, NINTENDO GAMES AND FREE HBO
- COMPLIMENTARY LOCAL TELEPHONE CALLS
- IRON, IRONING BOARD AND HAIR DRYER
- COMPLIMENTARY IN-ROOM COFFEE
- MINI REFRIGERATORS
- LARGE DESK & CHAIR
- TEN SUITES WITH FULL KITCHENS
- OUTDOOR SWIMMING POOL AND SUNDECK
- COMPLIMENTARY SHUTTLE SERVICE TO AND FROM THE BURBANK, GLENDALE, PASADENA AIRPORT
- OLIVE'S BISTRO & LOUNGE SERVING BREAKFAST, LUNCH AND DINNER
- ROOM SERVICE FROM OLIVE'S BISTRO & LOUNGE
- FITNESS ROOM & GUEST LAUNDRY FACILITIES

Safari
INN

LOCATED MIDWAY BETWEEN
HOLLYWOOD & UNIVERSAL CITY.

1911 West Olive Ave. Burbank, Ca 91506
818-845-8586 fax 818-845-0054

Chateau Marmont Hotel

8221 Sunset Blvd.   (323) 656-1010
Hollywood, CA 90046

Eclectic blend of '20s, '30s and '40s Old Hollywood glamour with a refined European sensibility. Medieval castle poised at the foot of the Hollywood Hills, heralding one's arrival to the Sunset Strip. 63 rooms, some occupied by permanent celebrity residents. Elegant lobby area and garden conducive for relaxation and socializing.

Citrus Suites

425 Broadway   (800) 410-0409
Santa Monica, CA 90401   (310) 392-9922
Web: www.citrussuites.com

The place to call home when you have an extended stay in the LA area. Luxurious corporate housing suites offer ocean views and the best of upscale hotel living. Fully furnished, kitchens, personal fax machines, and Internet access provided. Best of all, its on the beach and far less expensive than a hotel.

Embassy Suites Mandalay Beach Resort

2101 Mandalay Beach Rd.   (805) 984-2500
Oxnard, CA 93035   (800) 362-2779
Web: www.embassymandalay.com

Just 60 minutes north of Los Angeles, this all-suite oceanfront resort resembles the tropics with its lush gardens, waterfalls, and lagoons. Every room is a two-room suite with two marble baths and micro-kitchen. Every guest enjoys a complimentary full, cooked-to-order breakfast and hosted evening beverages daily. Onsite recreation includes an outdoor pool, tennis, bike rentals, two whirlpools and exercise room. Nearby golf, water sports, outlet shopping and other local entertainment. Special packages available.

Furnace Creek Inn

Highway 190, P.O. Box 1   (760) 786-2345
Death Valley, CA 92328   (800) 236-7916
Web: www.furnacecreekresort.com

Four-diamond resort hotel inside a fully restored original adobe brick, Mission-style structure. Sixty-six rooms, many with balconies offering palm garden views. Splash in the natural spring-fed pool, hit a few balls on one of four lighted tennis courts, go horseback riding on trails or take a romantic evening carriage ride. Home of the world's lowest golf course at 214 feet below sea level.

The Grafton

8462 Sunset Blvd.   (323) 654-6470
West Hollywood, CA 90069   (800) 821-3660

This intimate European-style hotel is within walking distance of many of the city's most exciting clubs and restaurants on the Sunset Strip. Corner rooms offer panoramic views of the city. The Georgian-influenced decor lends a touch of the traditional to this warm, hospitable hideaway on one of the world's most legendary boulevards.

Hilton Garden Inn Valencia Six Flags

27710 The Old Rd.   (661) 254-8800
Valencia, CA 91355
Web: www.hilton.com

Closest hotel to two popular amusement parks, Six Flags Magic Mountain and Hurricane Harbor. Oversized guest rooms are airy and restful, comfortably spacious, technologically efficient workspaces complete with ergonomic chairs and easy access, desk-level outlets. It's this attention to detail coupled with standard amenities like coffee makers, microwaves and refrigerators that make it like home – only better. Because your success doesn't shut down at 6pm, 24-hour complimentary business center is ready to work when you are. Boasts fitness facilities, outdoor heated pool and restaurant, as well.

Hotel Bel-Air

701 Stone Canyon Rd.	(310) 472-1211
Los Angeles, CA 90077	(800) 648-4097
Web: www.hotelbelair.com	

Nestled In a wooded canyon just outside of Beverly Hills, Hotel Bel-Air is a California oasis, with 11.5 acres of lush gardens and soaring trees. Intimate shaded courtyards, stone fountains and wrought-iron terraces accentuate the pink stucco mission-style structure of the 1920s. The hotel has 92 rooms including 40 suites, many of which have wood-burning fireplaces, private patios and jacuzzis. Offering California-French cuisine, The Restaurant is a popular setting for hotel guests and nearby residents.

Hotel Oceana

849 Ocean Ave.	(310) 393-0486
Santa Monica, CA 90403	(800) 777-0758
Web: www.hoteloceana.com	

Beachside property offers the utmost in luxury, comfort and elegance. Bright and open, the hotel maintains the true essence of Southern California with a sun-drenched lobby and private lanais facing the pool. Designer Cheryl Rowley has combined California architectural style with European splendor, from the wrought iron detailing welcoming you in, to the Cocteau inspired murals and Mediterranean gardens in the courtyard. Art Deco style suites contain executive work areas, high-tech media centers and gourmet kitchens (which will be stocked with any special requests). Fretted linens, thick comfy robes and marble bathrooms complete your relaxing experience.

Hyatt Valencia

24500 Town Center Dr.   (661) 799-1234
Valencia, CA 91355   (800) 233-1234
Web: www.valencia.hyatt.com

The newest California Hyatt and the only full service luxury hotel in the scenic Santa Clarita Valley, home to Six Flags Magic Mountain and many other local attractions. Situated in the heart of the entertainment district, the hotel overlooks splendid gardens and a championship golf course. Spacious guest rooms, some with private terraces, designed with a Mediterranean flair in rich woods are just part of the luxurious accommodations you'll find here. Add to this Vines Restaurant & Bar where you can dine on the fireside patio with its serene view of the pool and gardens and enjoy an international collection of wines with an artistically prepared menu to complement featured varietals. The fitness center, with its free weights, workout mat for floor routines and full selection of cardio machines, is an on-site state-of-the-art facility - yet another convenience to make your stay a true pleasure. Entertainment package available.

Hyatt West Hollywood

8401 Sunset Blvd.   (323) 656-1234
West Hollywood, CA 90069   (800) 233-1234
Web: www.hyatt.com

Nestled in the Hollywood Hills, the Hyatt West Hollywood has been a landmark on Sunset Boulevard for over 35 years. The recent renovation captures the art deco spirit of the city. In-wall fish tanks, featuring an assortment of tropical fish, adorn the walls of all suites. Take in the highest view of the Sunset Strip from the Hyatt's rooftop. Directly across the street from House of Blues.

Le Meridien at Beverly Hills

465 S. La Cienega Blvd.   (310) 247-0400
Los Angeles, CA 90048
Web: www.lemeridienbeverlyhills.com

Centrally located between the shore and downtown Los Angeles, and minutes from Rodeo Drive, the Beverly Center and the Wilshire business corridor, this hotel is perfect whether you are traveling for business or pleasure. Don't forget to stop by their restaurants Cafe Noir and Panagea Bistro which are quickly becoming industry hot spots.

Le Montrose

900 Hammond St.   (310) 855-1115
W. Hollywood, CA 90069   (800) 776-0666

Elegant European style hotel featuring 129 suites all furnished with refrigerators and fireplaces in sunken living rooms. Most boast kitchenettes and exhilarating city views from the balcony. In-suite dining, rooftop terrace dining, or dine at the Library Restaurant serving Continental cuisine. Facilities include lighted tennis court, rooftop pool and spa, health club and sauna. Private trainer, tennis pro, and masseur on staff. Fresh fruit and mineral water await each guest upon arrival, while those departing are offered complimentary chocolate chip cookies and milk.

Le Parc

733 N. West Knoll Dr.   (310) 855-8888
West Hollywood, CA 90069

Deluxe suites furnished in French decor, nestled on a quiet, tree-lined street but still close to West Hollywood hot spots. Services such as complimentary town car, and features such as gas fireplaces, tennis courts, and heated rooftop pool make this an outstanding stay. Cafe serves Mediterranean cuisine in an affable, living room setting with separate bar area. Perhaps the only upscale hotel in LA where pets are welcome.

Le Reve Hotel

8822 Cynthia St.   (310) 854-1114
West Hollywood, CA 90069

Charming French country 80-suite hotel offers the intimacy and personalized service its boutique status is noted for while offering all the luxury of the big guys. A welcoming fruit basket, room service 24/7, Internet access, a panoramic view from the rooftop pool plus dry cleaning and other on-site amenities, all in a quiet, residential setting but yet a block in any direction from dining, shopping, clubs and more.

Loews Santa Monica Beach Hotel

1700 Ocean Ave.   (310) 458-6700
Santa Monica, CA 90401

Beach front views, prime location and elegant dining are key features of this modern hotel. Offers the best of ocean-side living with private beach access, the convenience of the neighboring Santa Monica Pier and the all-encompassing Third Street Promenade. Restaurant Lavande features Provençal fare and is the toast of west side dining with its breathtaking panoramas. Set within a five-story atrium, The Lobby Bar offers nightly entertainment and weekend dancing. Indoor-outdoor pool also très deluxe.

The Luxe Summit Hotel Bel Air

11461 Sunset Blvd.   (310) 476-6571
Los Angeles, CA 90049   (800) 468-5411
Web: www.luxehotels.com

Centrally located near the Getty Center with special museum packages available. Offering large rooms, room service Luxe Summit Retreat full-service spa, fitness center, outdoor heated pool, tennis court, and shuttles to Rodeo Drive and UCLA. Lovely piano music in the elegant lobby drifts into the restaurants as you dine inside or under the stars. Conference facilities for up to 350.

Maison 140 Hotel

140 S. Lasky Dr.   (310) 271-2145
Beverly Hills, CA 90210

Charming 1930s hotel full of personality and with a European feel. Featuring a continental breakfast daily. Approximately 50 rooms nicely decorated with many original fixtures. Friendly and helpful staff. There's no place like home. Except maybe here.

● Mondrian

8440 W. Sunset Blvd.   (323) 650-8999
West Hollywood, CA 90069

Referred to by many as, "an oasis in the middle of the city," Philippe Starck's design blends muted whites and grays with white mahogany floors to create an airy, spacious, clean look. Spacious guest rooms bring the outside in with unique, glass-wall architecture. Asia de Cuba restaurant features inventive dishes from two disparate but somehow complimentary points on the globe. The Mondrian is home to the famed SKYBAR, the perfect place for a nightcap among the clouds.

Ojai Valley Inn & Spa

905 Country Club Rd.   (805) 646-5511
Ojai, CA 93023   (800) 422-6524
Web: www.ojairesort.com

Surrounded by a sprawling golf course and a skyline of the Topa Topa Mountain range, this renowned offers seclusion to those who seek it, and plays host to local championship golf tournaments, tennis and pontoon fishing excursions. Numerous nature trails for horseback riding, leisurely walks or bike riding. Two swimming pools, and full spa. Recently completed renovation of the 80-year-old Mara Villa Restaurant.

Pacific Shore Hotel

1819 Ocean Ave.   (310) 451-8711
Santa Monica, CA 90401

Fine resort hotel boasts 168 guest rooms with either panoramic views of the ocean or the Santa Monica Mountains. What a wonderful way to greet the day. All rooms have standing balconies. Close to Third St. Promenade, so you get the best of every world. Shoreline Grill is open for breakfast, lunch and dinner. Meticulous service, impeccable accommodations.

Peninsula Beverly Hills Hotel

9882 S. Santa Monica Blvd.   (310) 551-2888
Beverly Hills, CA 90212
Web: www.peninsula.com

Amazing five-star, five-diamond hotel. The Belvedere restaurant serves California cuisine with a French twist. Rooftop garden cafe is more laid back. Rooms adorned in pastels and showcase a collection of Asian art. Facilities include expanded fitness center, health spa with hydrotherapy bath and vichy shower, and 60-foot, heated lap pool. Massage and other healthful, restful treatments are also available.

● Radisson Huntley Hotel

1111 Second St.   (310) 394-5454
Santa Monica, CA 90403
Web: www.radisson.com

Boasting the best value at the beach, selected upper level rooms offer coastal views. All guest quarters have been newly renovated and are European-themed. This lively locale is just one block from Third Street Promenade. Its popular rooftop restaurant and cantina, Toppers, offers Mexican and Continental food served with a panoramic view of the Pacific from 18 floors above the world.

Ramada West Hollywood

8585 Santa Monica Blvd.   (310) 652-6400
West Hollywood, CA 90069   (800) 845-8585
Web: www.ramada-wh.com

Armada West Hollywood captures the spirit of one of the world's great cities with its Contemporary design. Its elegant loft suites and nicely appointed guest rooms offer quality accommodations and exemplary guest service. The hotel is conveniently located between Los Angeles, Beverly Hills and Hollywood and only minutes from the Pacific Design Center, Rodeo Drive, Universal Studios, Getty Museum and the beaches of Santa Monica.

RE / MAX Santa Barbara
Diana Fornas/Dani Burkhardt

                                   (805) 969-2282

Diana Fornas has been working in the Santa Barbara area since 1977 and has represented the full range of market - celebrities, executives, first-time buyers and company relocations. She is fluent in Spanish and English. She teams with Dani Burkhardt who began her career in 1974. Having been active in local theater, she is very experienced in the Santa Barbara area. She interacts well with first-time buyers as well as in the luxury home market for both buyers and sellers.

Regent Beverly Wilshire Hotel

9500 Wilshire Blvd.   (310) 275-5200
Beverly Hills, CA 90212

Fully renovated high-end hotel now boasts 395 rooms, 118 suites and balconies for captivating views of the LA skyline. Caters to corporate clients. The Dining Room showcases the best in continental cuisine in a formal setting. In walking distance to Rodeo Drive, The Regent is in close proximity to maximum swanky shopping. Full-service fitness club offers complete spa facilities, such as sauna and steam room. Ask about spa packages.

● The Safari Inn

1911 W. Olive   (818) 845-8586
Burbank, CA 91506   (800) 782-4373

A mecca for '50s aficionados and neophytes alike. Pull up to the door of your spacious room or suite (jungle-themed, of course) in your '56 Chevy convertible and dig the creature comforts. Refrigerators, coffee makers and data ports. Are you up for the challenge of the heated lap pool? Or get your workout on dry land in the fitness center. Laundry and dry cleaner on premises.

San Vincente Inn/Resort

845 N. San Vincente Blvd.   (310) 845-6915
West Hollywood, CA 90069
Web: www.gayresort.com

West Hollywood's only gay guest house, the San Vincente Inn/Resort offers a relaxing, intimate retreat just steps away from the shops, restaurants and exciting nightlife of Santa Monica Boulevard. It is centrally located in the pulse of the gay community. Quiet, comfortable cottages and rooms overlook the lush tropical gardens surrounding a tranquil heated pool and clothing optional sundeck.

Shangri-La Hotel

1301 Ocean Ave. (310) 394-2791
Santa Monica, CA 90401
Web: www.shangrila-hotel.com

Charming 55 room hotel, circa 1939, is right across from the Santa Monica Beach and offers unlimited ocean views. Sit down to a relaxing complimentary breakfast with such offerings as croissants and coffee, then later for afternoon tea in the garden patio. Free newspaper delivered to your doorstep.

Shutters on the Beach

One Pico Blvd. (310) 458-0030
Santa Monica, CA 90405

The only Santa Monica hotel actually situated on the beach, this is the place for ocean lovers who like to roll out of bed and splash into the surf. Retro-decor captures the stylish elegance of '30s and '40s Pacific beach front mansions (coastal room views included!) but with ultra modern conveniences like fully-appointed business and fitness centers. Fine dining at One Pico restaurant, while Pedals Cafe is less formal. For fun and convenience, rent a bike from the hotel and ride the path in the ocean breeze.

The Standard

8300 Sunset Blvd. (323) 650-9090
W. Hollywood, CA 90069
Web: www.standardhotel.com

Ditch conformity without crucifying your budget. De rigeur here means a front-desk dj, performance art, groovy furniture, in-room high-speed Internet access and music electronics, big stuff in the mini bar, laundry service, a barber shop/tattoo/piercing studio, a cocktail lounge and 24-hour eatery. And you won't wake up to a 7am vacuum cleaner.

Summerfield Suites Hotel

1000 Westmount Dr. (310) 657-7400
West Hollywood, CA 90069 (800) 833-4353

Tucked away on a quiet, tree-lined street, this boutique-style hotel is a few blocks south of the Sunset Strip, one block north of Santa Monica Boulevard and minutes from Beverly Hills. Tailored to the needs of the 90s style of life with spacious suites and a casual, cosmopolitan atmosphere, Summerfield Suites offers a relaxing retreat in the heart of West Hollywood.

Sunset Marquis Hotel & Villas

1200 N. Alta Loma Rd. (310) 657-1333
West Hollywood, CA 90069

World-renown for their extraordinary service, accommodations and location, location, location. All suite hotel with 12 private one and two bedroom villas which were originally estate homes and are now linked by 4 1/2 acres of lush gardens. The hotel's black slate entryway leads into the Modern interior filled with contemporary stylishness. Rooms are decorated in sophisticated taupes and rich chocolate browns. Spacious living areas contain business amenities disguised by minimalist cabinetry. Every detail is of the highest caliber down to the tiger's eye wood in the make-up area. The intimate restaurant is welcoming, with overstuffed couches and seating. An onsite commercial recording studio with screening room is available. The hip Whisky Bar is first-serve exclusively for guests of the hotel.

Surf & Sand Hotel

1555 S. Coast Hwy (800) 524-8621
Laguna Beach, CA 92651 (949) 497-4477
Web: www.surfandsandresort.com

Imagine a place that rises up from the beach, where the view is always of the ocean, you're serenaded by surf, and your room is a well-deserved luxury that feels like home. Someone has read your mind because this is it. Elegance and bleached wood, sea-washed palettes of color, a crystalline pool and deck seemingly floating above the ocean, gracious Mediterranean dining and world-class accommodations with an inimitable flair. Minutes from many noted attractions. If you can tear yourself away.

Santa Barbara

Bacara Resort & Inn
8301 Hollister Ave. (805) 968-0100
Santa Barbara, CA 93117
Web: www.bacararesort.com

Bacara Resort and Spa is a newly created oceanfront destination resort of Spanish Colonial architecture in a village setting. 311 luxury guest accomodations and 49 specialty suites, all with private balconies or patios, many with fireplaces and ocean views. Full service spa, three restaurants, golf, banquet and meeting facilities.

Captain Don's Cruises
219 Stearns Wharf, Box G (805) 969-5217
Santa Barbara, CA 93101

Sail the ocean blue amid abundant marine life with a Coast Guard-licensed captain for a whale watching excursion. Boats leave at daily at 8am and return by 2pm, June through September for blue whale season in which you're guaranteed a sighting. Gray whales migrate between February and May and tours are two hours long, launching at 9am, noon, and 3pm. Offers dinner and dance, sunset and holiday cruises and charters, too.

Circle Bar B Stables
1800 Refugio Rd. (805) 968-3901
Santa Barbara, CA 93117

Start off through back canyons, ford through streams, pass waterfalls, circle around mountains to Lookout Point and view valleys, the ocean and Channel Islands for 90 minute rides. Trotting and loping offered for experienced riders. Lunch ride leaves at 9 am and gets back at 1pm, with lunch under a eucalyptus grove with incredible views stretching to Santa Barbara.

Citronelle California-French
901 E. Cabrillo Blvd. (805) 963-0111
Santa Barbara, CA 93103

As noted for the sunsets coloring its three walls of windows atop the Santa Barbara Inn as it is for Chef Michel Richard's California French cuisine. His signature is the sauces: saffron dressing over blue crab salad, cider sauce on roasted duck, chardonnay sauce with asparagus crusted chicken. Can't decide? Chef's five-course menu offers a feast of variety. Extraordinary breakfasts and lunches enhanced by the light and airy European style room hued in Scandinavian blue and yellow.

Cold Springs Tavern
5995 Stagecoach Rd. (805) 967-0066
Santa Barbara, CA 93105

Original 115 year old stage coach stop now houses this romantic retreat housed in a canyon just twenty minutes outside of Santa Barbara. Lit by kerosene lamps and fireplaces, the menu features wild game (alligator, rabbit, buffalo, black bear) though other choices are available, even vegetarian. Live music weekends.

The Condor
301 W. Cabrillo Blvd. (888) 779-4253
Santa Barbara, CA 93101

Private charter boat (which also works with top researchers and museums) will take you on the trip of a lifetime. Summer is Blue Whale season, the largest animal ever to roam the face of the earth (its tongue is larger than an entire elephant). The only other place to see a Blue Whale is Costa Rica. During the rest of the year, view grey whales, dolphins, sea lions and harbor seals. Tours leave at 8am and return between 3-5pm. Weekday and weekend excursions.

Firestone Walker Brewing Co.
620 MacMurray Rd. (805) 686-1557
Buellton, CA
Web: www.firestonebeer.com

Their beers utilize oak barrel fermentation, giving them a unique fruitiness and fullness to the palate. Sample their hand-crafted ales and munch on brew snacks in their old world taproom.

Four Seasons Biltmore, Santa Barbara
1260 Channel Dr. (805) 565-8241
Santa Barbara, CA 93108
Web: www.fourseasons.com

The American Riviera's premier resort has it all: 20 acres of oceanfront vistas; an array of multi award-winning dining experiences including the exotic and the health-conscious with an emphasis on local produce and seafood; fitness club, two pools, tennis courts; and rooms, suites and cottages that capture and express the rich, Mediterranean history of the Spanish Colonial architecture but with very modern conveniences like data ports and two-line phones with voice mail. Casual luxury all the way.

RE / MAX Santa Barbara/Rose Ogden

(805) 687-7903
(805) 687-2232

With over 20 years experience in the Santa Barbara, Montecito and Goleta areas, Rose Ogden is highly skilled and intuitive to Buyers' tastes and needs and encourages positive client interaction and involvement. With a background in the entertainment and music industry, she is adept at finding the perfect luxury home for principal residence or vacation needs. She offers creative and dynamic marketing for her Sellers. Rose is an associate Realtor with RE/MAX Santa Barbara and Montecito, and RE/MAX International offering relocation and referral services globally.

San Ysidro Ranch

900 San Ysidro Ln.   (805) 969-5046
Santa Barbara, CA 93108

Exclusive rustic retreat ranch nestled in the majestic Santa Ynez Mountains, and surrounded by flower gardens and citrus groves. Twenty-one separate cottages (one with its own private pool). Tennis courts, heated ocean view pool, Ayurvedic spa services, nanny service, children's pool and special children's menu. Privileged pet program allows your pooch to select gourmet meals ranging from N.Y. Steak to Veggie Biscuits.

Santa Barbara Botanic Garden

1212 Mission Canyon Rd.   (805) 682-4726
Santa Barbara, CA 93105
Mon - Fri 9am - 5pm, Sat - Sun 9am - 6pm

Wind your way up the hills of Santa Barbara to sixty-five acres of native plants. Enjoy the redwood forest, historic dam and panoramic views of the neighboring Channel Islands. Five and a half miles of walking paths. Friendly gift shop.

Santa Barbara Conference & Visitors and Film Commission

12 E. Carrillo St.   (805) 966-9222
Santa Barbara, CA 93101

Santa Barbara Orchid Estate

1250 Orchid Dr.   (805) 967-1284
Santa Barbara, CA 93111
Mon - Sat 8am - 4:30pm, Sun 11am - 4pm
Web: www.sborchid.com

Old-fashioned nursery in business since 1957 allows the public to come in, wander around, enjoy the beauty of the orchids and select a variety. Situated just 500 feet from the ocean with over 1000 different species of orchid, visiting the nursery is like a mini-trip to Hawaii.

Santa Barbara Polo & Raquet Club

3375 Foothill Rd., Ste. 1200   (805) 684-6683
Carpinteria, CA 93013
Web: www.sbpolo.com

Polo, anyone? Or perhaps tennis. Whether you you play this lightning quick sport of 'hockey on horseback' or are an avid spectator, and whther you have a wicked serve or like fine service, there are four memberships to suit your style. A social membership gets you into Sunday polo matches, golf and retail discounts, dinner parties and other events. A tennis membership includes social privileges, access to eight championship courts, two staff pros, pool, jacuzzi and other amenities. There's also a swimming membership and, of course, the mack daddy of 'em all - a polo membership.

Simpson House

121 E. Arrellaga St.   (805) 963-7067
Santa Barbara, CA 93101

The first and only AAA Five Diamond North American Bed and Breakfast Inn. All rooms in this Victorian house are lavishly appointed (including antiques) but the Old Barn guest rooms and Cottages are truly magnificent, offering a "hayloft" with streams of natural light, antique pine floors and Oriental rugs. French doors open onto private decks overlooking the gardens.

Upham Hotel

1404 De La Vina St.   (805) 962-0058
Santa Barbara, CA 93101   (800) 727-0876
Web: www.uphamhotel.com

The oldest continuously operating hotel in Southern California, this 129 year old B & B style hotel was originally built as a New England-style boarding house. The original Lincoln building is Victorian and Craftsman cottages surround the gardens with fireplaces and views. Continental breakfast served daily with wine tastings in the afternoon and Oreo cookies and milk before bedtime. The hotel has all modern amenities for the business traveler including meeting rooms. Louie's restaurant serves California cuisine, is popular among the locals and has won many accolades.

Visitor Information Bureaus

Arroyo Grande
800 Wets Branch (805) 489-1488
Arroyo Grande, CA 93420

Cambria
767 Main St. (805) 927-3624
Cambria, CA 93428
Web: www.cambriachamber.org

Los Angeles Visitor Information Center
685 S. Figueroa St. (213) 689-8822
Los Angeles, CA 90017
Web: www.lacub.com

Mexican Goverment Tourism Office
2401 W. 6th St. (213) 351-2069
Los Angeles, CA 90057
Web: www.mexico-travel.com

Morro Bay
880 Main St. (805) 772-4467
Morro Bay, CA 93442

Ontario Convention And Visitor's Authority
2000 Convention Center Way (909) 937-3000
Ontario, CA 91764 (800) 455-5755

Oxnard
200 W. Seventh St. (805) 385-7545
Oxnard, CA 93030

Palm Springs Tourism
333 N. Palm Canyon Dr., #114 (800) 347-7746
Palm Springs, CA 92262
Web: www.palm-springs.org

Pasadena Convention And Visitors Bureau
171 S. Los Robles Ave. (626) 795-9311
Pasadena, CA 91101
Web: www.pasadenacal.com

Paso Robles
1225 Park St. (805) 238-0506
Paso Robles, CA 93446

Sacramento Convention And Visitors Bureau
1303 J St., Ste. 600 (800) 292-2334
Sacramento, CA 95814 (916) 264-7777
Web: www.sacramentocvb.org

San Diego
401 B St., Ste. 1400 (619) 232-3101
San Diego, CA 92101

San Luis Obispo
1037 Mill St. (805) 541-8000
San Luis Obispo, CA 93401

Santa Barbara Conference &
Visitors and Film Commission
12 E. Carrillo St. (805) 966-9222
Santa Barbara, CA 93101 (800) 676-1266
Web: www.filmsantabarbara.com

Ventura Visitors Bureau
89-C S. California St. (800) 333-2989
Ventura, CA 93001

West Hollywood Convention & Visitors Bureau
8687 Melrose Ave., Suite M-25 (310) 289-2525
West Hollywood, CA 90069 (800) 368-6020
Web: www.visitwesthollywood.com

Beckman Vineyards

2670 Ontiveros Rd.　　　　　　(805) 688-8664
Los Olivos, CA 93441
Mon - Sun 11am - 5pm

Loll in a gazebo while enjoying this hillside winery complete with duck pond and rose gardens. Wines include a rich and spicy Sauvignon Blanc, an approachable, full-of-fruit Syrah, creamy Chardonnay with citrus highlights and a soft, ready to drink Cabernet.

Bedford Thompson Winery

9303 Alisos Canyon Rd.　　　　(805) 344-2107
Los Alamos, CA 93440
Web: www.bedfordthompsonwinery.com

Hand-crafted wines produced at this traditional winery specializing in an elegant Chardonnay, a rich Viognier, a spicy Syrah and a lush Cabernet Franc. Picnic grounds under old oak and pine trees.

Buttonwood Farm Winery and Vineyard

1500 Alamo Pintado Rd.　　　　(805) 688-3032
Solvang, CA 93464　　　　　　(800) 715-1404
Mon - Sun 11am - 5pm
Web: www.buttonwoodwinery.com

Former horse ranch now houses organically farmed winery. Taste a Marsanne which is a Rhone varietal rarely found in California, a lush Sauvignon Blanc, exceptional Bordeaux-style reds or a classic Vintage Port.

Byron Vineyard and Winery

5230 Tepusquet Rd.　　　　　　(805) 937-7288
Santa Maria, CA 93454　　　　(888) 303-7288
Web: www.byronwines.com

State of the art winery designed by LA architect Scott Johnson (designer of the Transamerica Building in San Francisco). Picnic areas overlook gorgeous Tepusquet Canyon. Many wines produced here including Pinot Blanc, Pinot Gris, Chardonnay and Pinot Noir.

Cottonwood Canyon Winery

3940 Dominion Rd.　　　　　　(805) 937-9063
Santa Maria, CA 93454
Mon - Sun 10:30am - 5:30pm
Web: www.cottonwoodcanyon.com

On Foxen Canyon Trail, this modern winery can accommodate medium size groups for special events in their tasting rooms overlooking the valley or underground in the wine caves. Chardonnay and Pinot Noir are their specialty.

Edna Valley Vineyard

2585 Biddle Ranch Rd.　　　　(805) 544-5855
San Luis Obispo, CA 93401
Mon - Sun 10am - 5pm
Web: www.ednavalley.com

Sip their crisp Chardonnay with hints of tropical fruit at the 35 foot cherry wood tasting bar. Banquet facilities overlook rolling vineyards. Huge retail floor with wearables, wine accessories, paintings, and gourmet marketplace.

Fess Parker Winery

6200 Foxen Canyon Rd.　　　　(805) 688-1545
Los Olivos, CA 93441
Mon - Sun 10am - 5pm

Family owned and operated, Fess Parker's son Eli is the on-premises winemaker (sometimes you can even catch a glimpse of Fess working). Most known for their medium to full-bodied Syrah and Rhone varietals, their Chardonnay and Pinot Noirs have also won awards. An ultra-premium winery with beautiful grounds and picnic tables. Tastings include souvenir glass with Fess' trademark coonskin hat.

Firestone Vineyard

5000 Zaca Station Rd.　　　　(805) 688-3940
Los Olivos, CA 93441
Mon - Sun 10am - 5pm
Web: www.firestonevineyard.com

Third generation run company owns 600 acres of vineyard with a rustic tasting room decorated in Spanish tile and stone. Their Riesling is off dry and soft with tropical flavors.

The Gainey Vineyard

3950 E. Highway 246　　　　　(805) 688-0558
Santa Ynez, CA 93460
Mon - Sun 10am - 5pm
Web: www.gaineyvineyard.com

Tours offered daily through the shiny high-tech winery or just skip straight to the tastings. Gourmet food counter for those who have forgotten picnic baskets. Specialties include Chardonnay, Pinot Noir and Sauvignon Blanc. Beautiful upscale location.

Laetitia Vineyard and Winery

453 Tower Grove Rd. (805) 481-1772
Arroyo Grande, CA 93420 (888) 809-8463
Mon - Sun 11am - 6pm
Web: www.laetitiawine.com

Formerly Maison Duetz, this busy winery specializes in award-winning Pinot Noir, Chardonnay, Pinot Blanc and sparkling wine created by Methode Champenoise (natural aging process in the bottle). Special event center and family-friendly picnic area. Located right off the 101 freeway.

LinCourt Vineyards at the Santa Ynez Winery

343 N. Refugio Rd. (805) 688-8381
Santa Ynez, CA 93460
Mon - Sun 10am - 5pm

Former college transformed first into a dairy and then converted to its present day winery. Lovely lawn and deck for picnics. Try the medium-body, peppery Pinot Noir or the Chardonnay.

Los Olivos Vintners/Austin Cellars

2923 Grand Ave. (805) 688-9665
Los Olivos, CA 93441 (800) 824-8584
Mon - Sun 11am - 6pm

Turn-of-the-century tasting room. Featured wines are a full-bodied Chardonnay, a Sauvignon Blanc with a touch of oak, a red Cabernet Sauvignon, a Merlot and a Pinot Noir. Sweeter white wines include Muscat Canelli, white Riesling, Port, and botrytis Sauvignon Blanc.

Sunstone Vineyards and Winery

125 N. Refugio Rd. (805) 688-9463
Santa Ynez, CA 93460 (800) 313-9463
Mon - Sun 10am - 4pm
Web: www.sunstonewinery.com

Transport yourself to Provence on the banks of the Santa Ynez River. Two barrel aging caves carry you back in time. Browse the new wine library. Taste the soft fruity Chardonnay, mellow or outstanding Merlot. The entire vineyard is certified organic.

Talley Vineyards

3031 Lopez Dr. (805) 489-0446
Arroyo Grande, CA 93420
Mon - Sun 10:30am - 4:30pm
Web: www.talleyvineyards.com

Estate-grown Chardonnay and Pinot Noir are the specialties here. Their tasting room is inside an old adobe house built in the 1860s.

Zaca Mesa Winery

6905 Foxen Canyon Rd. (800) 350-7972
Los Olivos, CA 93441
Web: www.zacamesa.com

A picnic area beneath shady oaks, scenic hiking trails and estate grown Rhone varietal wines await you. Sample Syrah, Z Cuvee, Roussanne, Viognier and Z Gris along with Chardonnay in the wine tasting room. Group tours available by prearrangement.

Luxuries & Pleasures

Erotic Wear

Condomania
7306 Melrose Ave.   (323) 933-7865
Los Angeles, CA 90046
Sun - Thu 11am - 8pm, Fri - Sat 11am - 10pm
Web: www.condomania.com

From "Kiss O'Mints" to "Bareback Singles," nothing is more fun, safe and erotic to wear than a condom. Over 300 styles and varieties from around the world. Flavored gels and lubricants. Gift items and novelties. Call (800) 9-CONDOM for mail orders.

Dream Dresser
8444 Santa Monica Blvd.   (323) 848-3480
West Hollywood, CA 90069
Mon - Sat 11am - 8pm
Web: www.dreamdresser.com

Into themes? At Dream Dresser, become a Saturday Night Cowgirl, complete with leather chaps and riding crop or a fabulously slinky feline in a body-hugging catsuit. Or for a more traditional approach to setting the mood, there's always a classic boned corset or barely there G-string.

Frederick's Of Hollywood
6608 Hollywood Blvd.   (323) 466-8506
Los Angeles, CA 90028
Mon - Fri 10am - 9pm, Sat 10am - 7pm, Sun 11am - 6pm

An institution for over 50 years, offering push up bras for those women (and men) with the desire to feel more endowed. Turning lingerie into fashion and offering everything from classic feathered mules to edible underwear. Stylish casual wear, too. Friendly staff is always ready to assist with one's flight of fancy. Historic bra museum next door is worth a peek. Dare to be a diva.

Hustler Hollywood
8920 Sunset Blvd.   (310) 860-9009
West Hollywood, CA 90069
Mon - Sun 10am - 2am

Macy's it ain't. Erotic department store where the shopping experience is trés sexy. Delight in its collection of leather and lingerie. Make a statement with its provocative T-shirts and hip clothing lines. Or get down to the nitty gritty in the adult videos, DVDs and novelties sections. If it's hot, it's here. Also features a café hangout, international newsstand, adult film starlet appearances, celebrity book signings, poetry readings and other events. Café and newsstand opens at 8am.

Ida's Fashions
165 S. Fairfax Ave.   (323) 933-2787
Los Angeles, CA 90038
Mon - Sat 10am - 4:30pm

Right next to K-Mart in the Fairfax district is one of the last of a dying breed of lingerie shops. The kind of shop where sales clerks fit you to your chosen brassiere. Many unique panty girdles, long-line bras, boned bustiers and peignoirs in styles from the '50s and '60s.

Insideout
363 N. Camden Dr.   (310) 247-8477
Beverly Hills, CA 90210
Mon - Fri 10:30am - 6:30pm, Sat 11am - 6pm

Fine lingerie establishment catering to men and women. Cutting edge imports from The Netherlands, France, Italy, Germany, Spain and the U.K. Onsite bra fitting and bridal registry.

Jim Bridges Transformation Boutique

12457 Ventura Blvd., Ste. 103   (818) 761-6650
Studio City, CA 91604
Tue - Fri 12pm - 6pm, Sat 12pm - 10pm
Web: www.jbridges.com

Raison d'etre of this trés chic, reasonably-priced boutique is cross-dressing men, transvestites, transsexuals and fit-challenged women. The only designer/manufacturer in the U.S. that has dresses for men, perfectly proportioned, beautifully made. Custom corsets, shoes and boots, wigs and jewelry, stockings and prosthetics. Makeovers available. Femininity forward.

Lacy Lady Lingerie

1309 Montana Ave.   (310) 451-8115
Santa Monica, CA 90403
Mon - Fri 10am - 7pm, Sat 10am - 6pm, Sun 12pm - 5pm

Complete range of lingerie from ultra-feminine silks to fine cottons. Exquisite line of bridal and honeymoon intimates make registry a must. Helpful gift service for men records dates to remember (Lacy Lady will mail out reminder cards). Second location at 4708 Admiralty Way, Marina Del Rey.

Only Hearts

1407 Montana   (310) 393-3088
Santa Monica, CA 90403
Mon - Sat 10am - 6:30pm, Sun 11am - 5pm

A "shop for the shameless romantic," celebrate your daring with lingerie and candles, jewelry, gifts and fragrances. Wear your heart on your sleeveless with something from their own line of sexy "inner outerwear" featuring velvet camisoles and elegant cotton chemises complemented by dainty European handmade shoes. Also carries lines by other notable designers.

Petticoats

115 N. Larchmont Blvd.   (323) 467-1730
Los Angeles, CA 90004
Mon - Sat 10:30am - 6:30pm, Sun Noon - 5pm

Specializing in sleepwear (from the comfy two piece flannel kind to elegant special occasion). From extravagant to conservative, every style of bra and panty set imaginable is available.

The Pleasure Chest

7733 Santa Monica Blvd.   (323) 650-1022
Los Angeles, CA 90046
Sun - Wed 10am - Midnight, Thu 10am - 1am, Fri - Sat 10am - 2am
Web: www.thepleasurechest.com

Looking for a leather corset? How about matching chaps and cycle cap? Or just pour some liquid latex on your body wait till it dries and you're dressed for the night. PVC undies for gents and ladies. All of the above, plus cards, magazines, videos, lubes, condoms and many toys. Shop to your heart's content.

Shrine

7574 Melrose Ave.   (323) 655-1485
Los Angeles, CA 90046
Mon - Sat 11am - 8pm, Sun Noon - 8pm

Live your gothic Victorian fantasies ensconced in velvet, lace and other luxurious original clothing designs. Both genders are well-represented among the sexy, billowy shirts, well-tailored waste-coats, hand-crafted rings, and finely beaded pendants and chokers. Unusual artifacts to set the mood of dark romanticism in any sanctuary.

Trashy Lingerie

402 N. La Cienega Blvd.   (310) 652-4543
Los Angeles, CA 90048
Mon - Sat 10am - 7pm
Web: www.trashy.com

The best dressed dolls in town flash their plastic with pride in their monthly, holiday and seasonally themed display windows. You'll find every style of eroticwear, all designed and produced on-site, from red leather studded corsets to Barbie look-alike dresses. Now offers an original swimwear line. After paying a two dollar membership, shop til your libido's content.

Exotic Cars & Limousines

AAA Limousine Service
19710 Ventura Blvd., Ste. 108   (818) 704-4746
Woodland Hills, CA 91364   (800) 232-4133

Wherever you go, arrive in style. Getting there is half the fun in a private club disguised as a 10-passenger longbody with state-of-the-art sound and lighting. Extensive fleet also features eight-passenger super stretch limos, six-passenger presidentials and executive town cars, while club wagons accommodate up to 14. Special requests like champagne on ice, gourmet catering, current CDs and videos, and fresh flowers are accommodated with signature outstanding service. Available 24 hours a day to take you around the corner or across the state. When you're in a limo, you're going places.

Aria Limousine Services
8214 Foothill Blvd., Ste. A   (909) 949-8945
Rancho Cucamonga, CA 91730

Ride in elegant and palatial comfort inside a plush, tranquil stretch or sedan limousine. Ask about corporate accounts. Special Occasion Packages available. Service seven days a week, with 24-hour automated voice mail available. For Inland Empire service call: (909) 947-7135; fax: (909) 947-7386.

Autobooks, Etc.
3524 W. Magnolia Blvd.   (818) 845-0707
Burbank, CA 91505

Don't know the difference between your chassis and your catalytic converter? Then motor on down to Autobooks for videos, repair manuals, books and miniatures. An ample aerobook section for the novice pilot in you!

Bartel's Harley-Davidson And Buell
4141 Lincoln Blvd.   (310) 823-1112
Marina Del Rey, CA 90292
Web: www.bartels-hd.com

Full Harley dealership with clothing, collectibles, parts, service and bikes. Buell's for the sports rider or Harley's for the cruiser. Will outfit the new rider male or female. Rentals for movie shoots.

Beverly Hills Motoring Accessories
200 S. Robertson Blvd.   (800) 367-2462
Beverly Hills, CA 90211   (310) 657-4800

Luxury accessories for Mercedes and SUVs. From Momo shift knobs to custom car capsules. Go for that European look with clear turn signals.

Beverly Hills Rent A Car
9220 S. Sepulveda Blvd.   (800) 479-5996
Los Angeles, CA 90045   (310) 337-1400
Web: www.bhrentacar.com

One of the only places in town where you can rent a Ferrari, Porsche, BMW or even a Hummer for the day or weekend getaway. Passenger vans available for up to fifteen people. Delivery available anywhere in Southern California and "VIP Gate Meet" service at LAX. Studio rentals available.

Boyds Hot Rods And Collectible Cars
8400 Cerritos Ave.   (714) 220-9870
Stanton, CA 90680
Web: www.boydshotrods.com

Fifty cars available at all times. Buy, sell 'n trade (from $13,000-$300,000). Hot rods, Nomads, pickup trucks, Cadillacs, Buicks.

●Budget on Sunset
8789 Sunset Blvd.   (310) 652-1502
West Hollywood, CA 90069   (323) 222-1212
Web: www.budgetonsunset.com

Having served the entertainmnent industry's car rental needs for 30 years, they carry everything from sedans to exotics and specialty cars to trucks.

Budget Rent A Car
9815 Wilshire Blvd.   (310) 274-9173
Beverly Hills, CA 90212   (310) 821-1700
Mon - Fri 7am - 8pm, Sat - Sun 8am - 6pm
Web: www.budgetbeverlyhills.com

Beverly Hills style Budget car rental agency featuring the largest selection of luxury sedans in Los Angeles. Sport Utility Vehicles and exotic autos are available from Range Rover, Hummer, Jaguar, Porsche and Ferrari. Provides complimentary transportation to local Budget office. Cellular phones upon request.

Worldwide.
Coast to Coast.

Limousine Service

TCP801A ®

Worldwide Affiliates.
ll 50 states throughout the U.S.,
da, Mexico, England and Australia.
English-speaking chauffeurs in
Western and Eastern Europe,
Hong Kong and Japan.

s Angeles	Orange County	San Francisco	New York
0-255-4444	1-714-429-0166	1-415-357-5054	1-800-421-9494

body does better what we do best.®

Diva Limousine, Ltd.

1670 N. Sycamore Ave.   (323) 962-4712
Los Angeles, CA 90028   (800) 427-3482
Web: www.divalimo.com

With offices in Los Angeles, New York and San Francisco as well as world affiliates, will take you anywhere from Cannes, France to Miami, Florida. Their fleet includes Merecedes, Range Rovers, Suburbans, Mini-busses, Van, Town Cars and 6, 8 or 10 passenger limos. All vehicles are equipped with state-of-the-art computer tracking systems and up-to-the-minute airport information. Specializing in corporate and studio accounts.

Heritage Classics Motorbooks

8968 Santa Monica Blvd.   (310) 657-5278
West Hollywood, CA 90069

Gentlemen, start your engines please! This bookstore houses over 2500 books on every make of car, truck and motorcycle imaginable. Shop manuals and racing mags available. Get your copy of "Circle Track" here.

Ladies of Hogwash

     (877) 246-4927
Web: www.hogwash4u.com

A clean hog is a happy hog...Harley, that is. These sisters are experts in the science and art of big V-twin and HD detailing, providing meticulous service and the ultimate convenience: they come to you. Offering several packages, including bike-washing parties and preventive maintenance programs, they know immediately what needs to be done just by looking. Hog heaven all the way.

Malibu SpeedZone

17871 Castleton St.   (888) 662-5428
La Puente, CA 91748   (626) 913-9663
Web: www.speedzone.com

Fuel your need for speed in Top Eliminator (drag racing), Grand Prix (Indy cars), Slick Trax (sprint cars) or Turbo Track (road racing) competitions. 3/4 scale race cars on rails in which you gun the gas while automatic braking keeps you in line. Also offering 10-week competitions with cash prizes. Racing simulator game room, mini golf, and café. After 9pm, grown-up kids only.

Memory Lane Collector Car Dismantlers

11311 Pendleton   (800) 281-927
Sun Valley, CA 91352   (818) 504-334
Web: www.oldautoparts.com

The essential connection for vintage and classic U.S. car pickups and parts from the mid-'40s to mid-'70s. Hug inventory. Expert staff. Excellent resource within a resource. they don't have it, they know where to find it. When film, vide or TV need to cruise it, wreck it or blow it up, this is where the get it. Phone and fax requests. On-site browsing of 900-vehic inventory encouraged but forget the tools; skilled mechani remove parts. Fully restored dream machines for sale or re upon request. Restoration projects available.

Midway Rent A Car

1800 S. Sepulveda Blvd.   (310) 445-435
Los Angeles, CA 90025   (800) 824-52€
Web: www.midwaycarrental.com

Make a B-line to Midway, not your ordinary car rental agenc Featuring over 60 foreign and domestic makes and mode including luxury convertibles, sedans, 4 X 4's, mini and 1! passenger vans, cube trucks and camera trucks. Late mod Mercedes, BMW, Porsche, Jaguar, Lexus and other prestigio autos available. "Meet and Greet" express service to hote home, office, or airport provided. Many LA area locations.

● Music Express Messenger & Limousine Services

2601 Empire Ave.   (323) 849-224
Burbank, CA 91504   (818) 845-15C

Providing 25 years of service. English speaking messenge and limousine drivers in hundreds of cities world wide.

NHRA Motorsports Museum

1101 W. McKinley Ave., Bldg. 3A   (909) 622-21?
Pomona, CA 91768
Web: www.nhra.com

New 28,000 sq. ft. National Hot Rod Association museum race cars and memorabilia from the late 1930s onwa including: Lake and Bonneville cars, sprints, midgets, stre rods, firesuits, helmets, trophies and dragsters. Located on tl Fairplex in Pomona.

Petersen Automotive Museum

6060 Wilshire Blvd.   (323) 930-2277
Los Angeles, CA 90036
Web: www.petersen.org

Embodying LA's love affair with the automobile is the largest auto museum in the country. Over 150 famous wheels (and wheels owned by famous people) and exhibits on how the automobile shapes the highway to our heart.

Pick Your Part

11201 Pendleton St.   (800) 962-2277
Sun Valley, CA 91352

Auto graveyard where do-it-yourself motorheads raise the dead. Acres of cars on stands and arranged by make for convenient dismemberment and transplantation. Bring tools and self-sufficiency. Parts prices posted, warranties sold. The only risk you run is getting grubby. Nine locations.

Regal Limousine

P.O. Box 11487   (310) 446-0041
Glendale, CA 91226   (818) 244-6581
Web: www.regallimoserv.com

Discreet, professional, punctual and courteous. Offering corporate flat rates and airport greeters. 24 hours a day, seven days a week. Nationwide networking service. Features Mercedes Benz, Lincoln Town Car and Limos. Service out of two locations: LA and Glendale.

Route 66 Rendezvous

                                       (909) 889-3980

The tenth annual rendezvous happens in '99, the third week in September along Route 66 in San Bernardino. Elevating classics to an art form, the free event features a cruiser car show with hall of fame ceremony, celebrity cruise, open header and burn-out contests, live music, vendors and exhibits. Thursday through Sunday crammed with half a million enthusiasts, including kids who are the future of cruising.

Victorian House Vintage Auto Sales, Inc.

                                       (800) 666-5343
                                       (909) 478-3377
Web: www.vintagecar.com

Antique, vintage, classic, streetrod, muscle. The car of your dreams could be just a phone call away at the most unique collector car showroom in the nation: a sprawling 1906 Victorian home. How 'bout a '21 Model T? Or a '49 Harley? Maybe a '62 Austin Healey to suit your fancy? Website lists detailed inventory and great photos. Guaranteed price to consignors. Cars shown by appointment. Serious inquiries only. Clients receive a tour of the five-bed/three-bath landmark. Not your average used car lot.

Flowers & Gift Baskets

Adeline's Gourmet Foods

5036 Venice Blvd. (323) 933-9959
Los Angeles, CA 90019
Web: www.adelines.com

Customize your gift baskets in unique reusable containers holding the best fruits, snacks, wines, confections and specialty items from around the world. Elegant presentations using carefully and creatively wrapped packaging of tulle or silk fabrics.

Basket Heaven

(888) 272-6737
Web: www.basketheaven.com

Gift baskets offering a wide assortment of quality gourmet foods. Say thank you with chocolate truffles, amaretto cakes, all natural chocolate chip cookies and more. Shipping & delivery services offered.

Eric Buterbaugh Flower Design

300 S. Doheny Dr. (310) 247-7120
Los Angeles, CA 90048

To give one of these European floral designs is to inspire pleasure. To receive one is to be awestruck and joyful. That's why celebs and such have their homes adorned with them weekly and important events are all the more special because of their presence. Expensive but worth it, imported blooms like orchids, roses and peonies are at home in pots wrapped in silks, taffetas and other fabric delicacies, the studio's signature equivalent to the Chanel suit: exquisite and always in good taste. By appointment.

FanciFull

5617 Melrose Ave. (323) 466-7654
Los Angeles, CA 90038 (800) 350-4437
Web: www.fancifull.com

Sumptuous snacks, gourmet gusto, splendiferous elegance. If you can think up the contents of a gift basket (or case, trunk, bucket, wagon), this is the place to make it real. If you're at a loss, the creatives will put something together and make you look like a hero. Champagne and chocolates, wine and cheese, cigars and brandy, even BBQ kits. Can also accommodate office parties and celebrations of all sizes with unique and appealing items like Le Cordon Bleu olives, sun dried tomato spread, smoked turkey, brie and crackers. Always to arrive at the perfect time: when they're hungry.

"Fancy Me" Gift Services

5042 Los Feliz Blvd. (323) 660-3395
Los Angeles, CA 90027
Web: www.fancymegifts.com

Custom-made gift baskets for every occasion. Time Capsules are available for graduations, weddings and new babies. Themed baskets may include an ice cream sundae kit with old-fashioned dishes and scoops or dozens of other possibilities. Gourmet foods, chocolates and all manner of themed merchandise make up these special gifts.

Floral Art

(310) 574-6700
(310) 392-1633

Venice studio offering imaginative custom garden and floral arrangements for events and TV/movie sets. Lush flora and fauna available in an array of signature containers. Go beyond the ordinary. By appointment only.

Humble Abode

519 N. La Cienega Blvd., Ste. 10 (310) 360-9300
West Hollywood, CA 90048

Extraordinary. Imaginative. Perfect. Once you give one (or give it to yourself), you'll never think of gift baskets in the same way again. Candles, fine skin and hair care products, customized in themes and colors for any occasion and any body. For him. For her. For them. When it has to be special, go to a special place.

Illume

8302 W. Third St. (323) 782-0342
Los Angeles, CA 90048
Mon - Sat 11am - 6pm, Sun Noon - 5pm

Just walking into Illume is an otherworldly aromatic experience. Hundreds of candles in every size, shape and scent. Gift baskets are customized based by occasion and the individual's personality - from elegant or earthy to feminine or masculine.

Jacob Maarse

655 E. Green St. (626) 449-0246
Pasadena, CA 91101
Mon - Sat 9am - 6pm

Specialist in Dutch, European and English garden flower arrangements and even Ikebana (Japanese-style arrangement). Everything from a simple mother's day bouquet to a stupendous hotel lobby display. Delivers worldwide, walk-in orders welcome. Second small downtown location in the Jonathan Club.

Joan's On Third

8350 W. Third St. (323) 655-2285
Los Angeles, CA 90048
Mon - Sat 10am - 8pm, Sun 11am - 6pm

Innovative and sophisticated gifts for every occasion-corporate and personal gift giving. Decadent sweets, imported cheeses and irresistible baked goods. Ask about the "show stopper," guaranteed to make the right impression.

● Leave An Impression

4221 Wilshire Blvd., Suite 220 (323) 936-5446
Los Angeles, CA 90010
Web: www.leaveanimpression.com

Elevate gift-giving to high art with a custom basket that will absolutely Leave An Impression. Exquisitely designed and generous presentations for every interest, occasion, theme and price range includes delectable edibles and fabulous finds not available in your average market or department store. Appeal to the gourmand with chardonnay-filled chocolate or apricot-champagne biscotti. For those with an appreciation for luxury, a basket of bath products based on 16th century Medieval recipes or a men's line of products from Portugal is the very thing. Even welcome a new baby or pamper a pooch with fun, practical presents. With an impressive list of high-profile clients, can easily accommodate corporate needs with everything from globes to robes, personalized for that special touch. Excite and delight with an artful gift that's as good to give as it is to get. Showroom visits by appointment.

Los Angeles Flower Market

754 S. Wall St. (213) 622-1966
Los Angeles, CA 90014
Mon - Sat Hours Vary

Open to the public for limited hours, call for times. Independent vendors sell in bulk so arrive early, but there will be bargains galore! Spring is always in the air with rare blooms and lush greenery.

Leave An Impression

CUSTOM GIFT BASKETS

Start of the season/wrap gifts • Personalized service • Corporate gifts • Gift wrapping

Order online:
www.leaveanimpression.com

Call for a color brochure
Phone: 323-936-5446 Fax: 323-936-7704

World-wide shipping/local delivery   VISA/MasterCard/AmEx

Mark's Garden

13838 Ventura Blvd.   (818) 906-1718
Sherman Oaks, CA 91423
Mon - Sat 9am - 7pm

One of the largest flower shops in the city and official florist for the Oscars Governor's Ball. English garden basket is their signature arrangement. Uses only the freshest cuts of the season and is a member of the prestigious Fine Flowers Network. Will deliver anywhere in the city.

● Mel & Rose Wine and Spirits

8344 Melrose Ave.   (323) 655-5557
West Hollywood, CA 90069   (800) 701-9463
Mon - Thu 9am - 10pm, Fri - Sat 9am - 11pm,
Sun Noon - 7pm
Web: www.melandrose.com

Abundance is the operative word, with custom-made-to-order gift baskets overflowing with international delights and true rarities. Gourmet crackers with quince and rose petal Elizabethan jelly add Old World charm to a vast array of specialty items, all in creative presentations to fit any occasion. Whether it's a thank-you to a client or an assortment of treats for a baby shower or wedding present, share the abundance - - all under one roof. Free delivery in a five-mile radius. Shipping available.

Mrs. Beasley's Muffins & Gift Baskets

16805 S. Central Ave.   (310) 276-6404
Carson, CA 90746
Mon - Sat 8am - 6pm
Web: www.mrsbeasleys.com

Gift baskets with an assortment of mini muffins, brownie bars and cookies. Servings for 4-80, available the same day by hand-delivery. Consistent winner of high ratings.

Pure Indulgence Basketiers

2821 S. Robertson Blvd.   (310) 559-1883
Los Angeles, CA 90034
Web: www.pureindulgence.com

Made to order from an extensive product line. Can accommodate even the most unusual or original requests. Imaginative designs and memorable presentations make it easy to understand why they're called 'basketiers.' Send someone a Tub Full Of Love or a Bundle Of Joy. The Complete Meeting Basket is a must-have survival tool for those office marathons. Among the many additional baskets (which are sometimes suitcases, sometimes boxes) for every occasion (or no occasion at all) are Chocoholic's Heaven, Laughter Is The Best Medicine, and Golfer's Paradise. Will accommodate late night gift emergencies and impossible schedules. Local delivery, global shipping.

Rebecca Clark of Los Angeles

8222 W. Third St.   (323) 655-2559
Los Angeles, CA 90048
Web: www.rebeccaclark.com

Specializing in unique gift baskets for bridal showers, anniversaries, dinner parties and corporate gifts for a wide range of budgets and personal tastes. The gorgeous retail store showcases handcrafted soaps and bath products, handmade journals, whimsical cards and aromatherapy products (which scent the air of the shop). Custom gift wrapping with elegant chiffon and ribbon or kitschy Chinese to-go containers-endless unique creations.

Regal Cake Gallery

1068 S. Fairfax   323-938-2286
Los Angeles, CA 90019
Web: www.regalcakegallery.com

Send your friends baskets of freshly baked cookies in customized packaging from this gourmet bakery.

Rita Flora

468 S. La Brea Ave.   (323) 938-3900
Los Angeles, CA 90036
Mon - Sat 8am - 8pm, Sun - Sun 9am - 7pm

Full floral selection and creative staff. Arrangements go beyond baskets: flowers can be arranged in concrete containers or floating in glass bowls. Specials offered during holidays. Dependable source for fresh roses, exotics and all cut flower needs.

Shani Desserts & Gifts

13222 W. Washington Blvd.   (310) 578-1441
Los Angeles, CA 90066
Mon - Fri 8am - 5pm

The sweetest gift of all? Fresh, gourmet treats generously proportioned and beautifully arranged in an irresistible, customized presentation and hand-delivered in the LA area or shipped nationwide. Graham crusted Divine Bars, Chocolatey Brownies, Outrageous Chocolate Chip Cookies. Smart tarts like almond and fresh fruit, and clever cakes like chocolate cream cheese layer. Event catering, too. Some items available in high-end cafés and markets.

Thorn & Thistle

236 West Mission Rd.   (323) 460-5133
San Gabriel, CA 91776
Mon - Sun 11am - 7pm
Web: www.thornandthistle.com

Unique arrangements using original containers fashioned from every possible material. One Halloween they spray painted callalillies red and black and set them in a green urn for a macabre studio party. Using only the freshest flowers (no carnations!), they will deliver anywhere in the city.

Velvet Garden

8327 W. Third St.   (323) 852-1766
Los Angeles, CA 90048
Mon - Sat 9am - 5:30pm

Tired of wicker baskets and clear glass vases? The Velvet Garden specializes in fresh flowers and greenery in unconventional containers such as faux fur holders, stainless steel boxes, oriental teapots, even beaded purses.

Romance & Weddings

Adamson House
23200 W. Pacific Coast Hwy.   (310) 457-8185
Malibu, CA 90265

Built by the original owners of Malibu Tile. Exterior grounds await your fantasy wedding with three different fountains, and landscape setups to choose from. Open April-October, Saturdays and Sundays for weddings of up to 200 guests. Tours of the home take place Wednesday-Saturday 11am-3pm.

Cliff House Inn
6602 W. Pacific Coast Hwy.   (805) 684-0025
Ventura, CA 93001   (800) 892-5433
Web: www.cliffhouseinn.com

Located minutes from Santa Barbara and just mere miles from downtown Ventura, The Cliff House is the perfect location for guests who want ocean view privacy but nightlife as an option. An ancient Royal Palm tree holds court and offers shade over an aqua blue swimming pool and rooms (all with an ocean view) start at $95.00. The in-house restaurant, The Shoals, offers local seafood cuisine.

Creative Scentualization By Sarah Horowitz
22561 Carbon Mesa Rd. GH   (310) 317-6858
Malibu, CA 90265   (888) 799-2060
Mon - Sat By Appt Only
Web: www.creativescents.com

Custom blended perfume at their gorgeous Malibu location, each made exclusively for you and never replicated without your consent. Sarah will create the perfect scent suitable to your chemistry from essential fragrance and oils. Perfect gift for a beloved or bride-to-be. Once your scent is established, she can dispense it as a spray, lotion, bath gel, massage oil or concentrate on the spot.

Duke's Malibu
21150 Pacific Coast Hwy.   (310) 317-0777
Malibu, CA 90265
Mon - Sat 11:30am - 2:30pm, Mon - Sun 5pm - 10pm, Sun 10am - 2:30pm

Oceanfront dining by night at Duke's is romance and charm personified. Listen to the crashing waves and view the vibrant foam against the moonlight while dining on lobster tails and sipping fine wines. During full moons, the tide brings the waves right up to the glass. Come dressed up or down and you'll feel equally comfortable and welcome. Planning a wedding? Duke's Malibu can accommodate up to 250 for sit-down affairs and will help you customize as much or as little as you desire. They will make any event special with the spirit of aloha.

Four Oaks Restaurant
2181 N. Beverly Glen Blvd.   (310) 470-2265
Los Angeles, CA 90077

Once a biker's bar favored by Steve McQueen, now a quiet cozy restaurant nestled in Beverly Glen, north of Sunset. Kissing couples and industry bigwigs share the leafy patio or interiors with fireplaces. Emphasis on farm-fresh ingredients. Popular prix-fixe Sunday brunch.

Geoffrey's
27400 Pacific Coast Hwy.   (310) 457-1519
Malibu, CA 90265

The most expensive view in LA, is perched high atop a cliff overlooking the Pacific, Geoffrey's exudes a Mediterranean ambiance. End of summer provides picturesque smog-enhanced sunset skies of deep reds and pinks.

Gondola Company Of Newport Beach

3400 Via Oporto, Ste. 102B   (949) 675-1212
Newport Beach, CA 92663
Web: www.gondolas.com

Traditional Venetian Gondola rides, through the canals around Newport Island. Continental breakfast cruise comes complete with coffee, juice, champagne, pastries, bagels and the morning paper.

Gondola Getaways

5437 E. Ocean Blvd.   (562) 433-9595
Long Beach, CA 90803
Web: www.clever.net/gondolas

Imagine gliding through clear narrow canals and secluded waterways next to beautiful homes while you listen to romantic music and nibble on bread and cheese. In Long Beach? It's all possible. Call in advance to assure a booking.

Greystone Park (Doheny Mansion)

905 Loma Vista Dr.   (310) 550-4654
Beverly Hills, CA 90210

Courtyard with mansion, pool area and formal garden with giant fountain. On a hillside with city views, picnic areas, koi and lily pond with turtles. Open to the public. Weddings held outside.

Il Cielo   Italian

9018 Burton Way   (310) 276-9990
Beverly Hills, CA 90211
All Major Credit Cards, Reservations: Yes

Undoubtedly one of the the most romantic restaurants in LA having performed almost 1000 weddings in the past 13 years, set in a Tuscan cottage nestled between two ivy-draped buildings. Sit out front on the tree-lined patio, or in the rear-garden resplendent with fountain and gazebo. On Valentine's Day, a "couples only" policy is enforced at their tables for two. For that special occasion, order the heart-shaped tiramisu with Belgian chocolate romantic writings in Italian.

Madonna Inn

100 Madonna Rd.   (805) 543-3000
San Luis Obispo, CA 93405   (800) 543-9666
Web: www.madonnainn.com

Built in 1958, this oddball inn has grown over the years and there are now 109 rooms each uniquely decorated. There are rock rooms with rock waterfall showers, hearts-and-flowers rooms, French, African and more. The inn features leaded glasswork throughout and a carved marble balustrade from Hearst Castle in the dining room.

The Restaurant At Hotel Bel-Air

701 Stone Canyon Rd.   (310) 472-1211
Los Angeles, CA 90077

Get away from it all within a stone's throw of everywhere. Situated on 11 acres in the woods off Stone Canyon, this magical dining establishment is situated amid exquisite gardens, a small lake, nature walks and terraces. Marriage proposals take place on a nightly basis. Sit-down brunch includes champagne. Choose from scrambled quail eggs, smoked salmon or eggs Benedict. The terrace floor is heated year-round. Chocolate covered strawberries to feed your beloved.

Wayfarer's Chapel

5755 Palos Verdes Dr. South   (310) 377-1650
Rancho Palos Verdes, CA 90275

Four acres of gardens in conjunction with a magnificent glass chapel designed by Lloyd Wright, Frank's son. Grounds have a breathtaking view of the Pacific Ocean. In spring the rose garden is majestic. Busy wedding location.

Vintage Clothing & Furnishings

Antique Stove Heaven
5414 S. Western Ave.   (323) 298-5581
Los Angeles, CA 90062
Mon - Fri 8am - 6pm, Sat 9am - 3pm

Specializing in restoring, rechroming, repainting, reinsulating and just about anything else your antique stove needs. Will service stoves of any age in any location. Sells O'Keefe & Merritt, Wedgewood, Magic Chef and more.

Blagg's
2901 Rowena Ave.   (323) 661-9011
Los Angeles, CA 90039
Thu - Sun 11am - 7pm, or by appointment

Eclectic blend of vintage and modern 20th century furnishings, rugs and objet d'art. From deco brush sets to '50s chrome dining tables.

The Button Store
8344 W. Third St.   (323) 658-5473
Los Angeles, CA 90048
Mon - Sat 10am - 6pm
Web: www.hushcobuttons.com

Gorgeous selection of vintage buttons and vintage reproductions. With over a million buttons to choose from including marcasite, pictorial and bakelite. In-store museum with rare collectors items. Prices run from 5¢ to $300. You, too, can sport buttons from the Titanic!

Chic-A-Boom
6817 Melrose Ave.   (323) 931-7441
Los Angeles, CA 90038
Mon - Sat 12pm - 6pm

Vintage wind-up toys, lunch boxes and board games from the '40s-'60s. Rock'n'roll memorabilia from over 5000 concert posters to Duran Duran purses with a large collection of Beatles merchandise. Ten thousand kitchen products.

Decades, Inc.
8214 Melrose Ave.   (323) 655-0223
Los Angeles, CA 90046
Mon - Sat 11:30am - 6pm
Web: www.decadesinc.com

High-end vintage couture boutique for men and women featuring rare fashions primarily from the '60s and '70s. Designer stock from Pucci, Gernreich, Galanos and more. Hermes leather goods and accessories. Studio friendly.

Four Your Eyes
12452 Venice Blvd.   (310) 306-5400
Los Angeles, CA 90066
Mon - Fri 9:30am - 5:30pm, Sat 9am - 6pm
Web: www.fouryoureyes.com

With an inventory of over 75,000 dead stock frames, you're sure to find the perfect pair of vintage specs. From the early 1900s through the early 1970s with lots of rhinestones in-between. Specialists in spare parts and repair work.

Gotta Have It!
1516 Pacific Ave.   (310) 392-5949
Venice, CA 90291
Mon - Sun 11am - 7pm

From '40s rhinestone jewelry to three-piece polyester men's suits, many items on consignment and in like-new condition. Want music to browse by? Some days the DJ upstairs pumps hip hop and underground music throughout the store.

Junk for Joy Vintage, Etc.
3314 W. Magnolia Blvd.   (818) 569-4903
Burbank, CA 91505
Tue - Sat Noon - 6pm
Web: www.junk4joy.com

Specializing in unused vintage clothing and accessories from the '40s-'70s. A mecca for film and TV stylists and wardrobe.

Liz's Antique Hardware
453 S. La Brea Ave.   (323) 939-4403
Los Angeles, CA 90036
Mon - Sun 10am - 6pm
Web: www.lahardware.com

Vintage hardware and lighting; from the early Victorian Eastlake style of the 1860s to the streamlined Modern styles of the 1930s and 1940s. Millions of pieces to choose from starting at $12. Need two extra mid-century English knobs for your antique dresser?

Meow

2210 E. Fourth St. (562) 438-8990
Long Beach, CA 90814
Tue - Sat Noon - 6pm, Sun - Mon Noon - 5pm

Tired of that second hand look in your vintage closet? Meow specializes in '40s -'80s dead stock, original clothing that has never been worn, complete with tags. Clothing, fabric, accessories and eye glass frames for men, women and children. Step feet first into their "whirlpool-o-shoes" for a fabulous selection of footwear.

Needed Things

2924 Rowena Ave. (323) 664-1935
Los Angeles, CA 90039
Tue - Sun Noon - 7pm

Eclectic collection of antique and custom-made furnishings. Everything from a 1960s psychedelic p-funk bar to a pair of classic chrome bar stools from the '20s. Other items such as slide projectors and kitchenware cram the shelves.

Old Focals

45 W. Green St. (626) 793-7073
Pasadena, CA 91105
Tue - Sat 12pm - 8pm, Sun 12pm - 6pm
Web: www.oldfocals.com

Isn't it time to find some focus in your life? Old Focals features a large collection of stylish designer reconditioned eye wear and sunglasses at inexpensive prices (no pair is over 100 bucks!). Period frames from 1700 to present available for rent.

Orange

8111 Beverly Blvd. (310) 652-5195
Los Angeles, CA 90048
Mon - Fri 11am - 7pm, Sat 11am - 5pm, Sun Noon - 5pm

Vintage refurbished furniture from '40s-'70s. Many fur, suede, wool and leather pieces available. Everything from a five-foot high brown shag couch to a vintage skating bench with chrome legs and pale green wool upholstery. Check out the 13-foot neon "Capri" movie marquee from the '30s. Rentals available for film shoots.

The Pasadena Antique Center & Annex

444 & 480 S. Fair Oaks Ave. (626) 449-7706
Pasadena, CA 91105 (626) 449-9445
Mon - Sun 10am - 6pm
Web: www.pasadenaantiquecenter.com

Southern California's oldest antiques mall boasts over 130 merchants with displays covering 33,000 square feet. All periods and styles of quality collectibles, from beads to bedroom sets, can be discovered. Plan on spending a few hours combing through the many stalls in this mall.

Plastica

4685 Hollywood Blvd. (323) 644-1212
Los Angeles, CA 90027 (323) 655-1051
Tue - Fri 11am - 6pm, Sat - Sun Noon - 6pm
Web: www.plasticashop.com

Putting fantastic back into plastic, the folks at Plastica not only sell but actually celebrate processed synthetic ware your mom packed your lunch in.

Playmates

6438 Hollywood Blvd. (323) 464-7636
Los Angeles, CA 90028
Mon - Sat 10am - 8pm, Sun Noon - 7pm
Web: www.playmatesofhollywood.com

From '60s baby dolls and '90s peek-a-boo bras to $300 designer bustiers and 99 cent garters, Playmates knows how to make your mate wanna play. Clear plastic dresses, sexy see-through evening gowns and head-turning club wear. All that is shiny, glittery, feathery and risqué available, including a complete line of skimpy bikinis and kinky S&M bondage wear.

Polkadots & Moonbeams

8367 W. Third St. (323) 651-1746
Los Angeles, CA 90048 (323) 655-3880
Mon - Sat 11am - 6:30pm, Sun Noon - 5pm

A choice selection of clothes from the turn of the century up through the 80's. Hawaii shirt collection too! Great jewelry, shoes and bags.

Practical Props

11100 Magnolia Blvd.   (818) 980-3198
North Hollywood, CA 91606
Mon - Fri 8am - 6pm, Sat 11am - 5pm

Yeah baby, Austin Powers shops here for his far out lamps and so can you. New, used and reproduction lighting and accessories. Find that perfect shade to go with your '50s panther lamp. Chandeliers, wall sconces, floor and table lamps. Will rewire those flea market finds.

Rufcut

11344 W. Pico Blvd.   (310) 473-5384
West Los Angeles, CA 90064
Mon - Sat 11am - 6pm
Web: www.rufcut.com

Exclusive dealer of used and vintage Levi's (mainly 501). Let Levi expert Robert Rifkin and his staff help you select the perfect pair of classic faded Levi's. Repair and alterations also available.

Squaresville

1800 N. Vermont Ave.   (323) 669-8464
Los Angeles, CA 90027
Tue - Sat 11am - 8pm, Sun - Mon Noon - 7pm

From Pendleton to Pucci, this small boutique offers a multitude of men's and women's vintage and designer garments including near-mint handbags and shoes; cute and glamorous dresses; lingerie and jewelry. Buy, sell, trade or rent.

Syren

7225 Beverly Blvd.   (323) 936-6693
Los Angeles, CA 90036
Tue - Sat 11am - 6pm
Web: www.syren.com

Latex couture for men and women. Designs and manufacturers all manner of second skin slink, including the notorious Poison Ivy catsuit and other high-profile projects plus dresses, gowns, shorts, tops, bottoms and suits in vivid greens, yellows, pinks and, of course, seductive black. Rubber clothier to the stars. Powder down and stretch it on.

Ten 10

1716 Silver Lake Blvd.   (323) 663-3603
Los Angeles, CA 90039
Wed - Sun Noon - 6pm

Vintage furniture store showcasing furnishings from the '30s-'60s. Everything from Danish modern headboards to stainless steel and tile floor lamps. Large warehouse ensures that what you see is what you get.

Vintage Plumbing & Bathroom Antiques

9645 Sylvia Ave.   (818) 772-1721
Northridge, CA 91324   (818) 420-1233
By Appt Only
Web: www.vintageplumbing.com

Authentic Victorian-era bathroom fixtures and appliances: tubs, toilets, showers, towel bars and soap dishes. Specializing in the extraordinary. When you can't find it anywhere else, this is where it's at. Worth the effort, worth the drive. Rentals for set designs available. By appointment only.

Wells Antiques and Collectibles

2162 Sunset Blvd.   (213) 413-0558
Los Angeles, CA 90026
Wed - Sat 11am - 5:30pm

Antique tile shop with one of the largest collections in the nation. Specializing in California tiles with such well-known names as Malibu, Catalina, Batchelder and Claycraft. Custom quality and will track down the tiles you need. Hillside pottery and garden pottery arts-will work with your landscaper to create an authentic Arts and Crafts garden. Museum quality tiles for murals, wall hangings or easels.

Wine & Cigars

Epicurus Wine
625 Montana Ave., Ste. B   (310) 395-1352
Santa Monica, CA 90403
Mon - Thu 10am - 8pm, Fri - Sat 10am - 9pm,
Sun 10am - 7pm

Diverse, complex wine collection. Prices run from a mere $4.99 to the high digits. Inventory from California and around the world. Tastings every Saturday from 2-5pm. Wine gift baskets available.

Flint's
3321 Pico Blvd.   (310) 453-1331
Santa Monica, CA 90405

Elegant '40s-style roadhouse with all the suave the era conjures. Lobster Thermadore on the menu says it all. Sip a Flintini, one of 14 specialty cocktails of the house and recline in the luxurious sofa lounge or take in the cool night air from the patio. Cigar Night the first Monday each month enhances the club's sexy persona. Tuesdays feature live jazz. No cover.

Los Angeles Wine Company
4935 McConnell Ave., Unit 8   (310) 306-9463
Los Angeles, CA 90066
Web: www.lawineco.com

In their 17th year, bringing the best and brightest wines at the lowest prices. Passionate staff gives out expert advice for free. 200-300 different cutting-edge wines offered each month. Second location in Palm Desert.

Mel & Rose Wine and Spirits
8344 Melrose Ave.   (323) 655-5557
West Hollywood, CA 90069
Mon - Thu 9am - 10pm, Fri - Sat 9am - 11pm,
Sun Noon - 7pm

Abundance is the operative word for cigar aficionados with a penchant for limited productions and those who appreciate rare wines and exotic champagnes - all appealing and appeasing to even the most discriminating palates. Hard-to-find varietals and vintages are this gourmet and specialty shoppe's raison d'etre, with more than 1000 from which to choose under one roof. Neighborhood-close but with worldly sophistication, international delights are at your doorstep with free delivery in a five-mile radius and shipping available. Complimentary gift wrapping upon request.

San Antonio Winery
737 Lamar St.   (323) 223-1401
Los Angeles, CA 90031
Sun - Tue 9am - 6pm, Wed - Sat 9am - 7pm

Can't make it to Edna Valley? Just east of downtown is a fully functioning winery producing the "Maddalena" label. Plan for lunch at the Italian restaurant and choose between a docent led or self-guided tour where the curious can witness the process from grape to cork. Many imported wines available for tasting, no tour needed. Altar wine made and bottled here.

Santa Monica Cigar Co., Inc.
2814 Main St.   (310) 581-8555
Santa Monica, CA 90405

Cigar shop/lounge/art gallery open to the public. 80 brands of stogies available including Paul Garmirian, Dunhill and Montecristo. Enjoy a full bodied smoke while absorbing Cuban artwork or cheering on your favorite team on the TV screen. Cigar motif gifts from coasters to ashtrays and practical essentials (cutters, humidors and finger cases). Available for location shoots, corporate events and seminars

The Tinder Box

8621 Santa Monica Blvd. (310) 659-6464
West Hollywood, CA 90069

Exquisite cigar, cigarette and pipe accessories. Pipe and lighter specialist.

Twenty-Twenty Wine Co.

2020 Cotner Ave. (310) 447-2020
Los Angeles, CA 90025
Mon - Fri 10:30am - 7pm, Sat 11am - 6:30pm

Old and rare wines for the private collector. Back room is filled weekly with new treasures, including vintages dating back to the mid 1800s. Avoid costly surcharges by placing a pre-arrival order (a future) early. Prices begin at $20/bottle and goes into the thousands. "Birthday wines" available from practically every vintage. Will ship anywhere in the world. Wine lockers rent annually and can store between 25-1000 cases.

The V Cut Smoke Shop

8172 Melrose Ave. (323) 655-5959
Los Angeles, CA 90046

Smoke shop and espresso bar with numerous cushiony couches. Try an earthy Fuente or powerhouse Padrone from their extensive line. Imported cigarettes.

VIP Cigar Room

8860 Sunset Blvd. (310) 652-3622
West Hollywood, CA 90069

The Viper Room's smokin' neighbor stocks over 200 premium cigars and boasts a walk-in humidor. Soak in full-flavored aromas while deciding between a Palmera or Romeo & Gulieta. Light up inside or outdoors on the patio, No membership required. Stocks fine spirits: scotch, cognac, vodka, port, French Bordeaux and grappa.

Virtual Vineyards

650 Airpark Rd., Ste. D (800) 289-1275
Napa, CA 94558 (707) 265-2860
Web: www.wine.com

Wines via the web. Let your keyboard do the shopping for California and international wines. Product page lists tasting profile (oak, tannin and body), text description and additional info about the winery. Corporate gift wines with company logos available.

Wally's

2107 Westwood Blvd. (310) 475-0606
Los Angeles, CA 90025
Mon - Sat 9am - 8pm, Sun 10am - 6pm
Web: www.wallywine.com

Savor that black market Partagas with a fine vintage. Wally's stocks the largest stock of old and rare wines in Southern California. Knowledgeable and non-intimidating staff will help you start your own wine cellar or just select that one bottle for a special occasion.

The Wine House

2311 Cotner Ave. (310) 479-3731
Los Angeles, CA 90064
Web: www.winehouse.com

Vino made easy. Old and rare, obscure and affordable, there are 7,000 labels, a high-end spirits department, 300+ microbrews, a humidor, and gourmet delights across 18,000 sq. ft. Browsing is a pleasure, questions are encouraged, service is as abundant as selection. Wine classes are offered, and singles actually meet and marry (!) as a result of Friday Nights At The Wine Bar, an effective alternative to the bar scene. Call for busy event schedule and convenient hours.

resources

Resources

Astro's
2300 Fletcher Dr.   (323) 663-9241
Los Angeles, CA 90039

Breakfast 24 hours a day. Incredibly diverse crowd (from punks to families). Recently reupholstered booths don't take away from the original '60s diner feel. Laid back atmosphere. Greek style eggs fit for the gods are worth going gaga over.

Beverly Oaks Animal Hospital
14302 Ventura Blvd.   (818) 788-7860
Sherman Oaks, CA 91423

Cat got a 3am hairball attack? Rush in to Beverly Oaks, which specializes in treating canine and feline ailments and provides round-the-clock emergency ward services.

Bob's Big Boy
4211 Riverside Dr.   (818) 843-9334
Burbank, CA 91505

The only Boy in town without a bedtime. Opened in 1949, it's the oldest remaining Big Boy in America. Informal car shows Friday nights; burgers and fries forever. Polish those chrome bumpers, round up your best girl and take a big bite of tradition.

Coffee House
8226 Sunset Blvd.   (323) 848-7007
Los Angeles, CA 90046

Bored? Hungry? Need a place to converge with fellow insomniacs? Open 24/7, this homey yet hip hangout has a health conscious menu of distinctively Cal cuisine. Enjoy cornflake French toast at fireside or contemplate the moon over a cup of coffee on the patio. Sprawl on a sofa with a fresh scone and just dig the excellent music. The CD collection even includes local indie bands.

Denny's
7373 W. Sunset Blvd.   (323) 876-6660
Los Angeles, CA 90046

Early birds and night owls flock to feast on "Moons Over My Hammy," and the famous "Dingle Bird" sandwich at this American institution. Find out why it's called 'Rock & Roll...'

Fred's 62
1850 N. Vermont Ave.   (323) 667-0062
Los Angeles, CA 90027

Retro diner/noodle shop with decor and grub hip enough to lure the Eastside 24-7 crowd, but with a price range to fit anyone's budget. Food brought to you by Fred Eric the same creator of the famed VIDA. Try their Thai cobb salad, served with a spicy sesame dressing or their homemade apple crisp a la mode. What ever you are craving the folks at Fred 62 can satisfy it.

Hollywood Boxing Gym
1551 N. La Brea Ave.   (323) 845-1420
Los Angeles, CA 90028
Web: www.hollywoodgym.com

Got some evening rage to vent? Kick some punching bag butt, lift the world's weight off your shoulders with veritable tons of free weights or stretch out before bedtime at this 24-hour haven of hard bodies. Rock climbing, martial arts, saunas, spa and even a chiropractic facility will put you in motion.

The Home Depot
5600 Sunset Blvd.   (310) 822-3330
Los Angeles, CA 90028

Leaky faucet keeping you from your beauty rest? Avoid the daytime "do-it-yourselfer" crowds and head over to the 24-hour Home Depot. Take a midnight stroll through Bob Villa's fantasy aisles. Piped-in pop music helps keep customers and employees peppy during the wee hours of night and may keep you psyched to tackle that paint job instead of your pillow.

Izzy's Deli
1433 Wilshire Blvd.   (310) 394-1131
Santa Monica, CA 90403

People have been getting dizzy over Izzy's overstuffed sandwiches for a quarter century. One of Santa Monica's favorite Jewish-style delis. Rumor has it Bob Dylan penned poetic prose here. Very inspiring.

Johnie's Broiler
7447 Firestone Blvd.   (562) 927-3383
Downey, CA 90241

Forget about that joker Johnny (Rockets) and head out to Downey for the original '50s drive-in diner complete with glowing neon signs and surly gum-snapping bus boys. Greasy burgers stacked with your favorite condiments. Vintage hot rods and low riders show off nightly.

Krispy Kreme Donuts

1801 W. Imperial Hwy.   (562) 690-2650
La Habra, CA 90631

Drive-thru is open 24 hours a day, 365 days a year, while the store is open Sun-Thur 5:30am-11pm and Fri-Sat 5:30am-1am. 15 different varieties, but their signature donut is the hot-glazed-sweet, sticky and satisfying. (Also at 7249 Van Nuys Blvd., Van Nuys)

Lindbrook Bowl

201 S. Bruckhurst   (714) 774-2253
Anaheim, CA 92804

Become a kingpin hustler playing "Color of Money" Saturday nights as you knock down colored pins and win cold cash. Snack shop serves pizza, subs and dinner specials. Karaoke bar nightly until 1:30am.

Mel's Diner

8585 Sunset Blvd.   (310) 854-7200
West Hollywood, CA 90069

After-hours club scene where you can throw back a cup of joe as you ponder pivotal scenes from recent adventures. Order the pancakes; everyone else does. Or share a plate of crispy French fries. Cuisine Americana at its groovin' best. Extensive menu may even reverse the side effects of a night on the town. Definitely worth a try.

Norm's

470 N. La Cienega   (323) 655-0167
Los Angeles, CA 90048

Storm into Norm's for that late night stack of jacks or the crack-of-dawn-spaghetti special. Mighty good omelettes overstuffed with fresh ingredients and prepared to exacting specifications so go ahead - be picky. Thick steaks, thin prices. (Also at 1601 Lincoln Blvd. in Santa Monica.)

Novel Cafe

212 Pier Ave.   (310) 396-8566
Santa Monica, CA 90405

The perfect end to a late-night stroll. Two-level European style cafe with indoor/outdoor seating welcomes locals and tourists alike. Writers linger over the latest script while dining on eggs salsa brava. Open 24 hours, breakfast served round the clock.

Ordonoz

872 Garfield Ave.   (323) 724-6386
Montebello, CA 90640

Craving a taco at 3am? No problema! This Mexican restaurant is a welcome sight for Inland Empire dance floor refugees and insomniacs alike. Burritos and nachos galore plus other authentic favorites.

Original Pantry

877 S. Figueroa St.   (213) 972-9279
Los Angeles, CA 90017

Since 1924, this landmark, now owned by Richard Riordan (who sold the air rights so no one would ever tear it down), is quality comfort food: meaty BBQ ribs, sirloin tips, hamburger loaf, chicken fried steak and mac'n'cheese. You won't leave hungry.

Pacific Dining Car

1310 W. Sixth St., (Near Witmer St.)   (213) 483-6000
Los Angeles, CA 90017

All aboard! Make this the last stop of the evening for perfect, mouthwatering mesquite grilled baseball steak or indulge in eggs Benedict or sardou, your choice. Modeled after an authentic dining car except bigger, the Pacific rolled into Sixth St. station 78 years ago. (Also at 2700 Wilshire Blvd. in Santa Monica, but closes from 2am-6am.)

Pix

211 S. La Brea Ave.   (323) 936-8488
Los Angeles, CA 90036

Are you a shutterbug who can't get shut eye? Rents cameras, light meters and sells and processes film. Large, medium and small format cameras, and some grip equipment. Creativity never sleeps.

Security Couriers, Inc.

12828 Victory Blvd., PMB. 315   (818) 509-9500
N. Hollywood, CA 91606   (888) 863-7736
Web: www.securitycouriers.com

Fast, dependable messenger service for over 20 years. Bonded and insured. Available 24 hours a day, 365 days a year, featuring airport pickup and delivery, plus priority, rush and economy services so no matter what the deadline, it will be accommodated.

Spa Hotel and Casino

100 N. Indian Canyon Dr.   (760) 325-1461
Palm Springs, CA 92262

Is Luck too much of a Lady to travel to Sin City? Try your hand in the more staid Palm Springs, and roll the die at this always-open casino where the sweet sound of success is heard in jackpot slots and triumphant cheers at the Spa 21 tables. Fun and gaming this side of the border.

The Standard

8300 Sunset Blvd.   (323) 650-9090
W. Hollywood, CA 90069
Web: www.standardhotel.com

Few hotels serve food 24/7, but here you can eat where you sleep without watching the clock. Make the scene in the restaurant after hours or make your own behind closed doors. Either way, modern comfort food will quell that ravenous 4am appetite. But your name doesn't have to be on the guest registry to grab a table.

Super K-Mart

500 Carson Town Center   (310) 533-0285
Carson, CA 90745

The place to go for after-hours shopping. Who can resist the Blue Moon Light Specials? If you need something to wear to work tomorrow, the dilemma is solved. Ode to everything bizarre about America, from commuter mugs to fashion wear to lawn darts.

Kids

Archaeology Workshops

Skirball Cultural Center,   (310) 440-4636
2701 N. Sepulveda Blvd.
Los Angeles, CA 90049
Web: www.skirball.com

Children 8 and up and their parents learn the science of archaeology and discover mysteries beneath the sand during a simulated archaeological dig at the Skirball Cultural Center. Wear closed-toe shoes and play pants. Held the second Saturday of the month. $5/per child. Reservations required.

Bob Baker Marionette Theatre

1345 W. First St.   (213) 250-9995
Los Angeles, CA 90026

Since 1963, oldest legitimate house in the city. Ever-changing unique shows. Plays year-round, and you must call ahead for reservations for this one-of-a-kind theatre experience. Fun for kids of all ages.

California Science Center

700 State Dr.   (213) 744-7400
Los Angeles, CA 90037
Web: www.casciencectr.org

Interactive science and technology exhibits sure to keep kids so fascinated they won't realize they're learning. Two multifaceted permanent displays plus traveling installations that change every 4-6 months. Also contains IMAX Theater showing nature, astronomy, marine biology and other edutaining films in spectacular panoramic view and digital sound. You're never too old to learn, especially when it's fun.

Camp $tart-Up

126 Powers Ave.   (800) 350-1816
Santa Barbara, CA 93103

Entrepreneurial camp for girls 13-19. Camp in session last two weeks in June. Seminars and business plan contests run throughout the year. Cosponsored by Independent Means, a California company committed to educating young women about business and financial independence. Scholarships offered.

Children's Book World

10580 1/2 W. Pico Blvd.   (310) 559-2665
Los Angeles, CA 90064

Largest kids' book store in Southern California with over 70,000 titles. Offers wide selection of hard-to-find books and multicultural materials from smaller publishers. Knowledgeable staff can help pick out the right gift for your nephew or create a reading list for teachers. Videos, cassettes, CDs, and jigsaw puzzles available.

Cornerstone Music Conservatory
3107 Santa Monica Blvd.   (310) 447-5440
Santa Monica, CA 90404

Specializes in kids classes but all ages welcome. "Harmony Road" teaches piano and musicianship. "Baby's First Music" for 10-20 months. "Lil Tunes Pajama Club" weeknights. Voice lessons.

Dance Studio No. 1
1803 Pontius Ave.   (310) 446-4443
Los Angeles, CA 90025
Web: www.danceno1.com

Originally in Sweden, this multifaceted studio with a European sensibility is a prestigious Royal Academy of Dance school where students may take the exam, or learn ballet, tap, jazz, Expressercise and more for the fun of it. Small classes assure individual attention. Private dance and singing classes upon request. Summer mini camps available. Adult belly dance, Flamenco, salsa and others.

Didio's   Bagels, Coffee & Desserts
1305 Montana Ave   (310) 393-2788
Santa Monica, CA 90403

Neon colored Italian ice. Delightful flavors like grapefruit, mango, lemon; the kids will love cherry and blue raspberry. Sells candy like you once got at the five'n'dime: candy necklaces, dots on paper, wax lips and nickel nips.

Dinosaur Farm
1514 Mission St.   (626) 441-2767
South Pasadena, CA 91030
Mon - Sat 10am - 6pm, Sun 11am - 5pm
Web: www.dinofarm.com

For ages 0-99, educational toy and bookstore. Lots of specialty dinosaur items: skeleton models, stuffed animals, PVC and dinosaur digs (archaeological kits). Personalized, hands on service and hard-to-find toys. Twice a week craft classes.

Doulas Association of Southern California

(877) 423-6852

Free referral program offers a pool of qualified, educated, emotional support specialists who "mother the mother" in prenatal, labor and/or postpartum situations, protecting the woman's best interests and individual needs during the birthing procedure, acting as experienced liaison to the medical community.

Every Picture Tells A Story

7525 Beverly Blvd. (323) 932-6070
Los Angeles, CA 90036

Featuring original art from children's books, plus storytelling and celebrity book signings. Fantastic selection of titles for your favorite tot - Not just for kids! Unique toys from faraway lands, including hard-to-find Tin Tin merchandise.

Lee Strasberg Theatre Institute

7936 Santa Monica Blvd. (323) 650-7777
Los Angeles, CA 90046
Web: www.strasberg.com

Full curriculum includes: acting, dancing, singing and production. Classes run for 12 weeks on Saturdays during fall, spring and winter. In summer classes run four days a week for six weeks. Ages 7-17. Year round.

Mad Science of Los Angeles

8107 Orion Ave. (888) 251-1220
Van Nuys, CA 91406 (818) 909-6777
Web: www.madscience.org

Bubbling potions, lasers, rockets and slime are just a few of the hands-on science activities geared to 5-12 year olds. Scientists in lab coats entertain and educate at birthday parties, after school and camp enrichment programs, or any other special event where kids gather in the greater LA area.

Magicopolis

1418 Fourth St. (310) 451-2241
Santa Monica, CA 90401
Web: www.magicopolis.com

Reveal your inner magician as top flight national and local performers dazzle the eye and boggle the mind in an intimate theater setting. The Hocus Pocus room presents Quicker Than The Eye, a show of sleight-of-hand and other close-up tricks for a 40-member audience while the Abracadabra holds up to 150 for Witness The Impossible, spellbinding illusions on a large scale, though every seat affords an unobstructed view. Call for show times, featured acts and discounts. Available for private birthday parties.

Malibu Mamas

(310) 456-8113
Web: www.malibumamas.com

Behind every well-run household is a good nanny. Full-service domestic employment agency provides families with nannies, housekeepers, baby nurses, chefs and personal assistants. Prescreening, background checks, TB tests and trustline conducted on employees.

Nannies Unlimited

321 S. Beverly Dr. (310) 551-0303
Beverly Hills, CA 90212

Former industry insider now heads up this exclusive, ten-year old agency. All childcare providers must be over 21, fluent in English, possess a clean driving record and at least one-year consecutive experience. Live in or out. Part-time and full-time placements. One time fee with two-week trial period and 90-day replacement guarantee.

● Play Well

655 S. Raymond Ave. (626) 793-0603
Pasadena, CA 91105 (800) 585-0603
Web: www.play-well.com

Find all of your playground equipment needs in their showroom or catalog. They offer a diversity of systems in both redwood and douglas fir. Their sets emphasize safety and encourage social skills, physical develpment and hours of creative fun.

Pratesi Linens, Inc.

9024 Burton Way (310) 274-7661
Beverly Hills, CA 90211

Beverly Hills purveyour of fine Italian linens for the bed, the bath and table top.

The Pump Station

2415 Wilshire Blvd. (310) 826-5774
Santa Monica, CA 90403
Web: www.pumpstation.com

In addition to electric breast pumps available for rent, registered nurses certified in lactation education and consultation teach a variety of pre- and postnatal baby care classes. On-site boutique offers hard-to-find clothes for preemies plus mommie wear and custom gift baskets.

Seven Arrows

15332 Antioch St., PMB 313   (310) 454-7277
Pacific Palisades, CA 90272

Aiming to instill self-confidence, creativity, and spontaneity through private preschool, elementary school, summer camp and afterschool enrichment programs with classes in the arts and sciences for ages one to 12. Courses include such intriguing subjects as "Multimedia Art" and "Fairy Tale Theatre."

UCLA Bruins Sports Camps

     (310) 206-3550
Web: www.uclabruins.com

Camps for: baseball, basketball, football, gymnastics, golf, soccer, softball, throwing, track, volleyball and water polo. Taught by championship coaches at the nation's number one athletic school.

Yellow Balloon

1328 Wilshire Blvd.   (310) 458-7947
Santa Monica, CA 90403

When the bowl doesn't cut it, take your kids to the premiere children's hair salon. If anyone can get Junior to sit still it's the staff of experienced hair stylists whose skills in the intricacies of youth hair development are as sharp as their scissors. Fun and friendly atmosphere with video games, toys and coloring books to keep waiting kids occupied and parents happy. Kids from 1-91 welcome.

Pets

1-800-HELP-4-PETS

     (800) 435-7473
Mon - Tue 6am - 7:30am

Founder Liz Blackman says her service, which she designed to protect her own dogs, is like "Medic alert and 911 for your pet." It works like a dog tag, but with sophisticated technology to instantly put anyone who finds your pet in touch with a trained operator any time of the day or night, nationwide. It's already saved hundreds of pets and gets results anywhere in the U.S. and Canada.

Animal Rights Attorney, Michael Rotsten Esq.

     (818) 789-0256
Web: www.angelfire.com/ca/arlopage

Has your four-legged friend bitten off more than he can chew? Is there a custody battle brewing over the feline? Irate landlord got a thing against Great Danes? Need an attorney to work it out? Handles everyday legal problems involving animals and their people and is dedicated exclusively to animal rights law and general animal law. Animal rights lawyer devoted to activities that advance the welfare, protection, and rights of animals. Also legal advisor and consultant to the media and entertainment industry. When the fur flies and things get hairy, there's a legal beagle to soothe the savage beast.

Aquarium Stock Company

8070 Beverly Blvd.   (323) 653-8930
Los Angeles, CA 90048
Mon - Fri 9am - 8:30pm, Sat - Sun 10am - 6pm

Freshwater and saltwater fish plus supplies like fish tanks and food. Variety of small animals for companionship and ambiance including turtles, birds, mice, rats and rabbits. Aquarium set up and maintenance.

Aunt Patty's Pets

     (310) 820-4738
     (310) 838-1624
Mon - Sat 10am - 5pm

Premium supplies and gourmet foods. Mobile grooming van brings a pet salon to your door - sweet relief for car-weary animals. Pet sitting available at your pad, or take your doggie to Aunt Patty's for Canine Camp!

Casitas Hotel For Cats

3519 Casitas Ave.   (323) 664-7115
Los Angeles, CA 90039
Mon - Sun 9am - 6pm

Thirty private rooms at this 5-star cat hotel. Indoor/outdoor play areas with scratching trees. Individual attention is their specialty; unusual dietary requirements and medications easily accommodated.

The Dog House

5959 W. Third St.   (323) 549-9663
Los Angeles, CA 90036   (323) 549-9792
Mon - Fri 8am - 6pm
Web: www.hollywoof.com

Doggie day-care is offered here for the spayed/neutered pet that is current with all vaccines. Your dog must be friendly and non-aggressive. 2000 sq. ft. facility with a backyard area. Overnights by appointment only. Full-service grooming and shuttle service available. Canine boutique features cool accessories.

Ellen's Blue Ribbon Grooming

12047 Ventura Place   (818) 761-8799
Studio City, CA 91604   (888) 426-7764
Mon - Sat 8am - 6pm

Dog and cat grooming, specializing in all and rare breeds. Lifelong show grooming background and renowned reputation in the winner's circle assures the correct haircut for a specific breed, though your Fifi doesn't have to be a competitor to look like a champ and receive best-of-show treatment. Pick up and delivery service available. Sunday onsite pet-sitting for Farmers Market shoppers. Specialty gift boutique carries unusual and rare figurines (including horses), handmade leather leashes and collars. Appointments recommended.

Hollywood Hounds

                  (323) 650-5551
Mon - Sat 8am - 6pm
Web: www.hollywoodhounds.com

Pamper your pet with a "pawdicure" or massage. Let the friendly staff organize a birthday party or bark mitzvah. Muttrimony is a serious thing though, so prepare to book at least a month in advance. Retail shop specializes in canine clothes, including formal attire, chapeaux and sunglasses so high fashion is just a leap and a bound away. Expert training, grooming and daycare offered.

Hound's Lounge

12745 Ventura Blvd.   (818) 980-7666
Studio City, CA 91604
Mon - Fri 7:30am - 7pm, Sat 9am - 5pm
Web: www.houndslounge.com

Doggie day-care by avid doggie lovers. Homey space for your beloved companion. Couches, doggie videos, slides tunnels, outdoor patio (half-shade, half-sun) and complete grooming facility specializing in hand-scissoring and pet massage. At home services include dog-walking and sleep over sitting. Pickup and drop-off service including the major studios.

Kennel Club/LAX

5325 W. 102nd St.   (310) 338-9166
Los Angeles, CA 90045
Web: www.kennelclublax.com

Treat your four-legged friend to the largest indoor pet accommodations in Los Angeles. Luxurious theme cottages in the ultimate pet hotel, complete with TV and VCR in each room. 24-hour companionship available. Doggy aerobics, agility training, massage, daycare, spa, geriatric program, pool time, picnic in the park, and catnip parties. Limo transport. Pet relocation on both domestic and international flights.

Koi Pond World

10000 Indiana Ave., #7   (909) 343-5880
Riverside, CA 92503

Achieve absolute clarity -- at least in your water -- with advanced filtration supplies and systems. Owner and designer Jay even turned a 348,000-gallon pond from murk to crystalline. Need a school of koi for your pond? A pond for your koi? This is the destination. Economic and efficient pool filtration without chlorine. Even fiber optic lighting, trick fountains and portable water-based displays are all part of this world. Provided supplies for notorious "Ally McBeal" mud wrestling scene.

Los Angeles Pet Memorial Park

                  (818) 591-7037

Offering an alternative, this not-for-profit, group- owned organization provides private burial and cremation services for all pets large and small since 1928. Rolling hills and a lush memorial garden are the in perpetuity setting for more than 40,000 pets, many of them actors. Selection of urns, engraved head stones, floral arrangements, and 24-hour pickup service available. Make your loyal friend's departure as special as the relationship you shared.

The Loved Dog Co.

2100 Pontius Ave.　　　　　　　(310) 914-3033
Los Angeles, CA 90025
Mon - Sun Hours Vary
Web: www.theloveddog.com

6,000 square feet of cage-free play space for daycare and cage-free kennel featuring slides, tunnels, sandbox and couches, where pooches can frolic. Overnight accommodations include pine-covered suites with plush couches and music that will calm the most savage beast. Pick up and delivery, grooming, dog-walking and sitting services available. Training uses leash-free positive reinforcement.

Pampered Birds

　　　　　　　　　　　　　(323) 662-7807
Mon - Sat 10am - 7pm, Sun 10am - 5pm

Specializing in hand fed baby exotic birds that are people-friendly and won't bite. Everything from Macaws to African Greys to Cockatoos. Offering supplies including food and cages, along with such services as grooming, boarding and training.

Paradise Ranch Country Club And Bed And Biscuit Inn

10268 La Tuna Canyon Rd.　　　　(818) 768-8708
Sun Valley, CA 91352
Web: www.paradiseranch.net

Pet ranch on 1.5 acres of land. Socialized dogs play together. Two homes serve as the "Bed and Biscuit Inns." Dogs sleep in bedrooms; there are no institutional cages or kennels on the grounds. Rooms are $45.00/night. Limo service available.

Lori Peikoff/Urban Jungle Dog Training

　　　　　　　　　　　　　(310) 837-6397

Lori is to dog trainers what PBS is to FOX. Training all breeds and temperaments, she will work with the owner to establish status with the dog. Trains the untrainable and brings you into the world of your dog. She will come to your home anywhere in Los Angeles and has established a loyal celebrity following.

Petagree Pet Sitting

　　　　　　　　　　　　　(323) 225-0031

Leave your pet in capable, experienced hands in the comfort of home. TLC and attention to your pet's special needs including walks, litter box cleanup and good ol' companionship. Serves Eagle Rock, Mt. Washington, Glendale, Pasadena and surrounding area. Call for complimentary acquaintance interview.

Preventive Care

　　　　　　　　　　　　　(949) 722-3563

There's nothing quite like a face full of doggie dragon breath to spoil the moment between you and Rover. Experienced, gentle and oh so patient oral hygienist uses a hand scaler (like humans) without anesthetic to give canines and felines fresh breath and bright smiles. He wins their trust (even aggressive, small dogs), places them in a safe, comfortable position and eliminates tartar buildup. Checks for abnormalities and waives fee if problems are discovered. Gives free tooth brush and useful demonstration. Makes house calls anywhere between San Diego and San Francisco.

Puppy Pals Doggy Hikes & Socials

1764 Palisades Dr.　　　　　　　(310) 573-0245
Pacific Palisades, CA 90272
Web: www.home.earthlink.net/~puppypals

Doggie day camp featuring a private dog ranch in Topanga Canyon. Door-to-door service picks up your canine in their company vans with safety bolted cages from the Palisades, Brentwood & northern Santa Monica. Monday-Friday by membership. Must be at least 4 1/2 months old.

Van Nuys Pet Hotel

　　　　　　　　　　　　　(818) 787-7232
Mon - Fri 8am - 6pm, Sat Hours Vary

Deluxe accommodations for dogs and cats featuring spacious climate controlled quarters. Private apartment and patio leading to individual dog runs. Feeding twice daily, plus snacks and desserts. Grooming once a day and many playtimes for your feline friend and canine crony.

VCA Animal Hospital

　　　　　　　　　　　　　(310) 473-2951
Mon - Sun 8am - 11pm
Web: www.vcai.com

Dog get sick lapping toilet bowl water while you slumber? Kitty o.d. on the nip? Cat and dog pet hospital featuring 24 hour care. Specialists on duty include ophthalmologists, cardiologists, radiologists, surgeons, and internists. Emergency rates begin at 11pm.

Video Rentals

Cinefile

11280 Santa Monica Blvd.   (310) 312-8836
Los Angeles, CA 90025
Mon - Sat 10am - Midnight, Sun Noon - Midnight

Great selection of independant and foreign films at this alternative store. Find your favorite John Cassavettes films in their auteur section or the classic Kung Fu film you've been looking for in their foreign film section.

The Continental Shop

1619 Wilshire Blvd.   (310) 453-8655
Santa Monica, CA 90403
Mon - Sat 9:30am - 6pm, Sun Noon - 6pm

6,000 British videos, movies and TV series with 2000 rentals. Mostly work produced from the '30s through the '70s, including "The Professionals," "The Persuaders" and "The Forsythe Saga." Stocks audio cassettes, CDs, packaged foods, jams, jellies, sausages, cheeses, English butter, tea, and egg cups.

Dave's Video, The Laser Place

12144 Ventura Blvd.   (818) 760-3472
Studio City, CA 91604
Mon - Sun 10am - 9pm

Known for its celebrity signings of remasters, it deals exclusively in laser discs and DVDs with a complete sales and rental library of over 10,000 titles (many hard-to-find). Follow Dave's motto of "friends don't let friends watch VHS!"

Eddie Brandt's Saturday Matinee

5006 Vineland Ave.   (818) 506-4242
North Hollywood, CA 91601
Tue - Fri 1pm - 6pm, Sat 8:30am - 5pm

Looking for "Curse of the Demon" or the original "Avengers" (released for the first time in seven years). These are just a few of over 45,000 titles available. Film noir, silent, foreign and TV classics are abundantly represented at this family owned store; in business for over 30 years.

Jerry's Video Rerun

1904 N. Hillhurst Ave.   (323) 666-7471
Los Angeles, CA 90027
Mon - Sat 10am - 11pm, Sun Noon - 11pm

Jerry's reputation as a movie maven is legendary in the industry. Over 26,000 videos; many horror (including European), sci-fi, film noir and adult titles. "Phantom Lady" is one of their most sought-after film noir videos. Don't forget to ask about their humongous Hong Kong collection.

Laser Blazer

10587 W. Pico Blvd.   (310) 475-4788
Los Angeles, CA 90064
Mon - Sun Hours Vary
Web: www.laserblazer.com

LA's largest laser disc source carries over 10,000 titles in this format and over 1500 on DVD. 20% off on laser sales. Discs and DVDs contain supplemental features such as director commentaries and production notes. "Song of the South," a Disney title never released in the US and now a Japanese import, is available here. Buy or rent.

Now Playing Video

4718 1/2 Admiralty Way   (310) 306-3336
Marina Del Rey, CA 90292
Mon - Sun 10am - 10pm

Fun family atmosphere at this small store boasting 7,000 titles and many DVDs. New releases, foreign, drama and excellent kids section stocked with Disney, Sesame Street, Barney, Nickelodeon and Rugrats.

Odyssey Video

11910 Wilshire Blvd.   (310) 477-2523
Los Angeles, CA 90025
Mon - Sun 9am - Midnight

Not for the faint of heart, Odyssey carries an "offensive" section including banned-for-TV, gruesome and outlandish videos. Their huge Hong Kong section includes over 40 Jackie Chan and 10 Jet Li titles. Rare Japanese animation and huge adult sections. Among the largest and best priced DVD and laser disc rental sections around. (Also at 4810 Vineland Ave. in N. Hollywood.)

Rocket Video

726 N. La Brea Ave.   (323) 965-1100
Los Angeles, CA 90038
Sun - Thu 11am - 10pm, Fri - Sat 11am - 11pm
Web: www.rocketvideo.com

While their store contains over 20,000 rental videos, their website features over 100,000 for purchase. Titles ranging from the "Abbott and Costello Show" to "Zorro's Black Whip" and everything in between. Foreign, classics, cult, sci-fi, horror and adult titles. Many laser discs and DVDs in stock.

Video Journeys

2730 Griffith Park Blvd.   (323) 663-5857
Los Angeles, CA 90027
Mon - Sun 10am - 10pm

Over 20,000 titles specializing in documentaries, foreign, silent, and classics. Stocks the entire "Prisoner" series, "Grey Gardens" and all of Ken Burns' work. Showcase section rents out independent and student films free of charge. Friendly and knowledgeable staff. DVD and laser discs available.

Video West

805 Larabee St.   (310) 659-5762
West Hollywood, CA 90069
Mon - Sun 10am - Midnight

Out-of-print tapes and a gigantic television section can be found here including Brit hits like "Prime Suspect." Stocks dramas, classics, musicals, fine arts, westerns, foreign and the most up-to-date selection of gay, erotica and adult titles in town.

Vidiots

302 Pico Blvd.   (310) 392-8508
Santa Monica, CA 90405
Sun - Thu 10am - 11pm, Fri - Sat 10am - Midnight

Alternative video store featuring foreign, art, documentary and other hard-to-find titles. Stocks Chet Baker in "Let's Get Lost" and the Beatles "Let It Be." Performance art videos of Lydia Lunch, Bill Viola and Rachel Rosenthal. Filmmakers events have included guest speakers Angelica Houston, Michael Apted and more. Full line of DVDs.

Volunteering

Alisa Ann Ruch Burn Foundation

3600 Ocean View Blvd., Ste. 1   (818) 249-2230
Glendale, CA 91208
Web: www.aarbf.org

Provides outreach and assistance to burn survivors through innovative programs and services. Educates fire prevention and safety in community events and schools. Volunteering opportunities from office assistants to fundraising coordinators to "Champ Camp" counselors.

The Alzheimer Association

1339 Del Norte Rd.   (805) 485-5597
Camarillo, CA 93010
Web: www.alz.org/ventura

Support group educates and creates public awareness of Alzheimer's. Assists families with treatment and hospital referrals, and lends informative literature and videos to those in need. Various volunteer opportunities range from participating and planning the annual Memory Walk to contributing to the monthly newsletter.

American Red Cross

(213) 739-5200
Web: www.redcross.org

Relief organization assisting victims of natural disasters and other hardships. Call local chapter for volunteer opportunities such as answering phones for a day and training for disaster relief work. Help local fire victims or blood drives.

Animal Legal Defense Fund

127 Fourth St.   (707) 769-7771
Petaluma, CA 94952
Web: www.aldf.org

National nonprofit organization that implements laws for animal rights and defends against abuse and exploitation. Campaigns include "Zero Tolerance for Cruelty" plus protecting wild horses, challenging treatment of primates in labs and roadside zoos. Needs volunteers for written materials, videos, PSAs (live and animation) for national distribution and airtime. Attorneys and law students are in constant demand.

Big Brothers of Greater Los Angeles

1486 Colorado Blvd.   (323) 258-3333
Los Angeles, CA 90041

Big Brothers of Greater Los Angeles needs active and positive-minded adults (ages 18+over) to serve as role models and mentors for disadvantaged children (ages 6-12). Be the support system and make a difference in someone's life while retracing your own youth: saving the universe at an arcade or getting doused in a watergun fight with your new little brother.

Big Sisters of Los Angeles

6022 Wilshire Blvd., Ste. 202   (323) 933-5749
Los Angeles, CA 90036

Seeking women 21 and older to help as role models in one-to-one relationships with young girls.

The Braille Institute

741 N. Vermont Ave.   (323) 663-1111
Los Angeles, CA 90029   (800) 272-4553

Organization offers many important positions to be filled, including readers and hotline representatives, instructors (art, music and English as a second language) and office assistants. Training provided Monday-Friday 8:30pm-5pm. Tours 10am daily.

Girls Incorporated of Los Angeles

5855 Green Valley Circle, Ste. 305   (310) 670-6091
Culver City, CA 90230
Web: www.girlsinc.org

Dedicated to nurturing girls to become strong, smart and bold. Premier program is media literacy (9-11 years). Promotes career awareness in the film and entertainment industry. Volunteers needed to present how the industry can work for a girl's future career.

Greenpeace

    (800) 326-0959
Web: www.greenpeace.org/~usa

Committed to protecting the earth's resources by promoting biodiversity, global disarmament and international peace.

Handicapped Scuba Association International

1104 El Prado   (949) 498-4540
San Clemente, CA 92672
Web: www.hsascuba.com

The world's leading authority on recreational diving for those with physical disabilities. This non-profit corporation operates as an independent diver training and certifying agency. The "Dive Buddy Program" offers able-bodied divers a chance to gain diving experience while helping disabled persons dive. HSA organizes two or three accessible dive trips per year.

Inner-City Filmmakers

3000 W. Olympic Blvd., #1436   (310) 264-3992
Santa Monica, CA 90404
Web: www.innercityfilmmakers.com

Targeting graduating inner-city high school students with limited funds, this program seeks to provide a free education in developing a career in visual communications. Needs instructors in any aspect of filmmaking. Also seeks to place eager, conscientious youths in internships and entry-level positions.

L.A. C.A.N.

8709 La Tijera Blvd.   (818) 895-7380
Los Angeles, CA 90045

Volunteer service organization based on the power of doing. Bi-monthly newsletter ($20 annual fee) lists 60-90 community and charitable events requesting volunteers and is a nice alternative to the traditional singles scene. Activities include assisting at silent auctions, fundraisers, serving meals to the homeless and clearing brush from hiking trails.

L.A. Works

Web: www.la-volunteer.org

Nonprofit organization placing volunteers on a variety of community service projects for other non-profits and public institutions: planting trees along city streets, helping homeless people, community organizing and more.

LA Coalition To End Hunger And Homelessness

548 S. Spring St., Ste. 339   (213) 439-1070
Los Angeles, CA 90013
Web: www.lacehh.org

Volunteers needed for everything from stuffing envelopes to providing direct service in the campaign to end hunger and homelessness.

Los Angeles Commission On Assaults Against Women

605 W. Olympic Blvd., Ste. 400   (213) 955-9090
Los Angeles, CA 90015   (213) 626-3393
Web: www.lacaaw.org

Short and long term opportunities available. Help prevent violence against women by volunteering one-on-one crisis intervention and counseling services over the phone or conducting teen abuse prevention programs in public schools. Training provided.

Los Angeles Studios
Of Recording For The Blind And Dyslexic

5022 Hollywood Blvd.   (323) 664-5525
Los Angeles, CA 90027   (800) 499-5525

Devoted to the education of the visually impaired and dyslexic. Help record textbooks from first grade to graduate level and beyond. Minimum of two hours per week required. Two other LA area studios in West Hills and El Segundo.

National Multiple Sclerosis Society

                                    (800) 344-4867
Web: www.cal.nmss.org

The mission of the National MS Society is to end the devastating effects of multiple sclerosis. The largest non-governmental funder of multiple sclerosis research in the world, and the largest provider of services for individuals impacted by MS in Southern California. A wide range of volunteer opportunities exist in client programs & services, office administration, public affairs, fund raising, and special events.

Project Angel Food

7574 Sunset Blvd.   (323) 845-1800
Los Angeles, CA 90046
Web: www.angelfood.org

Prepares and delivers food to people living with HIV and AIDS. Offer your skills in the kitchen or as a driver for this essential organization. Food is love and getting it to where it needs to go is a gift, as well.

Santa Monica Mountains Trails Council

                                    (818) 222-4531

Promotes public awareness of recreational trails, and maintains a public trail system throughout the Santa Monica Mountains. Volunteers meet a trained leader each Saturday morning from January through November, except for August, for trail maintenance. Tools are provided. No experience necessary. Various trails are worked on each week. Periodic workshops are offered in conjunction with overnight camp outs.

Special Olympics

6071 Bristol Parkway, Ste. 100   (310) 215-8380
Culver City, CA 90230

International non-profit program offering year round sports training and athletic competition for over one million physically and mentally challenged individuals. Teach and develop activity skills and be a coach of the best kind, offering encouragement and hope.

The Streetlights Production Assistant Program

650 N. Bronson Ave., Ste. B108   (323) 960-4540
Los Angeles, CA 90004

Trains and places economically disadvantaged men and women and those with barriers to employment as production assistants in film and TV. Volunteer in job development, accounting, general office work and more. Or hire one of its ready, willing and able individuals.

TreePeople

12601 Mulholland Dr.   (818) 753-4600
Beverly Hills, CA 90210

Internships available in recreational park and nursery maintenance, urban forestry and environmental education. One-day volunteer opportunities available in the office or outdoors, no experience necessary.

United Farm Workers of America

                                    (213) 381-5611
Web: www.ufw.org

Seeks to provide workers with a living wage, clean drinking water, bathroom facilities and job security. Volunteer positions available in the office or in the field.

The Women's Care Cottage

6040 Vineland Ave.   (818) 753-4580
North Hollywood, CA 91606

Meets the immediate needs of homeless women and children, including temporary housing, food and life skills training. Vocational program encourages women to reach their full professional and personal potential. Volunteers needed to serve hot meals, provide child care, teach art, music or cooking classes, speak at or coordinate special events and offer clerical support.

Websites

ArtScene
Web: www.artscenecal.com

Culture is a click away with the electronic version of Southern Cal's leading art guide to fine galleries and museums. Links to a monthly calendar of events, maps, images, listings, articles and an art forum.

The Body: An AIDS And HIV Information Resource
Web: www.thebody.com/help.html

Website lists every major AIDS and HIV research, education and help group. Contact the organization of your choice; volunteer opportunities range from short to long term.

Cool Site Of The Day
Web: www.cool.infi.net

Cool 101 from activism to television, dolphins to zebras. and everything in between. Tap into the various links to discover the hipper, and dare we say it?, more useful side of cyberspace. Check in daily so you don't miss the big pick. Use with caution; you caould learn something.

DogFriendly.com
Web: www.dogfriendly.com

Dogs are people, too. If your dog wants to be included in more aspects of your life and so do you, then don't leave home without consulting this comprehensive website. Features designated hotels, beaches, shops, events, restaurants and even employers where canines are welcome throughout the U.S. and Canada. Links to additional indispensable resources like housing, rescue and insurance. Could end up being your second-best friend.

Feed
Web: www.feedmag.com

Feed your brain with well written, thought provoking articles covering global events, social issues and cultural (de)evolution. "Technology" and "Other Media and Culture" spotlights are especially tasty treats. Or scathing commentaries, depending on your brainbuds.

LA 411 Online
Web: www.la411publishing.com

LA 411's own website featuring an online version of our highly regarded production resource directory and a rich variety of resources for film and video industry pros.

@LA - Guide To Sites Of Greater LA
Web: www.at-la.com

Looking for something to do or see in the City of Angels? This online directory connects you to thousands of links that give the low down on what you want to know about what's hip, cool and decidedly LA.

LA Weekly
Web: www.laweekly.com

Selected articles, contents of current issue, subscription info, the infamous personals, LA/NY nightlife and an essential calendar of events.

Los Angeles.Com
Web: www.losangeles.com

Subtle, handsome site with links to music, dining, art events, movies, shopping, outdoors, media, the week's top picks and much more.

Where Los Angeles Goes to Play

Dining
Nightlife
Event Calendar
Real Estate
Surf Report
Message Board
Recreation Guide

Manhattan

Hermosa

Redondo

Palos Verdes

SOUTHBAYLIFE.COM

Los Angeles Times/Calendar Live

Web: www.calendarlive.com

Contains feature articles, a beach guide, weekend events, coffee house page, shopping in LA, Hollywood hotspots, a biking guide and weekend escapes.

MovieLink

Web: www.movielink.com

Sick of fumbling through the newspaper just to find movie times and locations? Try Mr. MovieFone's (777-FILM) website devoted to a more efficient method of finding what's playing where, and when. Never be late to a matinee again. Or at least know what time late is.

● The South Bay

Web: www.southbaylife.com

For the best the South Bay has to offer, visit the leading online guide to its glorious beach scene. This site features restaurant listings and insider info on the hottest nightspots. A calendar of world-renowned sporting events assures that you won't miss Gabrielle Reece in action. Something for everyone, whether you're a seasoned surf guru or a novice just planning a weekend coastal getaway.

Suck

Web: www.suck.com

Cutting edge, crisp commentary and dark humor on the state of the world, offering an alternative perspective to mainstream headlines.